The Duchess of Richmond's Ball

15 June 1815

THE DUCHESS OF RICHMOND'S BALL

15 JUNE 1815

by

David Miller

SPELLMOUNT
Staplehurst

British Library Cataloguing in Publication Data:
A catalogue record for this book is available
from the British Library

Copyright © David Miller 2005
Maps copyright © Spellmount and David Miller

ISBN 1-86227-229-8

Published in the UK in 2005
by
Spellmount Limited
The Village Centre
Staplehurst
Kent TN12 0BJ

Tel: 01580 893730
Fax: 01580 893731
E-mail: enquiries@spellmount.com
Website: www.spellmount.com

1 3 5 7 9 8 6 4 2

Typeset in Palatino by MATS, Southend-on-Sea, Essex
Printed in Great Britain by
T.J. International Ltd
Padstow, Cornwall

Contents

Introduction

History books abound with stories of victory and defeat in war, and of elections, riots, pestilence, political machinations and crime in peace, but few social events, such as balls or banquets, merit more than a passing mention. There is, however, one that stands out for its unique mixture of splendour, drama, poignancy and a sense of impending doom – the Ball given by the Duchess of Richmond in Brussels on the evening of Thursday 15 June 1815.

That Ball conjures up pictures of young officers dancing with their beautiful partners while anxious messengers stand at the doorway, trying to deliver the latest news of Napoleon's advance. Then, the mood of gaiety palpably ebbs as messages are passed from one officer to another; and, following hasty farewells to their partners, the officers slip quietly away into the night, duty calling more powerfully than the entreaties of the bewildered and sobbing ladies. With the makeshift ballroom lying empty, the scene shifts to the moonlit countryside, where officers gallop to reach their regiments, some of them arriving so late that they are still in their ball uniform and dancing pumps throughout the next day's battles – one even dying in them.

Charlotte, fourth Duchess of Richmond will forever be associated with the Ball, but little is actually known about her, while her husband, Charles, is generally relegated to historical footnotes either as a one-time lord-lieutenant of Ireland or as a shadowy figure in civilian dress, glimpsed galloping across the battlefield of Waterloo. Both were, however, interesting people in their own right.

The Ball and its hostess are mentioned in passing in many histories of the Waterloo campaign and of Napoleon's 'hundred days', but have seldom been examined in any detail, leaving many questions unanswered. Why did it take place, and where? Who actually attended and what happened? Indeed, who were the Duke and Duchess of Richmond, whose names are forever linked with that Ball? This book answers all of those.

It is important to an understanding of the Ball to appreciate that it was a *social* and not a military occasion, and that it was the Duchess of Richmond's *private* party, not an official event; thus, who was invited –

and who was left out – was entirely up to her. She was a duchess and socially by far the most senior English lady in Brussels, so she did not have to concern herself with pleasing or displeasing any individual or section of society, nor was she under any obligation to achieve a balance between military and civilian guests, between nationalities, or between this or that regiment. She seems to have invited a very few out of a sense of duty, for example, the mayor of Brussels and a few of the diplomats, and some others because she was returning their hospitality, but many were there simply because they were her friends.

She also went to a great deal of trouble to invite a proportion of army officers, and was even helped by Captain John Gurwood with the military arrangements. Thus, just over half her guests were military officers, of whom the majority were from the British Army, including one from the King's German Legion. There were a small number of Dutch Army guests, almost exclusively aides-de-camp (ADCs), whom she would have met when entertaining their generals, one officer from the Nassau contingent, several from Brunswick, just one from the Prussian Army and none from Hanover, despite its close links with the English Crown.

When historians reconstruct events in bygone battles they are able to consult the official reports and returns from regimental, divisional and army commanders of both sides, and to correlate these with personal accounts in journals, letters and biographies. Who was present, how they all moved, the timings and the detailed sequence of events can be reconstructed with a fair degree of accuracy. In the case of the Ball, however, there are no official records to be consulted; instead, there are only some personal reports of the period, and these tend to be dominated by the battles of Quatre Bras and Waterloo and the subsequent advance to Paris. As a result, many of these personal reminiscences of the Ball were recorded long after the event, some of them over fifty years later, and not surprisingly they frequently contradict each other over matters such as timing and the sequence of events.

Nevertheless, the Ball is an important historical occasion and has a significant place in the history of the Waterloo campaign. And, as will be shown, many of the comments about it are either inaccurate or unfair. This book sets the record straight.

The English community in Brussels, in general, and the Ball in particular did not exist in isolation and have, therefore, to be viewed in the context of the history of Belgium and its people and of the city of Brussels. In particular, there were many adverse comments made by English observers, both at the time and subsequently, about the ambivalence of many local people's feelings towards Napoleon. But, as will be explained, Belgium was a country which had been conquered so often and ruled by foreigners for so long that it is unsurprising that some, at least, hedged their bets during the Hundred Days.

The author has adopted the following conventions:

- English social custom at the time was that all Army officers junior to captain were referred to as 'Mr'. However, I have used their military ranks (e.g., lieutenant, ensign, cornet), both to indicate their correct military status and to differentiate them from civilians.
- To save repeated use of 'sic' all quotes are spelt and punctuated as in the original document.
- Nothing creates greater difficulties for an author – and gives rise to greater offence – than national titles. In the period covered by this book the people of the British Isles were known to foreigners as 'the English' and sub-divisions into English, Irish, Scots and Welsh were largely ignored as a domestic issue. Indeed, the vast majority regarded themselves as being English and that is how they are referred to in this book.
- Similarly, in 1815 there was no such political entity as Belgium; it had recently been either the Austrian Netherlands or an integral part of France. There is, therefore, no convenient title for the country, while its people were a mixture of Flemings and Walloons. However, in the absence of any other convenient and simple designation I have used the words Belgium to denote the country and Belgians, its inhabitants.

Acknowledgements

No book such as this could be researched and written without the help of a large number of friendly and cooperative people. In particular I am most grateful to Rosemary Baird, Keeper of the Goodwood Collection, whose help, advice and knowledge of the Richmond family history have been a constant encouragement.

Some of those involved in the events of 1814–15 kept journals or wrote letters in which they recorded day-by-day accounts of events and which, fortunately for posterity, have been preserved. Some have been published, others remain in private hands. The Dowager Countess of Uxbridge received regular letters from her daughter and grand-daughters in Brussels. These give an unparalleled insight into family life in the Belgian capital in 1814–15, with many snatches of gossip unavailable elsewhere. These have been published (*The Capel Letters*, Jonathan Cape, London, 1955) and I am most grateful to their editor, the Marquess of Anglesey, for permission to quote from them.

Spencer Madan was a young man appointed tutor in 1814 to the three youngest sons of the Duke and Duchess of Richmond. Like the Capels, Madan wrote regular letters home, which have also been preserved and published (*Spencer and Waterloo*, edited by Beatrice Madan, Literary Services, London, 1970). These fascinating letters take the reader right into the heart of the Richmond family, and give an unparalleled view of working with the Duchess. I am indebted to the editor's son, C W Brocklebank, Esq., for permission to quote from them and to use the silhouette of his ancestor.

Sir Hew Hamilton-Dalrymple sent me a copy and gave permission to quote from the diary of his ancestor, Lady Jane Dalrymple-Hamilton; it is quite electrifying to read the words of someone who sat beside the Duke of Wellington at the famous Ball. Similarly, Lady Anne-Louise Hamilton-Dalrymple gave permission to quote from the diary of Captain Arthur Shakespear.

Another treasure among these journals is that of Captain Digby Mackworth, who not only cast a refreshingly sardonic eye on the events around him, but also wrote up his journal almost every night, giving it a great sense of immediacy. He even found time to make his daily entry on the evening of 18 June: 'And so ended this ever memorable day. Lord Hill and Staff returned to a small cottage where we now are. We have but one room between nine of us, including him. All but myself are now asleep. Good-night.' I am indebted to the present Sir Digby Mackworth, Bart, for permission to quote from this document.

Fellow historians of the period are constantly generous with the time they are prepared to give to help a beginner among their ranks. In particular, I would like to thank Garry Cousins, now resident in Germany, Alice Dodge, Philip Haythornthwaite, John Hussey and Sally Smith. I am also greatly indebted to Philippe de Callateÿ, the distinguished Belgian historian, for his invaluable help and advice on the Brussels aspects of this story.

I have tried to track down as many modern-day descendants of those at the Ball as possible, in order to enquire whether they still possess any documents or artefacts relating to the Ball. Sadly, in most cases, they do not, but without exception they took the time to trawl through their family records and replied most courteously. I am grateful to them for doing so.

Others I wish to thank are: Dr Claudia Reichl-Ham of the Heeresgeschichtliches Museum im Arsenal, Vienna; Martin Lanthier of the National Archives of Canada; and Stephen Green, Curator of the MCC Museum.

As described in the text, I managed to track down some clothes, reputed to have been worn at the Ball. Helen Nicholl of the National Museums of Scotland was very helpful over the uniform of Lieutenant Claude Alexander, arranging for photographs to be taken specially for this book. There are also two dresses in the Costume Museum in Bath, and the unstinting help from Penelope Byrd, Rosemary Harden and Dr Anne Saunders is greatly appreciated.

I consulted the National Army Museum, the National Museum of Scotland and many regimental museums for information on individuals involved in this story. Without exception they were quick to respond and as helpful as their resources allowed. In particular, I would like to thank historians at the museums of the Brigade of Guards, the Queen's Own Royal West Kent Regiment, the Royal Sussex Regiment (35th Foot), the Duke of Cornwall's Light Infantry, Royal Green Jackets and the Gordon Highlanders (92nd Foot).

As I live some distance from London, I frequently asked Pauline Eismark, a professional researcher, to visit the Public Record Office on my behalf. Her great skill, unerring sense of just where to look and speed of response have been as excellent as ever.

One of the great treasures of this country are its networks of archives, libraries and museums, and the most knowledgeable and ever-helpful people who staff them. In this context I would like to thank the staff at: The

National Archives (formerly the Public Record Office); British Library; National Army Museum; Prince Consort's Library, Aldershot; West Sussex Record Office, Chichester; Dorset County Record Office; Exeter County Library Reference Section; and last, but by no means least, my own local library in Newton Abbot.

I gratefully acknowledge all this help and advice, but the opinions expressed in this book are mine alone and if there are errors or omissions, then the fault too is mine alone.

David Miller,
December 2004

CHAPTER I
Belgium

The Duchess of Richmond's Ball did not take place in splendid isolation; it was held in a foreign country, Belgium, and in a particular environment where Europe was trying to readjust itself after over twenty years of conflict. In order to understand many of the events in Belgium and the attitudes of individual Belgians during the period January 1814 to June 1815 it is necessary to be aware of the troubled history of that country and its people, who had been ruled by outsiders for centuries and where many of the changes were driven by events and people far outside its boundaries.

At the start of the 16th century the Low Countries were part of the Duchy of Burgundy, which covered all of what is now The Netherlands, Belgium, Luxembourg, Artois and Franche-Comté. This was ruled by Duke Philip I (1478–1506) and his wife, Joanna, daughter of King Ferdinand II of Aragón and Queen Isabella of Castile. Philip's son and heir, Charles, was born in 1500 at Ghent and seldom has the accident of birth rewarded an individual so richly as it did this boy. Unfortunately, two of his inheritances caused a conjunction between Spain and the Low Countries which was to embroil the latter in almost constant conflict and untold hardship for over three centuries.

Joanna became Queen of Castile on her mother's death in 1504 and Philip became joint ruler with her in 1506, but then died suddenly, at which point Joanna, who was becoming increasingly insane, remained joint ruler of Spain, but now in partnership with her father, Ferdinand II. Meanwhile, Philip's title as Duke of Burgundy passed to his 6-year-old son, Charles, whose aunt, Margaret of Austria acted as his regent. When Ferdinand II died in 1516 Charles inherited Aragón, Navarre, Granada, Naples, Sicily, Sardinia and Spanish America, as well as joint kingship with his mother. Charles subsequently also became Holy Roman Emperor. These multiple inheritances resulted in Charles moving to Spain, leaving a viceroy – always a Spanish nobleman – to administer his duchy of Burgundy

The situation in the Low Countries was further complicated by the rapid but uneven spread of Protestantism. The northern people, pre-dominantly of Dutch stock, converted to the new faith, while those in the

1

south, mainly Walloons, remained staunchly Catholic. The first of the anti-Spanish, anti-Catholic uprisings took place in 1566 and was short-lived, but the divisions were formalised in 1579 when the Walloons declared their adherence to the Catholic faith and Spanish rule, while in the north, the *stadtholder*, the Prince of Orange, formed a confederation against the tyrannical oppression by Spain, and, in particular, of the then king, Philip II. This was formalised in the Union of Utrecht, in which the signatories declared their determination to maintain their independence and the primacy of the Protestant faith.

The resulting Eighty Years War dragged on until 1648, when the Treaty of Münster acknowledged the independence of the north, which became known as the 'United Provinces'; a loose federation, in which the individual provinces maintained a large degree of autonomy. This was administered by the States-General under a ruling prince, originally elected, but whose office became hereditary to the House of Orange from the mid-18th century onwards. There was, however, an anti-Orange, republican faction, which became so strong that in 1787 *stadtholder* William V was forced to invite a Prussian army to help restore his authority. Meanwhile, the south remained under Spanish rule until 1713, when the Wars of the Spanish Succession were finally resolved by the Treaty of Utrecht, one provision of which was the transfer of the Spanish Netherlands from one Habsburg monarch to another and the country became the Austrian Netherlands. The country was generally peaceful, except for the short-lived Brabançon revolt in 1789, which was quelled in late 1790 by a powerful Austrian army.

In the early months of the wars of the French Revolution, the French quickly overran the Austrian Netherlands, which thereafter became a part of France, being integrated into the French economic system and providing young men as both officers and soldiers for the French Army. The United Provinces had hoped to remain neutral, but once France had annexed the Austrian Netherlands, they joined the First Coalition against them. The French responded by invading in 1794, forcing William V and his family to flee to England, at which the Dutch 'patriotic party' established the Batavian Republic, but under French suzerainty. French control became tighter and more direct until in 1806 the country became the Kingdom of Holland, ruled by Napoleon's brother, King Louis. The latter, one of the more decent members of his family, tried his best for a generally ungrateful people, but abdicated in 1810, when the country was simply annexed and became an integral part of France. This state of affairs lasted until November 1813, when there was a general, if rather disorganised, Dutch uprising against French rule.

Following Napoleon's disastrous invasion of Russia in 1812, French forces were pushed steadily back across Europe and suffered a major, although by no means final, defeat at the Battle of Leipzig (16–19 October

1813). Napoleon managed to extricate most of his force and what remained of the Grande Armée continued its long withdrawal to France, forced ever closer to home by the Swedish Bernadotte (Army of the North), the Prussian Blücher (Army of Silesia) moving along the Moselle valley into Lorraine, and the Austrian Schwarzenberg (Army of Bohemia) advancing across Switzerland and through the Belfort gap. On 8 November the Allies offered peace to France, but when this was rejected by Napoleon, they decided on 1 December to invade and for all of them, there was only one goal – Paris.

English Military Operations in the Low Countries 1813–14

With Napoleon's days now clearly numbered, his empire began to collapse; the Confederation of the Rhine[1] disintegrated in early November and this encouraged the Dutch to rise against French rule on 15 November 1813. News of this uprising reached London on 21 November, and, ever eager both to encourage resistance to the French and to destroy enemy warships in the Scheldt, the English cabinet despatched a small force of some 6,000 men, together with 20,000 muskets to be issued to the insurgents. As commander, they appointed General Sir Thomas Graham, who had recently returned from Spain on the grounds of ill-health, but his protestations were swept aside and he was persuaded to take the job.

French garrisons panicked at the combination of the news of Napoleon's retreat and the Dutch uprising, and precipitately abandoned the main towns to concentrate around Gorkum. They then recovered their nerve and sought to reoccupy the towns they had just left, but with limited success. At this stage there were three allied armies in the Low Countries. A Russian division (Benckendorf) was approaching the Hague, a Prussian division (Bülow) was thinly spread along the Rhine between Arnhem and Düsseldorf, and Bernadotte, with his Swedish army, was farther to the east but more interested, for national reasons, in Denmark than the Netherlands. Then, on 30 November, the Prince of Orange landed at Scheveningen, and the English expeditionary force under Graham started to land on 3 December.

The problem was that there was no commander-in-chief, and although there was some cooperation, it was the result of personal contact between commanders and mutual goodwill, rather than overall strategic direction. The Prince of Orange was unable to assert any central control over the Dutch population, and although there was considerable anti-French feeling, the uprising was spontaneous rather than the result of prolonged resistance and planning; as a result of which there was no organisation, either political or military. Indeed, Graham found the local situation nothing like so straightforward as he had been led to expect and it proved impossible to identify a responsible group to whom he could safely deliver the 20,000 muskets.

In the face of the initial English landings the French in the area withdrew into the fortress of Bergen-op-Zoom, although the English main force was delayed by adverse winds and did not arrive until 15 December. Graham's force was nominally 6,000 strong, but most units were well below strength and many of the soldiers actually present were either boys or unfit older men. To make matters worse, there were initially no artillery or cavalry, although some guns did arrive on the 25th. Understanding the English problems, Benckendorf generously lent some Cossacks, only to remove them without any warning on 2 January 1814.

In early January Graham was the senior officer in the area, while the Prussian Bülow, who had now arrived, was of lower rank, but had much the larger force, so the English general generously offered to subordinate himself to the Prussian. The two men met on 8 January and having agreed a plan, they started to move on 10 January. Despite their efforts at co-operation, however, their combined undertaking proved less than satisfactory; there were many missed opportunities and Bülow proved particularly inept. Finally, with the English only a mile from Antwerp, Bülow unilaterally decided to leave the area altogether, leaving his English allies in a very exposed position from which Graham had no choice but to withdraw. Graham did, however, manage to persuade Bülow that they should both make a second attempt on Antwerp, which was launched on 1 February. The conditions were very wintry, with snowstorms and deep drifts; the English ships were icebound at Willemstadt and to make matters worse, the siege train had still not arrived. Despite all this, the Anglo–Prussian force made progress, but failed in the major English objective, which was to capture the Dutch fleet. At this juncture Bülow was given an unequivocal order to join Blücher for the advance into France, and he departed on 6 February.

Graham's force was too weak to undertake operations on its own, so he now turned to Bernadotte for help, but then, to make matters even worse, he was warned that the English government needed most of his men elsewhere and was about to despatch them either to America or to bolster Wellington's forces in southern France. Faced with all this, Graham decided on an attempt to take Bergen-op-Zoom in an audacious night assault, without preliminary bombardment or trenchworks. This duly took place on 8 March 1814, and after an initial setback the English were on the verge of total success when the whole plan began to unravel. There was confusion among the troops already inside the town, mainly as a result of communications difficulties between units in strange surroundings, at night, and in the face of an enemy who knew the streets well. Matters were not helped when the commander of a feint attack turned it into a major assault, thus depriving Graham of his reserve at a critical moment. As a result, some troops inside the town started to withdraw, leaving those still inside with little option but to surrender, while Graham was marooned outside, unable to help. It was a well-planned and initially well-conducted operation, which turned into a gallant failure.

Allied operations elsewhere were more successful: the Russian tsar and Prussian king entered Paris on 1 April 1814, Wellington took Toulouse on 10 April, and on the following day Napoleon finally abdicated and departed into exile on the island of Elba. The long, long war appeared to be over.

Post-War Belgium

The sudden collapse of the French left many power vacuums across Europe, not least in the former Austrian Netherlands. The Belgians had not risen against the French occupiers in the aftermath of the retreat from Moscow and it was the Allied advances that forced the French to leave. Brussels, in fact, fell as early as 1 February 1814, with the French rearguard leaving by the Porte d'Anderlecht as the Prussian advance guard entered through the Porte de Louvain; the first major elements of the Allied army, commanded by the Duke of Saxe-Weimar, arrived the following day.

The most immediate problem was that Belgium had been ruled by various foreign powers for several centuries and for the past twenty years had been an integral part of France. As a result, not only was there no group to form a government, but the indigenous administrative framework was weak. This left the Allies with no immediate alternative but to restore the Belgian provinces to Austrian control and on 29 March 1814 Emperor Franz Josef in distant Vienna appointed a military man, General Baron Karl Vincent, as governor-general. Having considered matters further, however, the Allies decided to form the Belgian provinces into a new political entity, which would then become an equal partner with the United Provinces in a new state to be named The Netherlands, which would be placed under the rule of the House of Orange; this was set out in the Treaty of Paris (Article VI) and confirmed in the Treaty of London (20 April 1814). Thus, the renewed Austrian control proved to be short-lived and the governor-general, Baron Vincent, resigned his office and transferred power to the Sovereign Prince of the Netherlands on 1 August 1814.

While all this was under discussion, the Continental troops, mainly Prussian and Russians, withdrew from the Low Countries, leaving only the English under Graham, now ennobled as Lord Lynedoch. As the United Provinces were secured by their own army, the English moved southwards into the former Austrian Netherlands. They were not, however, an army of occupation, their task being to ensure stability and to maintain the provisions of the Treaty of Paris, pending the finalisation of a comprehensive peace treaty at the Congress of Vienna. Lynedoch initially established his headquarters in Antwerp (5 May) but subsequently moved to Brussels. The English garrison, which consisted initially of three battalions of Guards and twelve battalions of infantry of the line, settled down to a peacetime routine, in which they were joined in the middle of the year by most of the King's German Legion and 15,000 men of the Hanoverian Militia. Lynedoch, however, was now aged 67 and, with twenty-two years of constant campaigning behind him, was anxious to retire. So, he handed over his command and left Brussels on 16 August, his successor being Sovereign Prince William's son, the 23-year-old Hereditary Prince of Orange, who was promoted to lieutenant-general in the English Army.

Even the arrangement agreed in the Treaty of London proved to be short-lived, and on 16 December 1814 the Congress of Vienna declared the new state to be a kingdom with William as king, which he personally proclaimed in Brussels on 23 February 1815. Then, on 31 May 1815 the kings of England, Prussia and the Netherlands, and the emperors of Russia and Austria formalised all these arrangements in a treaty. William, assisted by his son, made every effort to encourage his Belgian subjects to be loyal members of the new kingdom, although he did not help his cause by appointing a number of known 'Bonapartists' as senior members of his council for the Belgian provinces.

This, then, was the political background in which the English colony in Brussels and the military garrison found themselves. The situation for the people of Belgium changed regularly as the Great Powers, holding discussions well outside their borders, sought to work out what to do with them. Certainly, in that autocratic period there was little prospect of the wishes of the people themselves being taken into account and even if they had been it is difficult to predict what might have been the outcome. Some hankered for firm rule, whether by the French or the Austrians, while others were prepared to accept rule by the House of Orange and yet another faction wanted the country to pass under the English crown.

Everything changed, however, when Napoleon returned to power in Paris and threatened reimposition of French rule. In the days to come, some of the English criticised those Belgians who made clandestine preparations to come to terms with the French, but with Belgium's troubled history, a succession of foreign occupiers and Napoleon's previous record of success, it is not surprising that they hedged their bets.

NOTE

1   Formed by Napoleon in 1806, the confederation consisted of the kingdoms of Bavaria and Württenberg, the grand duchies of Baden, Berg and Hesse-Darmstadt, and several smaller principalities. It eventually embraced nearly all the German states except Austria and Prussia.

CHAPTER II
The Richmond Family

The Richmond title originated when King Charles II's mistress, Louise de Keroualle, Duchess of Portsmouth, gave birth to a son, who was named Charles after his father. That child, Charles Lennox[1] (1672–1723), was created Duke of Richmond and married Anne, daughter of Lord Brudenell. They had one son, also named Charles (d. 1750), who married Sarah, daughter of Earl Cadogan, before succeeding to the title. They had seven children – two boys and five girls.

The second duke's eldest son, Charles (1734–1806), completed the almost obligatory 'grand tour' and was then commissioned a captain in the 20th Foot. He succeeded as the third Duke of Richmond in 1750, but continued his military career. In 1758 he purchased a lieutenant-colonelcy and became commanding officer of the 72nd Foot, with which he undertook several expeditions on the French coast. He also distinguished himself as ADC to the allied commander-in-chief, Prince Ferdinand of Brunswick, at the great allied victory over the French at Minden (1 August 1759). The highest public office he held was that of Master-General of the Ordnance, a most prestigious position which was always held by one of the most distinguished generals of the day and carried with it an automatic seat in the cabinet. He held this post from 1782 to 1795 and died in 1806 at the age of 72. He had married Mary, daughter of the Earl of Aylesbury in 1757 but they had no children, although the duke fathered three daughters by his housekeeper and another, Henrietta le Clerc, by an unknown mother, who was brought up at Goodwood.

The third duke's younger sister, Lady Sarah Lennox (1745–1826), was very beautiful, but her marriage to Sir Charles Bunbury proved unhappy and in January 1769 she fell in love and eloped with Lord William Gordon (1744–1823), second son of Cosmo, third Duke of Gordon. This created a major scandal but after some months the lovers parted; Lady Sarah went to live in seclusion in a house on the Goodwood estate provided by her brother. Sir Charles and Lady Sarah were divorced in 1776 and in 1781 she married for the second time, her new husband being Colonel the Hon. George Napier. This proved a great success: three of their sons became famous generals, one of them achieving fame as the historian of the

Peninsular War.[2] The link between the Gordon and Lennox families, temporarily formed by William and Sarah was, however, to become more permanent in the next generation.

The Fourth Duke

Because the third duke had no son, his younger brother, Lieutenant-General Lord George Lennox, was the heir presumptive. Lord George's wife, Louisa, daughter of the fourth Marquis of Lothian, bore him one son and three daughters, but when he predeceased his elder brother in 1805, the succession fell to that son, Charles Lennox (1764–1819). This young man, the future fourth duke, was educated privately by a tutor, but once old enough was not prepared to sit idly by; he followed his father's and uncle's footsteps into useful employment. His first job was as secretary to his uncle as Master-General of the Ordnance, but he was then commissioned into the Army in 1785, exchanging to the 7th Foot in 1786 and, by now a captain, into the 35th (Dorsetshire) Foot in 1787.[3] Then, in 1789, the king agreed to a direct request from the third Duke of Richmond for his nephew to be given command of a company in the 2nd (Coldstream) Foot Guards.

The commanding officer of the Coldstream, the king's son, Lieutenant-Colonel the Duke of York, took great exception to this, possibly because he had not been consulted. As a result, when on 15 May 1789 both men attended a masked ball at the fashionable Daubigney's club and York met a figure he took to be Lennox, he told him in forthright terms what he thought of him. Because both were masked, however, York was mistaken: the man (whose identity was never established) was not Lennox, but, on the other hand, the latter did not know who had made these offensive remarks. Nevertheless, he did not hesitate to pass them on; they quickly reached Lennox and in those times any slur on a gentleman's character or reputation had to be dealt with immediately.

What then followed was rather complicated, with tempers rising and Lennox becoming increasingly frustrated as he attempted to discover who had made the comments. His first reaction came on the following morning's parade, where he marched up to York, told him what had happened, and demanded that, as commanding officer, it was his duty to discover who was responsible for such an insult to one of his officers. York refused and promptly ordered Lennox to resume his place on parade. As soon as the parade was over the officers held a meeting when Lennox repeated his request; again, York refused to take the matter any further. Frustrated by this, Lennox next wrote a personal letter to every member of Daubigney's asking for information, but received not a single reply. This led him to conclude (correctly) that the person making theses remarks could only have been the Duke of York and, in accordance with the accepted behaviour of the time, sent his second, the Earl of Winchilsea to call him out. York made no attempt to shelter behind his status, either as commanding officer or as a royal duke, accepted the challenge and named Lord Rawdon as his second.

The two men met on Wimbledon Common on 26 April 1789 where it was agreed between the seconds that the two principles would stand twelve paces apart and, on a given signal, fire simultaneously. When the signal was given, however, only Lennox fired, his round grazing a curl of York's wig, whereupon the latter lowered his pistol, declaring that he had never had any intention of firing. Lennox demanded that York fire, as agreed, but the latter refused either to fire at Lennox, fire into the air, or acknowledge that he had been in the wrong in the first place. Lennox declined to push the matter any further, but the two seconds took the unusual step of issuing a joint statement that evening, setting out the sequence of events and ending by saying: 'The seconds think it proper to add, that both parties behaved with the most perfect coolness and intrepidity.'[4]

The affair caused much public comment. The officers of Lennox's own regiment met on 30 May and resolved that: 'It is the opinion of His Majesty's Coldstream regiment of Guards, that Lieutenant Colonel Lenox, subsequent to the 15th instant, has behaved with *courage*, but, from the peculiarity of the circumstances not with *judgment*.' This was rebutted by a pamphlet written by 'The Captain of a Company in One of the Regiments of Guards' (from the text he appears to have been from either 1st or 3rd Guards) which generally supported Lennox,[5] while the author of another pamphlet, one Theophilus Swift, criticised him, was challenged to a duel, and wounded. However, the fuss was such that Lennox judged it wise to exchange back into the 35th Foot,

Lennox rejoined his old regiment in Edinburgh on 21 July 1789 as lieutenant-colonel in command, where he was given a hero's welcome, with the castle being illuminated in his honour. In return, he threw a banquet for the officers and gave ten guineas for the men of the regiment to drink his health. His affable nature and approachability made him popular with all ranks, one of the most noteworthy features of his command being that his devotion to the game of cricket led him not only to encourage his soldiers to play but also – very unusually for that era – to take part with his men on an equal basis.

Lennox had been in Scotland a mere seven weeks when on 9 September he married Lady Charlotte Gordon (1768–1842), the eldest daughter of Alexander, fourth Duke of Gordon, of which more below. The 35th Foot left Edinburgh in spring 1790 to spend a year in Hamilton, a small town south-east of Glasgow, before moving to Ireland. Four years later the 35th was under notice to go to the West Indies, a notoriously unhealthy station, when Lennox was offered another posting, but he refused on the grounds that he would be seen to fail to share the hardships with his men. They duly arrived in Barbados on 5 May, where Lennox immediately took a small force to San Domingo to assist in the capture of Port-au-Prince. The dreaded yellow fever struck during the short voyage and some 250 men died only for it to be discovered that Port-au-Prince had surrendered to another British force two days earlier. The 35th remained in the West Indies until July 1795 when Lennox took the survivors back to Europe where, after a short break in England, they were sent to join the garrison in Gibraltar. The Rock is, however, a very small station and Lennox clashed constantly with his superiors, so it was as well that he was promoted to colonel in 1796 and left. He had spent seven years in command and shared every privation with his men, but since he was an extraordinarily fit and healthy man there is no record of him ever being taken ill.

Lennox was promoted to major-general in 1798 and to lieutenant-general in 1805, but it would appear that he did not have any active military employment during these years. He certainly continued to hope for a high command in the field, but everything changed in 1806 when his uncle died and he succeeded to the dukedom. This included many properties, such as Goodwood House in Sussex and Richmond House in London, but also some £180,000 of debts, a very considerable sum equivalent to approximately £8 million at today's prices.

At this point, the fourth Duke of Richmond's career took an unexpected turn, as there was a vacancy for the post of Lord-Lieutenant of Ireland, and the government of the day could find no other suitable and willing candidate. Richmond was reluctant to go, saying that all he wanted was to continue to serve as a soldier, although, in view of the debts he had inherited, the prospect of a steady income may have been attractive.[6] Nevertheless, he was persuaded to take on what was described to him as a short-term appointment, although, as so often when this happens, he was kept in post until 1813.

The Richmonds arrived in Dublin in April 1807, where they found Colonel Arthur Wellesley, temporarily in civil employment, as Chief Secretary, thus starting a friendship which was to last the rest of their lives. Richmond had somewhat reactionary views, but disarmed many critics by walking about Dublin, even into the most dissident areas, accompanied only by an ADC, and stopping to hold friendly conversations whenever the opportunity arose.

Richmond was described by one commentator as 'irresistibly convivial', with a particular liking for claret and an ability to sit down with a group of cronies and drink them all under the table. Like many men of his standing he had affairs, although he must have regretted one incident when a loving letter to his mistress, Lady Augusta Everitt, was delivered through a servant's mistake to the Duchess – she was a forthright woman at the best of times and her reaction can only be imagined.

The Richmonds lived in great state in Dublin and entertained on a lavish scale, observers noting that the duchess particularly enjoyed her position and the trappings that went with it. The style that the Richmonds kept, however, cost them a great deal of money. When they arrived the lord-lieutenant's salary was set at £20,000 a year, but in 1810 Richmond managed to persuade the prime minister, Perceval, to raise it to £30,000, although he protested that this was still insufficient. When he left in 1813 he estimated his debts to be in excess of £50,000.

The main reason that Richmond stayed so long in Dublin was that Perceval, prime minister from 1809 to 1812, was politically too weak to find a successor and thus tended to appease Richmond over either salary or policies in order to persuade him to stay on. Richmond's tenure was marked by no great successes, but marred by no great failures either. Indeed, it was aptly summed up by an Irishman who said that Richmond's main achievement was that he had 'kept Ireland tranquil but unhappy'.

On their return to London in 1813 the Richmonds' financial situation, coupled with the large size of their family – their fourteenth child had arrived in 1809 – meant that they had little option but to undertake drastic economies. Thus, in June 1814 Richmond wrote to his friend, the Hon. John Capel, who was already living in Brussels in order to save money, '. . . to make enquiries about this place with a view to coming here with all his Family for a year on an Economical Plan'.[7] The reply was positive and, as a result the Duke set out with his two eldest daughters on 20 June, arriving in Brussels a few days later, where they took up residence in the Rue de la Blanchisserie, which Lady Caroline Capel described as '. . . a delightful House & Gardens in the Lower part of the Town, & delightful it ought to be, to at all compensate for the disadvantage of the situation . . .'[8] But the house had to be large to accommodate the Richmonds and their entourage; a family of fifteen, a tutor, governess and butler, and a domestic staff of some ten people, plus a regular succession of visitors – perhaps thirty in all.

No member of the Richmond family kept a journal, but, by chance, Spencer Madan, a well-educated and literate young man of good family, served as the boys' tutor in Brussels from September 1814 to December 1815, and wrote a series of letters to his family which describe life in the Richmond family in great detail.[9]

Richmond was an excellent runner and long-jumper, a horse-rider of repute, but above all a passionate cricketer. He excelled as a batsman and wicket-keeper, being reckoned to be 'first-class' standard for twenty-two years, and played at every possible opportunity. He and his friend, the Earl of Winchilsea (his second at the duel with the Duke of York) were instrumental in persuading Thomas Lord, the groundsman at an existing cricket field in central London, to open a new venue on the present-day site of Dorset Square. Lord opened his new ground in May 1787 and at one match Richmond met the Duke of York and the two men were reconciled. The ground was moved in 1809 to the present site in St John's Wood, but the name remains, as it always has been, Lord's.

All who knew him considered the fourth Duke of Richmond to be a genial and convivial man, who enjoyed nothing more than sitting with a group of friends into the small hours drinking, smoking cigars and exchanging news, views and stories. He was capable of great kindness and treated his younger sons' tutor, Spencer Madan, with great consideration, including him in family dinners and proposing him for membership of a Brussels gentleman's club. He also provided Madan with some protection against the worst rudenesses of the Duchess, although he could not be there all the time.

The Duchess

The Duke of Richmond may have been a relatively straightforward character, but his duchess, Charlotte, was a strange mixture, whose character, if mentioned in histories at all, is generally described as 'difficult'. Lady Charlotte Gordon (1768–1842) was the eldest daughter of Alexander, fourth Duke of Gordon and came of a line of feisty and forthright women. One example was her grandmother, Lady Catherine Gordon, who told her father, the second Earl of Aberdeen, that she intended to marry her cousin, the Duke of Gordon. Her father objected strongly and dispatched her under escort to the castle of her grandfather, the Duke of Atholl, for 'her protection', but Catherine escaped and got married anyway. She then judged that a head-on approach would be best and wrote her father a singularly uncompromising letter:

> My dear Father   September 3, 1741
> I beg to inform you that I was married this day to the Duke of Gordon. We propose in a few days to present ourselves at Haddo House, when I have no doubt we shall receive your blessing.

Charlotte's mother, Jane Maxwell, daughter of Sir William Maxwell, third Baron of Montieth, was famous for her beauty, great physical energy and forthrightness, coupled with the ability to speak to commoners without condescension or aloofness. She was a wild, precocious youngster, but well-educated in the best traditions of the Scottish Enlightenment. She met her future husband on what would be described today as a 'blind date' and they were soon in love and married, but without, on this occasion, the necessity of elopement. Jane bore her husband two sons and five daughters, but was on friendly relations with her husband's nine known illegitimate children (there may have been more), although she eventually moved to a separate house when his affair with his housekeeper's daughter became too intrusive.[10] She dealt with one potential difficulty in a characteristically forthright manner; one of each brood was named George (in honour of the king) so she simply described them as 'the Duke's George' and 'my George'. But he was not the only one to stray; on another occasion Jane assured one of her daughter's suitors that his beloved had 'not a drop of Gordon blood in her'.

Jane brought great energy to everything she did and was a skilled organiser, both in her family and in society at large. She was particularly keen on all things Scottish, including clothing, pipe music and, most importantly, dancing. One of her particular interests – which she shared with her husband – was the raising of the 100th Regiment of Foot in 1794. She rode to country fairs in the area wearing a Highland bonnet and regimental jacket, encouraging potential recruits to take the 'king's shilling' by placing a guinea between her lips and asking the young men to remove it with their teeth. Having been raised as the 100th Foot, the regiment was renumbered in 1798 as the 92nd Foot, but it was always better known as the 'Gordon Highlanders', not because it contained a large number of men bearing that name, but because it was a Highland regiment raised by the Duke of Gordon, and these links between the Gordon family and the Regiment were maintained for many years.

One of Jane greatest ambitions was to ensure that her daughters married well – and three of them duly became duchesses and another a marchioness.[11] Naturally her first thoughts were for her eldest daughter, Charlotte, and she took her to be presented at court and to see what London had to offer; she even made an attempt to make a match with William Pitt the Younger. That came to naught, but when Lieutenant-Colonel Charles Lennox arrived in Edinburgh on 21 July 1789, matters seem to have progressed at a breakneck speed, possibly with more help from nature than from the mother. Precisely when they first met is not known, although it might have been in London, but what is certain is that the 25-year-old Charles Lennox married Charlotte Gordon, then aged 21, on 9 September. The actual ceremony was performed in the Duchess of Gordon's dressing room, with the Duchess herself and two serving women as witnesses, and the fact that it had taken place was only publicly announced at a dinner party two days later. Thus, in a curious combination, the families of the ill-starred lovers of the previous generation were re-linked, as this was a case of Lady Sarah Bunbury's nephew marrying Lord William Gordon's niece

Jane separated from her husband in the 1790s. She visited the Richmonds twice during their time in Dublin in 1809 and 1811 and died in Pulteney's Hotel in London in April 1812 in the arms of her eldest daughter, Charlotte.

Charles and Charlotte Lennox were a fit, healthy and passionate couple, and she bore her husband fourteen children at almost annual intervals:

Child*	Date of Birth
Mary	15 August 1790
Charles	3 August 1791
Sarah	1792
George	3 October 1793
Georgiana	30 September 1795
Henry Adam**	6 September 1797
Jane	5 September 1798
William Pitt	20 September 1799
Frederick Seymour	24 January 1801
Sussex	11 June 1802
Louisa Maddalena	2 October 1803
Charlotte	4 December 1804
Arthur	2 October 1806
Sophia Georgiana	21 July 1809

Table I: Children of the Fourth Duke and Duchess of Richmond

It was not uncommon in those days for there to be miscarriages or for children to die in infancy, but it would appear that neither happened in Charlotte's case. Indeed, as will be described, her children seem to have been in far greater danger from family horseplay than from disease or pestilence.

Charlotte accompanied her husband to Hamilton in 1790–1 and to Ireland in 1792–4. It is not certain whether she went to the West Indies, but she definitely accompanied her husband to Ireland in 1806, where she

---

* On their father's succession to the dukedom in 1806, those children born prior to that event became Lord ... or Lady ..., according to gender, except for the eldest son, Charles, who became Earl of March.
**Lord Henry died as a midshipman whilst serving in HMS *Blake*. He fell from a mast and was drowned.

revelled in the power, influence and social kudos that accompanied the viceroy's post. One particular pleasure for the duchess was the presence in Ireland of the 2nd Battalion, 92nd Foot – her beloved Gordon Highlanders – and she called upon them on several occasions and also took her mother along during one of the latter's visits. However, she left the younger boys behind in London and there is no doubt that, without parental guidance, they rapidly got out of control.

The duchess was widely known in society as a difficult person, a good example being Madan's first interview with her, which started amicably enough, '. . . she received me in the most polite and civil manner possible, so that I felt myself at home immediately'. But then, 'after a short conversation her Grace observed that my bed was ready, that she dined at six, and that I probably had something to do . . . I took the hint and retired'.[12] The next day, however, Madan was summoned to Downing Street to meet Earl Bathurst, the Secretary for War and the Colonies, who was married to the Duke of Richmond's sister, Emily, and who proceeded to caution him '. . . against the temper of the Duchess generally, and in particular what she might say about the boys . . .'

The truth of Bathurst's remarks was quickly borne out, Madan remarking only a few days later:

> . . . she is one of the sourest most ill-tempered personages I ever came across in my life . . . a shade of ill-humour is superadded to her usual acidity of temper by the thoughts of going abroad, and every post brings her some news that she does not like . . . one day she was angry because she did not receive a letter from the Duke, another because she did.[13]

The duchess's reputation preceded her to Brussels, Lady Caroline Capel telling her mother on 7 October 1814:

> . . . the D[uche]ss is not yet arrived but is daily expected, I am afraid not with the feelings of delight which the arrival of a Wife and Mother ought to occasion. But her Temper is dreadful, tho' there is no denying that she has just cause for complaint.[14]

Unfortunately, that last enigmatic remark is never explained.

The duchess was, without any doubt, a serious snob, who was as ambitious for her daughters as her mother had been for her. Thus, according to a lady's maid working for the family, the duchess had told her older daughters that they were not to dance or talk too familiarly with any gentleman without a title, and preferably nobody less than a duke or a lord. Had she been asked, the duchess would almost certainly have added that even with the correct titles it was essential that any suitor should also have money. On the other hand, she clearly valued friends and in the correspondence of Sir Robert Peel in the British Library there are many letters from her written in a friendly way and regularly asking for news of mutual acquaintances. She also took some trouble to call on Lady Frances Wedderburn-Webster during the latter's visit to London in 1818.

During her time in Brussels the duchess clearly made great efforts to get to know the Belgian aristocracy and to include them in her dinner parties and balls. Some British ladies were undoubtedly stand-offish and rude about the Belgians behind their backs, but, whatever her other faults, the duchess seems to have kept well clear of such churlish behaviour.

There are occasional contemporary references to the duchess's liking for gambling, Joseph Farrington, for example, stating in 1819 that, '. . . the Duchess . . . has ruined him [the Duke] by gaming. He paid £30,000 to Marshal Prince Blücher which She lost to Him.'[15] This was not an excessive sum by contemporary standards – in 1804 the Hon. John Capel was found to have debts of £20,000[16] – but it was folly indeed to incur such debts at a time when the family was already seriously short of money.

Madan noted that she was a woman of contradictions. On some occasions she was extremely stingy and economised drastically in normal household expenses, but on others she wasted what appeared to him to be huge amounts on useless trinkets. Then, in her dealings with him, she was sometimes extremely rude and hostile, but she could also be very kind and considerate; thus, Madan, like many others, never quite knew where he stood with her.

The Children

The Richmond's eldest son, Captain the Earl of March, 52nd Foot, had followed his grandfather and father into the Army. He went to the Peninsula with the 13th Light Dragoons, and was then selected to be assistant military secretary and ADC to Wellington from 1810 to 1814. He went as a volunteer with the storming party at the siege of Ciudad Rodrigo – his companions in the adventure were the Prince of Orange and Lord Fitzroy Somerset. He then exchanged into the 52nd Foot and was with them at the battle of Orthez (27 February 1814) where he was hit by a bullet which lodged in his chest and could not be recovered. Despite this wound he remained in the service and was appointed extra ADC to his erstwhile fellow ADC, the Prince of Orange. The wound gave him continuing problems and Maria Capel reported in September 1814 that he '. . . still has a ball in him from the effects of which he has not recovered, but faints at the least transition from heat to cold'. Once his father had established himself at his house in the Rue de la Blanchisserie, March was given his own residence in a small house within the same grounds. He was a popular young man, liked by all who knew him.

Lieutenant Lord George Lennox, the Richmond's second son was a lieutenant in the 9th Light Dragoons, and had been one of Wellington's ADCs for some time. The other son in uniform was Lieutenant Lord William Pitt Lennox, who was ADC to Major-General Peregrine Maitland but had suffered a serious fall whilst racing at Enghien in April 1815. His injuries were such that he was thought at first to be dead, but he recovered, although Maitland refused to take him back until he was fully fit and found a temporary replacement, Ensign James, Lord Hay, borrowed from the 1st Foot Guards.

The Richmonds had seven daughters. On their arrival in Brussels the three eldest – Lady Mary (23), Lady Sarah (22) and Lady Georgiana (20) – played an adult role in the social events in the city. They were universally held to be charming and attractive young women, although their father disapproved strongly of their predilection for the waltz. The three youngest – Lady Louisa (11), Lady Charlotte (10) and Lady Sophia (5) – were too young for such adult pursuits and were looked after by a governess known as 'Mademoiselle'. That left Lady Jane (16) who was stuck somewhere in the middle. Spencer Madan was loud in their praises, telling his parents that they, '. . . are the most good-humoured unaffected girls I have ever met with, exceedingly highbred but without an atom of pride. They do not deserve to be coupled with the D(uche)ss, whom they resemble but in name.'[17]

When the tutor, Spencer Madan, took up his post on 9 September 1814, he was faced by Lord Frederick (aged 13), who had attended Westminster School for five years, but to little apparent benefit, Lord Sussex (12), who despite his brother, Lord Henry's, death was due to go to sea the following year, and Lord Arthur (8).

These younger Lennox boys were almost out of control and before they had even left London Madan had a number of adventures with them. On the first night he was there, a servant came to tell him that Lords Frederick and Sussex were in the kitchen throwing everything about and making such a riot that no servant could live in the house, while on another day they threw a ball at the bells in the passage, causing the servants to rush to answer calls which had not been made. Then on 13 September Frederick, Sussex and Arthur climbed over the railings separating the garden from the River Thames and slid down onto a coal-barge; Madan recovered them and gave them a telling off, but the next day Lord Arthur did the same thing again but this time miscalculated and fell into the mud, where he was quickly submerged up to his chin and had to be rescued by two bargees. The next day their aunt, Lady Bathurst, very misguidedly gave them £1 which they used to buy a brace of pistols and some gunpowder, but fortunately this was discovered before any damage was done!

The Journey to Brussels

The party set out on Wednesday 28 September, with the duchess in charge of a party of eighteen people in two carriages. The first carried the duchess, Ladies Georgiana, Jane, Louisa and Charlotte, and the duchess's maid, Mrs Smith, inside, and Mr Johnson, the butler, and the coachman outside. The second carriage, a barouche landau, carried Lady Sophia and her maid, plus Madan and the three boys (and a large number of parcels) inside, while outside were M. Gillet, who had been sent over from Brussels by the duke to make the payments during the journey, plus two lady's maids and the coachman.

This immense party took two days to reach Dover, where they were forced by adverse winds to wait until Wednesday 5 October before sailing aboard the Royal Navy sloop, HMS *Redpole*, which had been arranged by the duke. They sailed at noon and arrived off Boulogne at 8pm, but were so eager to leave the pitching and tossing ship that the duchess insisted on going ashore in rowing boats. On landing, however, they found that it was low tide, so they had to walk several miles along the beach to the nearest inn. After an arduous journey, they arrived in Brussels on Friday 14 October where the duke and his two elder daughters were waiting for them.

Madan makes much of the difficulties of the journey and of the behaviour of the duchess and there can be no doubt that on occasions she was decidedly eccentric. However, she must have been sorry to leave England and the London social scene and felt humiliated by the fact that they were leaving the country for 'economical' reasons. Further, little in her previous life can have prepared her for being in personal charge of such a large and disparate group on a long journey, which included crossing the Channel.

NOTES

1 The family name was usually spelt Lenox in the early 19th century and changed to Lennox sometime later. To avoid confusion, I have standardised on the more recent spelling.

2 Napier, General Sir William Francis Patrick, *History of the War in the Peninsula and in the south of France, from the year 1807 to the year 1814*, London, 1834.

3 The 35th was subsequently redesignated 35th (Sussex) Regiment in 1805.

4 Captain of a Company in One of the Regiments of Guards, *A Short Review of the Recent Affair of Honor between His Royal Highness the Duke of York and Lieutenant Colonel Lenox, with free and impartial strictures and comments upon the circumstances attending to it*, p. 26.

5 Ibid.

6 Letter Richmond–Bathurst dated Bruxelles, April 10, 1815. BL. Loan 57. NRA 20952. 57/9 f. 970

7 Capel Letters, p. 57.

8   Ibid., p. 71.
9   *Spencer and Waterloo*, the Letters of Spencer Madan.
10 Named Jean Christie, she bore him several children during Duchess Jane's lifetime and the duke married her in 1820.
11 Lady Susan, who became the Duchess of Manchester, eventually ran off with a footman, leaving behind two sons and six daughters. She was divorced by her husband, and emigrated to Australia – but that is another story.
12 Madan, p. 12.
13 Madan, pp. 23–4.
14 Capel Letters, p. 72.
15 *The Diary of Joseph Farrington* (ed. Kathryn Cave), Yale University Press, 1984, Vol. XV, p. 5210.
16 Capel Letters, p. 25.
17 Madan, p. 53.

CHAPTER III

The English Arrive

The great majority of the English civilians arriving in Belgium in 1814–15 had been confined to their homeland since the end of the 'Short Peace' in 1803, and for them the legendary 'Grand Tour' was but a distant memory. Some of the military had served in the infamous Walcheren expedition of 1809, but that had been farther north, and the majority were either newly-joined recruits, or were veterans more familiar with the Peninsula and Mediterranean countries. Thus, Belgium was a source of amazement to all and many letters and journals are full of wondering descriptions of this strange land and its quaint people.

For most of these travellers, the voyage across the English Channel was their first experience of the sea and was undertaken in small sailing ships, whose motion was upsetting for all but the steadiest stomachs. Indeed, generations of cross-Channel travellers will sympathise with Captain John Gray of the 10th Hussars, who was sick almost continuously from Ramsgate to Ostend. At one point he called out to enquire: 'How much longer before we get in?' and when he was told, 'Twenty minutes,' uttered the pitiful reply, 'Then I'm a dead man!'

Even when the vessel reached the far shore, the excitements were not over, as there were few port facilities. Arriving off Ostend on 11 April, Captain Cavalié Mercer was astonished when the pilot aimed their vessel straight at the jetty below the glacis wall of the town's defences, and was even more surprised when, as they hit the jetty, a rope was thrown ashore to be caught by a squad of soldiers. All became clear, however, when the soldiers used the rope, first, to prevent the ship falling back onto a sandbank and then to tow it farther until it could be beached alongside other newly-arrived vessels. Many, even people as exalted as the Duchess of Richmond and her family, were taken ashore by rowing boat and dumped unceremoniously on the beach, where they were left to find their own way to the nearest inn or coaching station.

Once ashore, the most popular form of travel was by canal, where huge horse-drawn barges conveyed large numbers – up to 200 in some cases – with what for the day was remarkable speed and comfort. Thus, Sergeant Wheeler's battalion (51st Foot) was wafted from Ostend to Bruges, and after a short stop, on again to Ghent, whence they marched to Brussels. To infantrymen all too used to going everywhere on foot this was, indeed, a blissful experience and as Wheeler remarked: 'Being old campaigners we made the most of the good things fortune threw our way, knowing from past experience that her ladyship is a fickle dame.'[1] Cavalry units and the artillery travelled of necessity by road. But, whatever the mode, it is clear from the various officers' and soldiers' accounts that there was an efficient and well-oiled machine operated by the Quartermaster-General's department, which ensured that units arriving at the various ports were moved rapidly and efficiently to their allocated cantonments near the border with France, with accommodation, rations and fodder available at regular intervals along the route.

Many civilians travelled by coach along the *chaussée* towards Brussels. They admired the paved road, which seemed to be one unending avenue of tall trees stretching as far as the eye could see, while on either side the aspect was peaceful and untroubled, the countryside covered with neat cottages, scattered hamlets and small farmhouses, and in the summer months the fields were filled with a tall, luxuriant crop of corn. The sight was idyllic; almost all the peasants wore rough clothes and sabots, working in the fields or at household chores, while the children went barefoot and bareheaded, and ran alongside the carriages turning cartwheels as they went.

Once beyond Alost, the landscape was no longer absolutely flat but became both slightly undulating and even richer. Finally, they reached Brussels, whose outskirts, like any large town's, were somewhat grubby but soon the tourists found themselves among fine looking houses in narrow, bustling streets. To the wondering English, everything was strange: the people, their appearance, their dress, the houses, the shops – even the fact that the signs were in French astonished them, a language most had met (if at all) only in plays, books or the schoolroom.

One of the major causes for remark by virtually all English travellers was the Catholic nature of the land. There were many churches and to those who knew only England there seemed to be a lot of priests, although the soldiers who had served in the Peninsula thought that by Spanish standards there were remarkably few! Most English ventured into at least one Roman church, which they considered to be very ornate by Protestant standards, although what struck many most forcibly were the people making oral confessions.

Harriet Capel wrote to her grandmother in July 1814 about the annual grand fête given in celebration of St Francis, patron saint of Brussels:

> . . . [the statue] had been previously traipsed round the town with the most astonishing pomp & splendour. We followed the procession the whole way, having first attended the Grand Mass in the Chapel – The

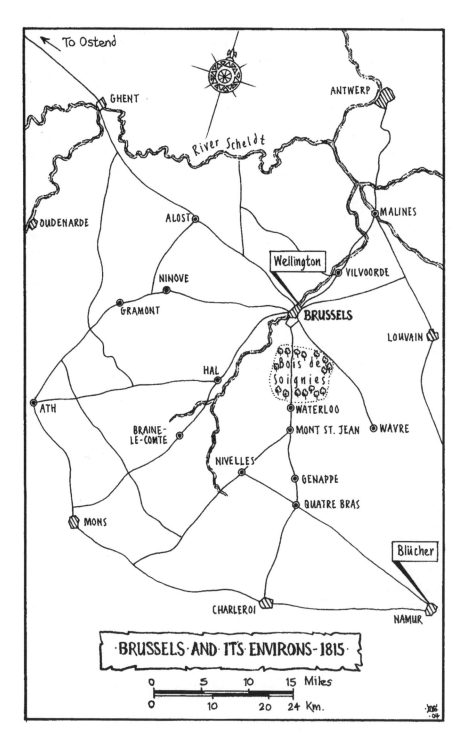

To Ostend

GHENT

ANTWERP

River Scheldt

MALINES

OUDENARDE

ALOST

Wellington

NINOVE

VILVOORDE

GRAMONT

BRUSSELS

LOUVAIN

Bois de Soignies

HAL

WATERLOO

ATH

BRAINE-LE-COMTE

MONT ST. JEAN

WAVRE

NIVELLES

GENAPPE

MONS

QUATRE BRAS

Blücher

CHARLEROI

NAMUR

·BRUSSELS·AND·ITS·ENVIRONS-1815·

0   5   10   15 Miles

0   10   20   24 Km.

service the music – the Cathedral – the magnificent habits of the Priests was certainly most impressive, but when it came to the procession in the open air, the folly of it really made one quite melancholy – the image of his Saintship had above 50,000 pounds worth of jewels upon it – he had a canopy of massive silver, trimmed with gold over his head – this was supported by 8 priests, & was preceded by about a hundred more carrying torches, all glittering with gold & jewels – St Francis marched to military music – there certainly never was so incongruous a medley – there was an alternate march or waltz from the Belgic band, and a hymn or Psalm from the Priests, & every five minutes, the whole cavalcade halted, the People (with whom the streets were lined) popt down on their knees in the mud – the Priests crossed themselves, & the last not least, poor old General Vincent (who by the bye was the principal performer) knelt down in a regular way, & prayed to the Virgin in a most audible voice for the good of the public.[2]

At that time Brussels was still a walled city, and for visitors it seemed to burst into sight as one approached, dominated by the immense twin towers of the Cathedral of St Michel and St Gudule. In the centre of the city they came across the Grande Place and the splendid Hôtel de Ville, and then wound their way up along La Montagne de la Cour to the high town of Brussels. At the summit there was the lightness, gaiety, and beauty of the Parc, which was quite unlike an English park, being a large rectangular piece of ground, enclosed by iron railings, and laid out with gravel walks between grass plots, shaded by trees, and ornamented with fountains and statues. It was only for promenading – horses were banned – and in the centre was a kiosk selling refreshments. It was surrounded by a wide street and enclosed on three sides by magnificent houses built of the finest freestone and on the fourth side by the old city wall, which dated back to 1044. It was generally rated by the English to be finer than any square in London, Edinburgh or Dublin.

Many visitors approached the city along l'Alée Verte, a mile-and-a-half long promenade by the banks of the Willebroeck Canal flanked by stately elms, whose branches had been trained to meet to form an archway. The water was usually covered by brightly-painted barges and the wide roads on either bank were crowded with carriages, riders and walkers.

Many of the English officers and soldiers were accommodated in civilian houses and the great majority of those were looked after exceedingly well. According to the Belgians, the British (and, in particular, the Scots) were ideal guests, being courteous and paying for everything, and were certainly preferred to the French of years gone by, while anyone was preferred to the Prussians, who were universally unpopular. Barrack-masters were charged with arranging billets for the troops; they worked in conjunction with the local mayor or magistrate and generally did their job fairly. If, however, a civilian made trouble or tried to refuse to take his fair share, then the barrackmaster took his revenge by allocating the more unpleasant soldiers to the house, and lots of them.

All visitors seemed to be obliged to visit the notorious 'manneken-pis' conveniently near the Grande Place, on the junction of rue de l'Etuve and rue de Chene. Then, as today, it attracted reactions ranging from amusement to shock; indeed, some years previously King Louis XIV of France had gone so far as to present the Brussels authorities with a rich set of special clothing to enable the infant to present a more decent appearance on ceremonial occasions.

NOTES
1   Letters of Private Wheeler, p. 160.
2   Capel Letters, pp. 53–4

CHAPTER IV
Brussels: 1814–March 1815

The events leading up to the Ball can conveniently be divided into three phases: from early 1814 to March 1815, from April to 14 June 1815, and the day of the Ball itself, the 15th. The first period began with Napoleon's first abdication on 11 April 1814 and his departure for Elba, news of which spread across Europe like wildfire. One of the many consequences was that English families, which had long been prevented from visiting 'the Continent', began to cross the Channel in droves. Many headed for Paris or the German spas, but a number went to Brussels, a city which offered two great advantages: it was within relatively easy travelling distance of London, and the cost of living was very low.

Among the earliest arrivals was the Capel family, who reached the city in June 1814. The Hon. John Capel (1769–1819), second son of the fourth Earl of Essex, was married to Lady Caroline Paget (1773–1847) and at the time of their arrival they had two sons and ten daughters. Once in Brussels, Lady Caroline and her eldest daughters wrote regular letters to Caroline's mother, the Dowager Lady Uxbridge, which gave a valuable insight into life in Brussels, and which, fortunately for posterity, have been preserved.[1]

The English colony soon discovered that the city possessed several additional advantages. One was that it was a convenient stopping-off point on the main routes between the Channel ports and places such as Hanover and the German spas, thus guaranteeing a constant stream of visitors, with whom news and gossip could be exchanged. Another was the presence of the English garrison which not only provided smart young officers to grace the parties, but also proved remarkably useful with help in such tiresome matters as transport. In addition, all except the most insular also started to make friends with their equals among the Bruxellois. As a result, there was soon an energetic social life and in July, for example, the presence of the Hereditary Prince of Orange encouraged private dinners and dances in his honour on three successive nights, the first given by Lady Capel, the second by Lady Mountnorris and the third by Lady Waterpark.

Nor was dancing the only social pastime, as official levees, picnics, assemblies, horse races, routs and dinner parties followed one after another at a breathtaking pace as the English families took full advantage of a lifestyle which they simply could not have afforded at home. The Reverend G G Stonestreet, chaplain to the Guards Division, described the goings-on to a friend in England, estimating that the English colony, excluding the military, was some 1,500 strong, and that the top echelon of this society of 'about seven or eight titles' kept the others at a distance. For all of them, however, '. . . the Theatre and Balls seem to constitute the greatest happiness of these people. There is scarcely a single quiet evening with a good family . . .'[2]

At the pinnacle of Brussels society were the three Princes of Orange: the Sovereign Prince William and his two sons, the eldest, the Hereditary Prince William Frederick, always known as William, and the younger, also Prince William Frederick, known as Frederick. Formally, they were known by their correct titles, but the English had a variety of nicknames for the first two, who were sometimes known behind their backs as 'the old frog' and the 'young frog', while the Hereditary Prince was also known to his English military friends as 'slim Billy' and to the English civilians in Brussels as '*Oranje boven*', the title of the Dutch national anthem. Both father and elder son were based in their traditional Dutch homes in the Hague, but travelled regularly to Brussels, where the Hereditary Prince was a constant feature of the city's social life, particularly with the English community. He had good reason for such visits as he was in command of all troops in the country, which included the English garrison, and held the rank of lieutenant-general in the British Army, which uniform he wore to the virtual exclusion of all others.

For many months the future of the former Austrian Netherlands was far from clear and there was a succession of wild rumours. One party yearned for a return to French rule and another wanted the country to become part of England, with the Duke of Cambridge marrying the Duchess of Oldenburg and ruling in Brussels as viceroy. A variation on the latter rumour was that, in return, the English king would transfer Hanover to the Dutch crown. There were even some (but not all that many) who wanted the country to be united with the Netherlands and it was in pursuit of that plan that in September 1814 the Sovereign Prince of Orange established the palace at Laeken as his Brussels residence. However, the prince still spent most of his time in The Hague, so he established a separate council of state for Belgium, to which he appointed three ministers who, to the surprise of the English, were known Bonapartists.

Balls

Balls took place with great regularity, sometimes two or three in a week, and often several on the same night. There were four main types, the first,

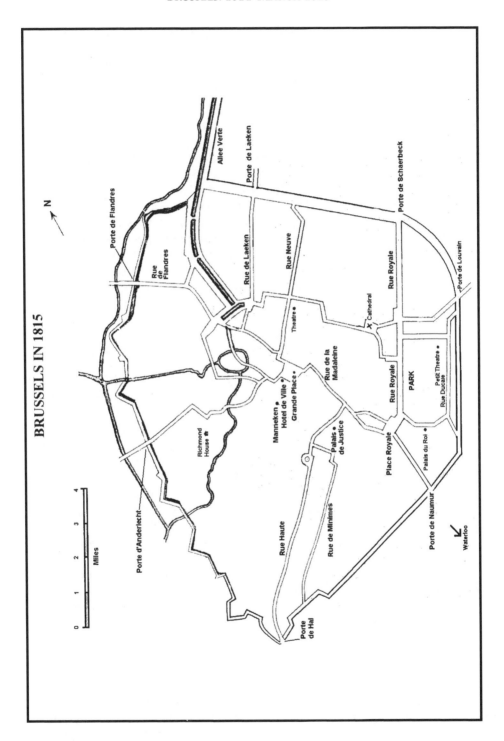

BRUSSELS IN 1815

and usually the largest and most lavish, being the official balls. These were held to mark a particular occasion such as a royal birthday, and were hosted by someone of the stature of the mayor of Brussels or the British ambassador. Guests were a mixture of civil and military dignitaries and those highly placed on the English and Belgian social ladder. The second type were private balls hosted by a particular person, who both paid for the entire evening and set the guest list; the Duchess of Richmond, for example, held a 'rout' for some 200 people on 12 November. The third type was organised by a group of ladies and an entrance fee was charged, one example being that held on 1 November 1814 under the patronage of the Duchess of Richmond, Lady Greville, the Duchesse de Beaufort and the Marquise d'Assche; tickets cost one Napoleon each.

The fourth type, 'subscription balls', were a feature of the winter months. Such events had been a popular feature of English society since the beginning of the nineteenth century and were intended to ensure a regular programme of entertainment without exorbitant expense for hostesses. A committee set the dates (usually a fixed day in each month) and made all the arrangements such as obtaining a ballroom, providing music and refreshments, and setting the price of the subscription. This was not all, however; the committee also determined the eligibility of applicants, ensured that 'suitable' newcomers were invited to join, that visitors (also 'suitable') passing through the city were given an oppor-tunity to attend, and, of course, ruthlessly excluded those considered 'undesirable'. The first was held on Saturday 10 December and caused some tension, as some of the English ladies

> ... caused great discontent to Belgian Cavaliers because we all refused them and pleaded engagements when they asked us to dance, and wrong as I know this was, you will I am sure allow & agree with us in saying that it is a great Bore to dance the whole Evening with Creatures who look like Shoemakers and Tallow Chandlers and with whom we are not acquainted even by sight, much less by name, for it is not the fashion to wait for an introduction.

Somebody clearly took these ladies to task, as the same writer continued, '... however we have all promised compliance at next Saturday's Ball'.[3]

The ladies were particularly enthusiastic about the balls, which generally ended at about 4 am, the Duchess of Richmond having the reputation of going early and staying late; she was rumoured to require at the most four hours sleep per night. The Rev. Stonestreet, however, took a characteristically jaundiced view of the behaviour at such balls.

> Whenever they get together the severest etiquette is present. The women on entering always salute on each side of the cheek; they then

set [sic] down as stiff as waxworks. They begin a Ball with a *perfect froideur* they go on with their *dangerous* waltz (in which all the Englishwomen join) and finish with the Gallopade, a completely indecent and violent romp.[4]

The waltz was, indeed, very popular. Apart from during the 'short peace' England had been cut off from continental ways and fashions for over twenty years, and in 1814 its dancing was still deeply rooted in the eighteenth century. As a result, foreigners looked at English dancing with a very critical eye, a German condemning it disdainfully as '. . . *charakterloses Getrippel, etwas pferdetrottmässiges, um ein recht plumpes Ding mit einem recht plumpen Worte zu bezeichnen*' (characterless tripping, something like a horse-trot – to call a coarse thing by a coarse name).

The waltz had its roots in a Teutonic country dance known as the *Ländler* and had steadily gained in popularity. By the early nineteenth century the centre of the waltz was Vienna, which possessed some huge dance halls dedicated almost exclusively to the waltz; the Apollo Palace, for example, contained five large and thirty-one smaller dancing rooms in which some 6,000 people at a time could dance the night away.

England held out against this fashion, which was both 'foreign' and new, longer than anywhere else. It was certainly being danced at some balls in 1790/1, but the upper echelons of society were resolutely opposed to it and when it was demonstrated at Almack's in 1812, the act of physically holding one's partner in public created such a scandal that even *The Times* felt moved to protest. Indeed, Lord Byron, who was certainly no stickler for decorum, described a couple waltzing as being 'like two cockchafers spitted on the same bodkin' and went on:

> Waltz – Waltz alone – both legs and arms demand,
> Liberal of feet, and lavish of her hands;
> Hands which may freely range in public sight
> Where ne'er before – but – pray 'put out the light'.

> ....thy subtler art,
> Intoxicates alone the heedless heart;
> Through the full veins thy gentler poison swims,
> And wakes to wantoness the willing limbs.[5]

Regardless of what went on at home, the English colony in Brussels could not escape this new phenomenon and were dancing it in the summer of 1814, mainly because of Belgium's long links with Austria, which were resurrected briefly between March and August. As Caroline Capel wrote at the time: '. . . the [Belgian] dancing however is beautiful, at least in the Women; the Men are all like a set of dancing masters – and dance as much

31

too well, as most of our Country Men dance too ill . . .'[6] and, of course, what the Belgians – both men and women – were dancing was the waltz and her daughter, Georgiana, was waltzing with the Hereditary Prince of Orange in July. There was some resistance from the older generation and, immediately following his arrival, the Duke of Richmond refused his daughters permission to join in this scandalous pastime; like so many fathers before and since, he was fighting a losing battle and was soon forced to admit defeat. Soon, even the English children were waltzing, with Jane Capel, aged 15, being described by her mother as 'very pretty & Waltzes very well'. Indeed, the influence of this dance was so pervasive that when Captain Samuel Burgess, the acknowledged beau of the 1st Foot Guards, was about to have his leg amputated after Waterloo, he announced in a tone of infinite regret: 'I fear this will cut short my waltzing.'

Special Occasions

Special occasions, such as investitures or anniversaries, were always good excuses for a party. In August 1814, for example, there were four major events in the course of two weeks. The first was the Prince Regent's birthday (12 August), which was marked by a magnificent parade, with British soldiers lining the perimeter of the park to fire a deafening and exciting *feu de joie*. The celebration was given added interest by the presence of the Duke of Wellington, who was passing through Brussels on his way to take up his post as British ambassador in Paris, while the British ambassador at The Hague, Lord Clancarty, came to Brussels to organise a ball for some 500 guests.

Only four days later the celebrations were for the Duke of York's birthday:

> . . . *The Guards* gave a Ball & Supper in the handsomest way possible – The Public Rooms in which it took place are really beautiful. The Dancing Room is as long as the Gallery at Beaudesert, brilliantly lighted, & two Collonades of Yellow Marble Pillars hung with Flowers extend the length of the Room. At the Top of the Room was a place raised 10 steps, furnished with Blue & Silver Turkish Couches – a Representation of *Peace* in the Centre. The Walls were hung with Banners, Standards & other Military Trophies which had a very good effect. The Supper Room was fitted up with Scenes to represent a Wood & hung with Flowers & lights . . .[7]

The Belgians were not to be outdone by these British celebrations and also held large parties. On 24 August the City of Brussels gave a Ball for the Sovereign Prince of Orange on his birthday. Two days later the Duke of

Cambridge and Lord Castlereagh, who were on their way to Hanover and Vienna respectively, visited Brussels in order to invest the Sovereign Prince of Orange with the Order of the Garter and the Hereditary Prince with the Order of the Bath. This was done at a grand ceremony where the Duke of Cambridge wore his full ceremonial robes, exciting the admiration of the Belgians, particularly the ladies. That night the two princes threw a grand ball to mark the occasion.

Yet another celebration took place on 18 November to mark the occasion of the birthday of the Princess of Orange, the wife of the Sovereign Prince. Again, the town was illuminated, there was a large military parade at which troops of the King's German Legion fired a *feu de joie,* and Mr St George, the British chargé d'affaires, gave a Grand Ball.

On 1 February the anniversary of the Allied entry into Brussels was celebrated with a *Te Deum* in the cathedral, an artillery salute, and a parade with troops from the Guards Brigade, the Hanoverian Hussars, and detachments from newly formed Belgian cavalry and infantry units. It goes without saying that there was a celebration ball in the evening!

Only a few days later, the Hereditary Prince threw a Grand Masqued Ball and the preparations occupied the intended guests and their servants for the preceding two weeks. The highlight of the ball was a quadrille involving no fewer than thirty-two people, carefully chosen and dressed in identical costumes. Naturally, the Hereditary Prince was personally involved and took part in the constant practice, which lasted for several days before the event.

Other Events

In July 1814 Lord Lynedoch, the English garrison commander, organised a grand picnic in the Forêt de Soigny, a large wood lying just south of Brussels and through which ran the road to Waterloo, a village whose name meant absolutely nothing to any of them at the time. The party was organised with military precision by the general's staff, and as there were twenty-six carriages, it appears that there must have been around a hundred guests, of whom the principal was the Hereditary Prince of Orange who was about to take command from Lord Lynedoch. It was a lovely day and the site was carefully chosen, with tents on a hillock overlooking a small lake. The regimental band of the 52nd Foot played a musical accompaniment, with the horn players scattered around the wood to heighten the effect. A very pleasant day out ended with Lord Lynedoch organising the carriages into a convoy and then leading them around the forest, finally reaching Brussels in the moonlight.

There was a wolf hunt (*Grande Chasse*) in early February 1815, organised by the Duke of Richmond, the Hon. Mr Capel and the Belgian Duc de Beaufort, who also made two of his Ardennes châteaux available to the hunters. Prussian cavalrymen served as escorts to the hunters and local villagers acted as beaters; the hunters killed six boars, one wolf and many smaller animals, all of which were put on public display in Brussels on their return.

One of the British Army's enduring passions was for fox-hunting, which had been energetically pursued in the Peninsula whenever the opportunity offered, but in Belgium even the intrepid British had to admit defeat. In the first place, the farmers could not understand the propriety of a large number of horsemen and hounds charging across their land and crops, as a result of which the Hereditary Prince, who was an enthusiastic participant, had to pay large sums in compensation for alleged damage. A greater problem, however, was that the local foxes declined to run when put up by the hounds, which completely spoilt the thrill of the chase. This was, Lieutenant Basil Jackson declared (tongue-in-cheek) because the '. . . Belgian foxes had no idea they were to run before the hounds, not being trained, I presume, to do so from birth like our own'.[8] Having failed in the open country, the would-be hunters tried the Forêt de Sognies, but when the foxes again refused to run, they gave up in disgust.

Horse racing was a constant feature of the Brussels social calendar, with, as in so many other spheres, the Duke of Richmond very much to the fore, both as senior steward and as an owner. The military were particularly enthusiastic, with Guards officers riding many of the entries, usually their own chargers, but with the young Prince of Orange again taking part. Races were held on 14 September, 10 October and 5 November, all at Brussels.

A much valued part of the social scene was the theatre, in which plays and concerts were regularly performed. Highlights were when famous English stars such as Mrs Jordan stayed in the city to give a few performances and to fill the houses.

Nor were the children forgotten. In November 1814 Lady Caroline Capel organised a concert performed by her own children, supported by Major Dawson and Miss Arden, daughter of Lady Alvanley. A number of Belgian and Dutch guests were invited to listen to Handel's music, which the English thought to be seriously under-appreciated by foreigners. Then on 30 November Lady Alvanley gave a dance for children, to which Lady Capel took no fewer than nine children. The Hereditary Prince, who seems to have put in an appearance at *every* party, not only attended but also joined in the quadrille and country dances.

Personal Relations with Belgians

Personal relations between the English and the Belgians seem to have been reasonably amicable at all levels, and the army officers and soldiers found that in almost all cases their involuntary hosts were pleasant and welcoming. At the top levels of society, some close friendships were formed, notably between the Capels and the Beaufort and d'Oultremont families, and between the Richmonds and the d'Assche family. Despite these contacts, many of the English were initially determined that they would strive to maintain their Englishness, which included their dress, language and social customs, although this sometimes had its disadvantages, as, for example, when insistence on leaving windows open, as was the custom in England, resulted in a spate of thefts.

The continental habits of kissing and seemingly continuous bowing caused some English mirth, while the different timings for meals and of arrival at and departure from social events took some getting used to. Soon after her arrival, Harriet Capel was assuring her grandmother: '. . . we reject every innovation even of the most trifling nature that in the slightest degree swerves from English dress, manners, or sentiments . . .'[9] Some, however, went to the opposite extreme, Lieutenant the Hon. Hastings Forbes of the 3rd Foot Guards being taken to task for becoming,

> . . . so completely foreignised that except by his language he might be taken for one, his Dress is quite à la francais, which as it is totally unlike the other officers of his Regiment, has given great discontent, and I think it a pity that some Friend should not tell him so.[10]

Religion

By far the most predominant religion among the English was Church of England and the English civilians in Brussels were served by the Reverend G G Stonestreet, the chaplain to the Guards Brigade, who was assisted by a sergeant in the Guards as his clerk. Stonestreet conducted Sunday worship and other ceremonies, such as baptisms and weddings, for both the military and civilian communities. The English viewed the Catholic churches and customs with some astonishment, and from 1 to 7 February 1815 most of them encountered carnival for the first time. Their reaction was reflected by Captain Bowles: '. . . the people are masquerading it & making fools of themselves to their heart's content. John Bull looks and wonders what the joke is.'[11] These pre-Lenten festivities provoked a number of duels and Hastings Forbes (he of the frenchified dress) was on the point of fighting one, although it seems never have come to the point.

In February the English visitors were treated to a much more macabre entertainment in the form of a public execution in the Grande Place. They were used to public hangings at home, but what made this much more interesting was that it was done using the French machine of which they had heard so much over the past twenty-two years – the guillotine. Four men were brought to the Grande Place in a tumbrel to be executed for murder, and three went to their deaths quickly and relatively quietly, but one added interest to the proceedings by singing, dancing and shouting, and then, to everyone's surprise, he was led into the Hôtel de Ville for further questioning, apparently in the hope of extracting a confession from him. When, after two hours, this had proved to be of no avail he was led out again, still shouting and mocking the priest at his side, and was duly executed.[12]

In July 1814 daily prices were very low: a pound loaf of bread cost the equivalent of one-and-a-half English pence and a bottle of claret just two shillings, all of which led Spencer Madan to describe living there as 'cheap as dirt'. By December, however, the exchange rate with the English currency was at such a very low ebb that Lady Capel described how '. . . every one is wanting money & nobody can bear to draw for it till the last extremity'. But the exchange rate was even worse in Paris and Lady Francis Bentinck arrived in Brussels to find somewhere more affordable. The following month the Rev. Stonestreet complained that 'an influx of English into Brussels, about 1500 not military, has deprived us of many of the advantages otherwise derived from our residence here. Expenses of all sorts have increased . . .'

One feature of life for the English families at the top of the social tree was the willingness of the Army and Navy to make life more pleasant for them. Mention has already been made of the cross-Channel passage for the Duchess of Richmond and family aboard a naval vessel, but the Army also helped its friends. Thus, when the Capels' baggage was lost, the Army found it for them and then provided four baggage wagons to bring it to Brussels, and later, when the Capels moved from one house to another in Brussels, the Army again provided the wagons. The Capels also made friends with Lieutenant-Colonel Lindsey, commanding officer of the 78th Regiment (the Seaforth Highlanders), with the result that the civilian family was able to have the services of the regimental pipe band whenever they asked for it.[13] A rather more unusual use of the military was to smuggle dutiable items, such as ladies' dresses and Brussels lace, into England, the hope being that their military uniforms would get them past the eagle-eyed customs officers at the Channel ports.

The Last Days of Peace

On 24 February the news reached Brussels that the Congress of Vienna had agreed to the union of the former United Provinces and the former Austrian Netherlands in a new Kingdom of the Netherlands and that the Sovereign Prince would become King William I. Two days later this was celebrated in a solemn *Te Deum* in the cathedral and a large military parade. The English community partied on, although a few, at least, of the stricter Belgian Catholics curtailed their social activities somewhat during Lent, but all were looking forward to Easter. A major concern among many in the English civilian community, however, was that as peace became more secure and lasting political settlements were made, the regiments of the English garrison would be posted away, depriving them of the central core of their social life.

But, unknown to all of them until many days later, an event took place elsewhere which dramatically altered the situation in Brussels for civilian inhabitants and military garrison alike, for Napoleon escaped from his exile on Elba on 28 February and landed at the Golfe de Jouan on 1 March. Suddenly, Brussels would no longer be a political backwater, but would find itself, instead, in the front line of the renewed European war – indeed, it would shortly become the first target of the dictator seeking to restore his empire and thus one of the most important strategic places in Europe. One thing that did not change, however, was the parties, which would continue right up to the last minute.

NOTES

1   They were published as 'The Capel Letters' (Cape, London, 1955).
2   Letter Rev. G G Stonestreet to G Trower, Esq., Brussels 11 January 1815. BL Add MS 61805.
3   Capel Letters, p. 79.
4   Stonestreet, op. cit.
5   'The Waltz, an Apostrophic Hymn' in *The Works of the Rt Hon. Lord Byron*, pp. 113–19.
6   Capel Letters, p. 66.
7   Capel Letters p. 67.
8   Basil Jackson, *Notes and Reminiscences of a Staff Officer*, p.6.
9   Capel Letters, p. 52.
10 Capel Letters, p. 79. Forbes was the second son of the sixth Earl of Granard. He attended the Ball on 15 June and was killed at Waterloo on 18 June.
11 Earl of Malmesbury, Letters, Vol. II, p. 430.
12 Stonestreet letter. February 1815.BL Add Ms 61805.
13 Capel Letters, p. 58.

CHAPTER V

Romances

Many of the British officers in Belgium in 1814–15 had spent most, if not all, of the previous six years in the Peninsula, where campaigning had been hard and continuous, and the opportunities for romance correspondingly few and far between. The cultural and religious differences between the Spanish and Portuguese on the one side and the English on the other were such that there were remarkably few romantic entanglements, let alone marriages, with young Iberian ladies. One of the few exceptions to this was Captain Harry Smith of the 95th Rifles who, with some friends, was standing helplessly watching the sack of Badajoz, when they were approached by two ladies fleeing from the city. The younger of these two sisters was the 14-year-old Doña Juana Maria de los Dolores de León, a member of an aristocratic Spanish family, and only recently released from a convent education. She and Harry fell in love on the spot and, despite her youth, Catholic faith and Spanish traditions, were wed within days, resulting in one of the most enduring and famous marriages in the history of the British Army. Harry's wife was universally known, respected and loved as Juana (or Juanita), and her name lives on in the South African town named after her – Ladysmith.

Few British officers in the Peninsula were so fortunate, although some did manage to get home to England for a short period of leave, where they had the opportunity to meet and fall in love, although marriage was usually out of the question due to the requirement to return to duty. One such was Lord Saltoun of the 1st Foot Guards, who, during a short home leave in 1813, met Catherine Thurlow, one of the three natural daughters of the Lord Chancellor, Edward Thurlow (1731–1806) and his mistress of many years, Mrs Hervey, whom Thurlow ensured were brought up well and were fully accepted in society. Saltoun and Catherine corresponded for the remainder of the war and were married on 6 March 1815, despite some initial objections from the groom's family, which were quickly overcome. Saltoun was on his honeymoon at Brighton when, on 1 April 1815, he received orders to rejoin his regiment with all despatch, which he did, leaving his bride hunting for a house in London.

Another officer whose honeymoon was disrupted was Colonel Sir

William De Lancey. This officer never once returned home during the Peninsular campaign but when Wellington's army was disbanded in 1814 he was posted to Edinburgh where, in a whirlwind romance, he met and wooed Magdalene, daughter of Sir James Hall, Bt, a wealthy Scottish landowner and savant. They were married in Edinburgh on 4 April 1815 and were on their honeymoon at the Hall country home at Dunglass when, like Saltoun, De Lancey received a message summoning him to Belgium. He and his bride travelled immediately to London, from where De Lancey went to Brussels, arriving on 25 May, followed by Magdalene on 8 June. They took an apartment in the house of Count de Lannoy on the park.

Lieutenant-Colonel Lord Fitzroy Somerset was the youngest son of Henry, fifth Duke of Beaufort and served throughout the Peninsular War as Wellington's ADC and Military Secretary. On his return from the Peninsula in 1814 he married Lady Emily Harriet Wellesley-Pole, the second daughter of William, third Earl of Mornington (Wellington's brother) and his wife, Katherine. Fitzroy Somerset spent some months at the British Embassy in Paris in 1814, but was posted back to his battalion, 1st Foot Guards, that October, when it was part of the British peacetime garrison in Brussels. Lady Emily was already pregnant when they arrived, and in the alarms of May 1815 she considered moving to Ostend or Antwerp to have the baby but was dissuaded by her uncle, the Duke of Wellington, and was safely delivered of a daughter in Brussels on 16 May 1815.[1]

Many of the bachelor officers in Brussels may have been looking for romance, but Captain Digby Mackworth (1789–1853) was not one of them. He had served in the Peninsular War, first with the 7th Foot, with which he was at Albuhera, and later with the 22nd. While with the latter, he was taken prisoner and sent to France, where he was lodged with a French general, Baron de Richepanse. The young English officer fell in love with his gaoler's daughter, the Baroness Marie Alexandrine Ignatie Julie de Richepanse, but he was exchanged before the war's end and had to leave. Nevertheless, they seem to have had 'an understanding', so that Mackworth's heart was elsewhere during the Waterloo campaign, which explains why his journal was written in such a detached manner.[2]

Brussels was also the scene of new romances, feverish match-making by mothers and a few marriages. Captain Lord John Somerset, temporarily on half-pay, caused some mirth in social circles, when, having spent a great deal of his time being particularly rude about Lady Catherine Annesley, suddenly did a complete volte face and proposed to her. She accepted and despite 'having not a 1,000 [pounds] between them & without a Prospect of more', they were married on 1 November 1814. Lord John was one of the Hereditary Prince's ADCs during the Battle of Quatre Bras and Waterloo.

Another to get married was Lieutenant-Colonel Sir George Berkeley,

35th Foot, who married a daughter of the late Sir Thomas Sutton MP, in late March. His bride's mother and sister were both present in Brussels in March–June 1815, but whether the marriage had been arranged earlier, or the Berkeleys met in Brussels is not known.

Unfortunately, not all outcomes of these Brussels romances were so happy. One of the most eligible and popular English bachelors was Major-General Edward Barnes, who arrived in September 1814 as Adjutant-General to the Hereditary Prince. He was a thoroughly nice man, had proved himself a dashing soldier, was very wealthy – and single. He quickly attached himself to the Capel family and proved most attentive, helping them in many ways, making military baggage carts available when the Capels moved house, sending their mail in the military courier's bag, and entertaining them with suppers or outings whenever they required. On 28 February 1815 Louisa Capel told her grandmother that Sir Edward (he had been knighted in January 1815) was the family's '. . . Best and Dearest Friend' and '. . . how much you would like him if you knew him . . .' But then – and completely out-of-the-blue – came two thunder-bolts: the first was that he proposed to Maria, the Capel's third daughter, and the second that she turned him down!

The parents had no objection; they liked him greatly and he was not only suitable but also wealthy. Nevertheless, albeit with some reluctance, they accepted their daughter's decision, but her sisters, all of whom doted on Sir Edward, were highly indignant, thought her very foolish, accused her of a 'want of taste' and repeatedly reproved her for her folly. Maria, who appears to have been taken totally by surprise by the proposal, was adamant in her refusal, writing to her grandmother:

> . . . on this subject I am not I think very Romantic, for I do not think *violent Love* necessary to one's happyness, but I think you will agree with me that a *decided preference* is absolutely so, and that, that preference even, I never could feel.[3]

Somewhat surprisingly, Sir Edward only took a couple of days to recover from this rebuff and was then at the Capels' house as often as before and being, as always, of great service to them. His aim was still matrimony, but he now turned his attentions to the eldest Capel daughter, Harriet, although he did not stand a chance with her either, but for a different reason – she was already deeply in love with someone else.

The man in this case was Lieutenant-Colonel Otto Trip, a 41-year-old officer in the 60th Foot, a Dutchman who had gone to England in the 1790s and transferred to the British Army in 1800. He served both Wellington, then plain Sir Arthur, and Lord Uxbridge as an ADC, and then Wellington again as a member of his Adjutant-General's staff. In 1814 he was appointed principal ADC to the Hereditary Prince of Orange and was welcomed into the Capel household in Brussels, not only because his general was a frequent visitor but also because of his long friendship with Lord Uxbridge, his one-time chief and Lady Caroline's brother. Harriet appears to have met him soon after his arrival in Brussels in September 1814 and by December was deeply in love and sending him regular letters. It gradually dawned on her, however, that her love was not returned – or, if it was, with nothing like the same ardour; her letters to him continued but with an increasingly desperate tone.[4]

Trip went to Paris in March 1815[5] but soon returned and then disaster struck when, on Thursday 14 April, Harriet's father became aware of what had been going on, accused Trip of behaving dishonourably and called him out. Capel went to considerable lengths to keep the news of the impending duel from his family, while his second, the Duke of Richmond, who was experienced in such matters, made the arrangements. At the meeting on Sunday 17 April Capel, as the aggrieved party, fired first and just missed his opponent's ear, whereupon Trip – against all normal etiquette and to the astonishment of both seconds – fired back, although, fortunately, he too missed.

Lady Caroline was overwhelmed with love for her husband, both for keeping her completely in the dark until it was all over, and for fighting for his daughter's honour. Meanwhile, Maria tried to resolve her sister's miserable situation by writing clandestinely to Trip to inform him that Harriet was due to inherit a sizeable amount on the death of their grandmother, the Dowager Countess of Wessex. This was an exceptionally touching and noble attempt to help her heartbroken sister, and one which would have incurred the wrath of both her parents had it been discovered. But Maria appears to have been mistaken in thinking that the problem was one of money – whatever the reason, her letter had no success. Harriet was one of those invited to the Ball who did not attend, presumably because she thought it possible that she might meet the lover who had treated her so cruelly. There can be no doubt that Trip treated Harriet very badly; he must have given her encouragement at the start, but then left her totally deserted, so that the remainder of her stay in Brussels was thoroughly miserable. He committed suicide in 1816 and whatever his reason for rejecting Harriet, he took it with him to the grave.

There are passing references to just two romances between British officers and Belgian ladies but there must have been others.[6] Lieutenant the Hon. Hastings Forbes of the 3rd Foot Guards was in love with Mademoiselle de Ghistelles who gave him a miniature of herself to wear around his neck when he left for war on 15 June – a sign of true love. He was killed at Waterloo and a friend fulfilled his dying request to return the portrait, which was 'almost shivered to pieces', to its original owner. She was seen by Muzzy Capel in July, looking distraught and 'the shadow of her former self'.

Lieutenant Henry Webster was engaged to Mademoiselle de Hamm. He survived the battle without a scratch but then rejected his fiancée, leaving her *'in the lurch in hystericks'*, and as such mountebanks often do, placed the blame (quite unfairly) at the door of his mother, Elizabeth, Lady Holland. This made him so unpopular in Brussels that he was forced to resign his post as ADC to the Hereditary Prince of Orange and return to England.[7]

Nor were officers the only ones to form attachments, for, as Sergeant Wheeler of the 51st Foot noted, there were some very pretty women in the country. 'Some of them,' he wrote to his father, 'are got very much attached to our men, and I doubt not when we move there will be an augmentation in the number of women.'[8]

One romance which must have started in Brussels was that between Major-General Peregrine Maitland and Lady Sarah Lennox. This couple eloped in Paris in September 1815, which suggests that they must have been entertaining romantic thoughts for each other well before that, although there was not one scintilla of gossip to link their names in Brussels. On 4 August, however, Lady Sarah wrote to her friend Lady Georgiana Bathurst:

> I am delighted by what you tell me about my friend Gen¹ Maitland . . . he is a most delightful person . . . He has sent me a Legion of Honor taken by his Brigade of Guards at Waterloo.

No great warmth, perhaps, but she had certainly been singled out for a special mark of affection.[9]

In such an atmosphere, it was fitting that the climax of this period should be one of the most romantic balls ever held.

NOTES

1 *Gentleman's Magazine*, 1815, Volume I, p. 561.
2 Mackworth returned and married Julie in 1816, she gave birth to their son in 1817 and died in 1818. Information supplied in 2003 by Sir Digby Mackworth, Bt.
3 Capel Letters, p. 88.
4 Many of her letters to him survive and are included in the Capel Letters, pp. 187–219.
5 He was on a spying mission for the Hereditary Prince.
6 Both the following examples are from the Capel Letters, p. 131.
7 Curiously both Baron Trip and the Hon. Hastings Forbes committed suicide, the former in 1816 and the latter in 1847.
8 The Letters of Private Wheeler, p.162.
9 They eloped on the evening of 15 October and spent the entire night travelling around Paris, asking one army chaplain after another to perform the marriage ceremony for them. Unfortunately, all these ministers found

good reason to decline and the farcical situation was only ended when the Duke of Wellington instructed his personal chaplain to marry them on the morning of 16 October. Letter, Revd G G Stonestreet to George Trower Esq. BLib Add Ms 61808 ff 77, 80.

CHAPTER VI
Brussels: March–June 1815

March 1815.

The first news of Napoleon's escape – 'the *Tyger* having broke loose' as Lady Capel described it – arrived in Brussels on 11 March, but was initially regarded with relative equanimity among the civilian population. Not so the military, however, and on 13 March 1815 the Hereditary Prince wrote to Earl Bathurst that Napoleon had reached Lyons in his march on Paris and:

> ... nothing but a combined and surprise movement of the British, Dutch and Prussian troops disposable in this neighbourhood can stop him and save Louis XVIII my opinion is that we ought to support him with all we can and move to that effect into France ...[1]

The prince sent Major-General Lowe to Aix-la-Chapelle (Aachen) to coordinate plans with the Prussian General Kleist and despatched one of his ADCs, Lieutenant-Colonel Baron Trip, on a spying mission to Paris, a rash act which aroused the fury of Sir Charles Stuart.[2]

Many in Brussels, including most of the English civilians, became apprehensive at the prospect of the Hereditary Prince of Orange commanding the army if military operations were to start, since, as a lieutenant-general in the British Army, he was the ranking officer in the kingdom. The prince was personally popular, was known to be brave, but he was just 23 years old, headstrong and his only military experience had been as an ADC in the Peninsula. The government in London ensured that he was surrounded by English staff officers, including Major-General Sir Hudson Lowe – Quartermaster-General; Major-General Sir Edward Barnes – Adjutant-General; Lieutenant-Colonel Sir John Colborne – Military Secretary; and Captain the Earl of March – ADC, but his royal status enabled him to issue orders which could not be gainsaid, as was to happen, with dire results, at Waterloo. The disquiet was felt even in the ranks of the infantry battalions, Sergeant Wheeler being of the opinion that the Prince of Orange '... is not the man for us. None but Wellington or Hill, or some one of the Generals who have served us in the late campaigns [in the Peninsula] can have our confidence.'[3]

The prince's talk of marching into France gave rise to considerable alarm in London, where it appeared possible that he might undertake a pre-emptive strike before the other allies were ready. This concern was further increased when it became known that the Sovereign Prince was proposing that his son should command a combined Anglo–Netherlands army in the forthcoming campaign against Napoleon; it would have been folly of the highest order for an inexperienced young man commanding a heterogeneous army to attempt the defeat one of the two greatest generals of the age.

Bathurst reacted quickly by insisting that the prince discuss every proposal with Lieutenant-General Sir William Clinton before taking any action. He also despatched an even more senior officer, General Lord Hill, to bring the impetuous young man under control, although the problem was only properly resolved when Wellington arrived. Even then the King of the Netherlands would accept no post lower than that of corps commander for his son, so the prince was placed in command of I Corps, which was by far the largest element of the Anglo–Netherlands Army.

In Brussels, however, most people's attention was devoted far more to the news that the Congress of Vienna had decided that the Sovereign Prince of Orange should become King of the United Netherlands, which was later formalised on 17 March by a proclamation from the balcony of the Hôtel de Ville read by the mayor of Brussels. Then, as Napoleon and his followers approached Paris, there was an exodus of English visitors from the French capital; some went home to England, but many others headed for Brussels, with the inevitable impact on accommodation and prices.

The news from Paris rapidly became more menacing, with Napoleon entering the city to popular acclaim on the 20th – and without one hostile shot having been fired – while the Bourbons and their supporters fled ignominiously on the 19th. Louis XVIII himself reached Lille on the 22nd. Louis then went to Ostend, possibly with the intention of returning to his old sanctuary in England, but was persuaded to establish himself in Ghent; other members of his court, including the Duc de Berri, Prince Condé and Marshals Victor and Berthier went to Brussels, but thence to Ghent.

The people of Brussels were starved of official information about both the situation in France and the allies' proposed responses, which resulted in a spate of rumours, some leading to panic reactions. There were repeated stories that Napoleon was advancing towards Brussels; some were vague, others specific. For example, a report reached Brussels on 22 March that Napoleon was at Amiens with 50,000 men, which prompted the Hereditary Prince to set out on a personal inspection of the frontier defences. All this caused such alarm that even an old soldier like the Duke of Richmond decided to issue instructions that his family should retire to Antwerp, although he countermanded this within hours when he heard that 40,000 Prussian troops were arriving in Louvain. Then the next day the English Foot Guards, part of the Brussels garrison, marched out of the city at 4 o'clock in the morning, heading for the frontier. The banks then closed, cutting off the money supply, and in the resulting panic the great majority of English families departed in considerable haste for Antwerp, although a more resolute few, including the Richmonds and Capels, remained behind. Another family to remain behind was the Suttons, as on 26 March, Lieutenant-Colonel Sir George Berkeley, a British officer on the Prince of Orange's staff, married Miss Sutton, daughter of the late Sir Thomas Sutton MP; the ceremony was conducted by the Rev. Stonestreet, chaplain to the Guards, with the bride's mother and sister both present.

Considerable amusement was caused by Lord Waterpark[4] who fled with his family to Antwerp and then some four or five days later sent his sister-in-law back to Brussels, dressed in French clothes and riding in a Belgian coach. Her mission was to reconnoitre the city in order to discover whether the French had arrived and what had happened to several heavy parcels which had been left behind. One of the Duke of Richmond's daughters met and recognised this lady in a shop, as a result of which the gallant lord's somewhat craven behaviour was exposed.[5]

Common sense soon returned and most were back in the city in time to see the new King and Queen of the Netherlands make a solemn entry on 10 April. Every house was covered with boughs of fir and larch tied together with orange ribbons; some were embroidered with scarlet thread, and all with national flags. The procession was some three miles long and the Reverend Stonestreet said that he had never seen anything like it, although he noticed that the people were '. . . wanting that enthusiasm which so strongly marks an English populace'. Indeed, even Lady Caroline Capel noticed that despite the apparent joy, '. . . the greatest jealousies [exist] between the Dutch & the Belgians' and predicted that the moment the British troops leave there will be trouble. '. . . their religion is different, their Manners & habits also & they say that a Constitution which may suit Holland will not do here . . .' In fact, the union was to last somewhat longer than she had forecast – fifteen years – but otherwise her observation was very perceptive.

The month ended with another development which was to have major repercussions on life in Brussels when the Congress at Vienna appointed the Duke of Wellington to be commander of the Anglo–Netherlands Army. He set out from Vienna on 29 March, accompanied only by two ADCs: Lieutenant-Colonel Fremantle and Lieutenant William Lennox (one of the Richmonds' sons). The trio overtook the courier who had left Vienna the day before they did and reached Brussels on 4 April.

April 1815

The officer tasked with bringing the Hereditary Prince to his senses was General Lord Hill, who embarked on 30 March and arrived in Brussels at 8pm on 1 April where he went straight to see the young Dutchman. Captain Digby Mackworth, Hill's ADC recorded:

> It appears that the Prince has made himself unpopular in our army, and that the present situation has a little turned his head, nor have flatterers been wanting to make him believe that he is as great a general as some of the ancient Princes of his house; which, judging from the present state of the army under his command, and from the mode in which everything is carried on by him, does not appear to be the case.[6]

Then, on 4 April, the Duke of Wellington arrived and immediately set about seizing the reins of command. He set himself up at No. 36 in the park, which became not only the military but also the social hub of the city. He met the King of the Netherlands and travelled to Ghent on the 8th to renew his acquaintance with Louis XVIII. One of his main tasks was to spread confidence and calm, which even extended to encouraging his pregnant niece, Lady Fitzroy Somerset, to remain and have her baby in Brussels. His arrival and assumption of command met with universal approval among the British soldiers, who told each other: 'Glorious news, Nosey [Wellington] has got the command, won't we give them a drubbing now.'

Wellington had to convert a peacetime garrison force and command structure into an efficient and effective field army, ready to face one of the finest generals of the age. To achieve this, he was constantly pestering the Horse Guards in London not just for more units, but also for more *experienced* units, preferably those from his victorious Peninsular army. British reinforcements soon started to flow into Belgium, being despatched mainly from Great Britain and Ireland, although these were joined in June by troops returning from the ill-fated campaign in North America. Typical of these was the 10th Royal Hussars which in early March 1815 was one of several cavalry regiments helping to put down the Poor Laws riots on the streets of London. As soon as word of Napoleon's escape became known, however, the rioting ceased and the regiments, mainly cavalry, were able to set out for the seat of war almost immediately. The 10th returned at once to their peacetime station at Romford, Kent, to collect their war equipment, and thence to Ramsgate. The voyage to Belgium was very rough and unpleasant, but once ashore at Ostend they set out for the front. The regiment was at Bruges on 18 March, Ecloo on the 19th, Ghent on the 20th, Oostakcer on the 22nd and at their destination, Oudenarde, on the 23rd.

Wellington set a fast pace. He toured the frontier between 17 and 22 April, accompanied the King of the Netherlands on the 24th to inspect the newly-established headquarters of the Reserve Army at Nivelle, which was commanded by the king's younger son, Prince Frederick. Then, on the 26th he went with the king and both his sons to Mons. By this time a degree of calm had been restored in Brussels, most of those who had fled in the March panic had returned and as a result, the parties began again. This time, however, there were two very significant differences: the presence of the Duke of Wellington and an ever-increasing military community.

Shortly after Wellington arrived there was a ball at the Hôtel de Ville for the king and queen, and among those present were the Duke of Wellington and General Lord Hill, as well as two French aristocrats, the Prince de Condé[7] and Monsieur.[8] On 28 April Wellington gave the first of his own entertainments, a grand concert, ball and supper, which was attended by the King and Queen of the Netherlands, the young Prince of Orange, the Duc de Berri, Sir Charles Stuart (the British Minister in Brussels) and as many visitors as could be accommodated. When there were no balls there were dinner parties – Wellington was at the Richmonds' on 6 April – or concerts such as that given by Madame Catalani on the 27th.

May 1815

The threat of military operations increased steadily throughout May, with most people under the impression that the Allies intended to invade France in early July. British reinforcements continued to arrive at Dutch and Belgian ports, and to move into cantonments in southern Belgium. British commanders carried out a rigorous programme of inspections, parades and field days in order to ascertain for themselves how ready the officers and their troops were for battle; it was also important for the troops to see who would be commanding them. Also, of course, in an era when most battlefield manoeuvres were simple drills, it was an opportunity for the commanders to see the troops practise their tactical moves.

The command arrangements also had to be sorted out. Thus, on 3 May Wellington went to Tirlemont to coordinate plans with the Prussian Field-Marshal Prince Blücher.[9] Then, on the following day, Wellington's appointment as a field marshal in the Netherlands Army was announced, thus resolving any lingering doubts about his relationship with the Hereditary Prince of Orange.

Also at this time the Prussian liaison officer at Wellington's head-quarters, Major-General von Roeder, was replaced by Major-General Friedrich Freiherr von Müffling. Roeder had not been a success and had made little effort to come to terms with English military customs, which were much less formal than those in the Prussian Army.[10] Müffling, on the other hand, quickly adjusted and became both respected and popular among the staff officers, and was highly thought of by Wellington, who gave every sign of trusting him completely.[11]

The inspections proceeded apace. Some were of individual units, such as Lord Hill's inspection of 71st (Highland) Foot near Liège on 12 May, and others of brigades, such as Lord Uxbridge's inspection of the British Hussar brigade on 6 May. Some inspections were on an even grander scale. Lord Hill inspected Prince Frederic's Corps, at Sotteghen on the 19th, which was some 10,000 strong; it was, incidentally, found to be in better order than expected, with the 'Brigade of the Indies' proving particularly impressive.

The Duke of Wellington's programme was especially busy. On 11 May he inspected British and Hanoverian troops in the Allée Verte in Brussels, and on the 22nd he was joined by the Hereditary Prince and the Duke of Brunswick to inspect Hanoverian and Brunswick troops at Vilvorde and watch their manoeuvres. Wellington often took one or more ladies on such inspections and on this occasion he was accompanied by Lady Georgiana Lennox, who was treated with particular courtesy by the Duke of Brunswick and who returned home wrapped in a soldier's greatcoat, which Lord Uxbridge had obtained for her, and escorted by General Alava.[12]

The pace of the social programme was also increasing. The newly-arrived Captain Shakespear of the 10th Hussars, which had now moved to Voorde some twelve miles from Brussels, was invited to a rout at the Richmonds' house on 1 May and to a dinner party there on the 7th. But the major events were the dances and Lady Caroline Capel wrote to her mother in June: 'Balls are going on here as if we had had none for over a year.'[13] On the 27th Field Marshal Prince Blücher visited Brussels and the Duke of Wellington gave a grand ball in his honour which was attended by so many of the city's high society that the gardens had to be opened and illuminated to accommodate the numbers involved.

Nobody in the British Army or the English colony in Brussels had anything but admiration for Wellington as a military commander, nor did they doubt, for one moment, his ability to defeat Napoleon when the time came, but his off-duty behaviour certainly excited some adverse comment. Captain Mackworth attended the ball on the 27th and noted in his journal:

> The Duke himself danced, and always with the same person, a Lady Frances Webster, to whom he paid so much attention, that Scandal, who is become Goddess here, began to whisper all sorts of stories, but we are not bound to believe all she says; not but that the well-known bad private character of His Grace would warrant any suspicions

whatever. There must have been something essentially bad in the education of the Wellesley family – on the score of gallantry not one of its members, male or female, is *sans reproche.*

At the same time Lady Caroline Capel was telling her mother that:

The Duke of W has not improved the *Morality* of our Society, as he has given several things & makes a point of asking all the Ladies of Loose Character – Every one was surprised at seeing Lady John Campbell at his House & one of his Staff told me that it had been represented to him her not being received for that her Character was more than Suspicious. 'Is it, by –, said he, 'then I will go & ask her Myself.' On which he immediately took his Hat & went out for the purpose.[14]

Horse racing continued to be popular, although the main venue had changed from Brussels to Grammont, the main centre for the British cavalry, with meetings on 16, 23 and 30 May.

At a cavalry review in late May the Duc de Berri made himself look ridiculous. The inspecting officer was Wellington, whose standards were very high, so as soon as the troops, some 6,000 of them, were lined up they busied themselves with last-minute preparations, checking each other's turnout and giving the horses' coats just one more brush. They were thus engaged when the Duc de Berri galloped up to the saluting base, stopped and turned to face the parade, clearly expecting some form of general salute. The British officers and soldiers simply glanced at him, noted that he was not Wellington, and carried on. Infuriated at being ignored, de Berri despatched one of his ADCs to Lord Uxbridge, the parade commander, to demand the salute due to a prince of the blood royal, to which the latter replied firmly that he had no instructions for such an event. On being informed of this, and clearly humiliated, the Duc de Berri galloped off the parade ground, followed by his suite, and the phlegmatic British soldiers smiled to each other and carried on preparing for the arrival of someone who, as far as they were concerned, was of infinitely greater importance.

June 1815

In the early days of June there was an increasing sense that something was about to happen, although nobody was sure what. Lady Caroline Capel wrote on 13 June:

I should suppose the Commencement of Hostilities (if they ever do begin) cannot be far distant – But Nobody can guess Lord

Wellington's intentions & I dare say Nobody will know he is going till he is actually gone. In the meantime he amuses himself with Humbugging the ladies, particularly the Duchess of Richmond.

Foreign troops arrived in increasing numbers throughout the first half of June, but the English civilians noted with some surprise that while Belgian civilians were obliged by law to provide billets for such troops, they, as foreigners, were not. As a result, a Belgian household could be compelled to accommodate English officers or soldiers while an English family living next door took none.

The military reviews continued apace, with the fourteen English, Dutch and Hanoverian battalions making up the Brussels garrison being inspected in the Alée Verte, whilst farther afield the plains around Grammont proved particularly suitable for cavalry drills, as a result of which Lord Uxbridge assembled the whole of the British cavalry there three times a week. These parades were interspersed by sporting events, with horse racing taking place at Grammont on 1, 11 and 13 June, while cricket matches took place at Enghien on 6 and 13 June. In both activities, the Duke of Richmond was, as usual, an active participant.

The feeling that only Wellington knew what was going on was widely shared, causing at least two people to check with him before they finalised their plans. One was Lady Georgiana Lennox, who was deputed by a group of Army officers in early June to seek the commander's advice about a picnic they were planning in the Tournay or Lille area. The duke's reply was instant: 'No; better let that drop'[15] – which, of course, they did.

Another was the Duchess of Richmond who was planning a ball for 15 June and spoke to Wellington directly about it:

Duke, I do not wish to pry into your secrets, nor do I ask what your intentions may be; I wish to give a ball, and all I ask is – May I give my ball? If you say, Duchess, don't give your ball, it is quite sufficient – I ask no reasons.

The Duke replied: 'Duchess, you may give your Ball with the greatest safety without fear of interruption.'[16]

Other balls followed in quick succession. Wellington held one on Saturday 3rd, Wellington's friend, Sir Charles Stuart, the British Minister in Brussels, on Monday 5th, and then Wellington another on Wednesday 7th. Wellington was also known to be planning yet another, on an even grander scale, for the 21st, the second anniversary of his great victory at Vittoria.

In the second week Captain Verner and Lieutenant O'Grady of the 7th Hussars were invited to spend a few days in Brussels with the Richmonds (Verner had been the duke's ADC in Ireland in 1807–8). At the end of their stay the duchess spoke to Verner about her planned Ball on the 15th and asked him to hand-carry the invitations to the cavalry officers and distribute them during the next field day at Grammont. The invitations were also being issued in Brussels and when the now heavily pregnant Lady Caroline Capel announced that she would not go, her daughters insisted that their father must go as their chaperone.

Thus, by the 14th it was clear that something must happen soon, but for the great majority in Brussels there was no certainty as to what form this might take and Wellington, as usual, was tight-lipped, giving not even his closest staff officers any major indication of his plans. The civilians could see couriers constantly on the move, either bringing the latest news from the frontier stations or being despatched to disseminate the latest intelligence to the field commanders. There was also considerable traffic between Wellington and his ally, Prince Blücher, with messages regularly exchanged between Brussels and the Prussian headquarters at Naumur. Prince Blücher also sent higher-ranking liaison officers to Brussels from time to time, one being Oberst von Pruel, who visited on 14 June.

As night fell on 14 June it seemed to everyone in Brussels that all that could be expected was another day of preparations for an invasion of France which would take place at some unspecified date in the future. Indeed, the event giving rise to the greatest expectation was the very select Ball hosted by the Duchess of Richmond that was to take place the following evening.

NOTES

1   Letter Prince of Orange to Earl Bathurst, Brussels 13 March 1815, B Lib Loan 57/9 f.949.
2   Letter Stuart to Bathurst, The Hague, 24 March 1815, B Lib Loan 87/9 f. 958.
3   Letters of Private Wheeler, p.160.
4   Richard Cavendish, second Lord Waterpark (1765–1830).
5   The Waterparks appear not to have returned to Brussels as Lord Hill and his staff took over their house on 6 April.
6   The Waterloo Diary of Captain Digby Mackworth, 7th Foot, ADC To Lt-Gen Lord Hill, *Army Quarterly*, October 1937, January 1938.
7   Louis Josephe, Prince de Condé (1736–1820).
8   It was French practice to call the eldest living brother of the reigning king, Monsieur. In this case it was Charles (1757–1836), who subsequently succeeded as King Charles X (1824–30).
9   Lennox, p. 109.
10 Müffling, p. 213.
11 The one occasion Wellington is known to have deliberately withheld information from Müffling was over the post of Governor of Paris. In July 1815 the Prussians wanted Zieten, a distinguished lieutenant-general, to hold this prestigious and demanding post, but Wellington, without discussing the matter with Müffling, went to see Blücher in person and secured the post for his Prussian liaison officer, a singular display of his trust. Wellington also

ensured that Müffling was awarded the high honour of Commander of the Order of the Bath in recognition of his services. Müffling p. 255.

12   Swinton (ed.), *A Sketch of the Life of Lady de Ros*, p 121.
13   Capel Letters, p. 102.
14   Capel Letters, p. 102.
15   Lady de Ros, p. 122.
16   *Reminiscences of William Verner (1782–1871), 7th Hussars.*

CHAPTER VII
Invitations to the Ball

There are three sources of speculation about the Ball: who was invited, who actually turned up, and where did it take place? This chapter addresses the first two of these, although, as will be explained, a final and definitive answer is impossible. Three lists are known to exist, which differ in certain details, but all are the same in principle – they are *invitation* lists. But, apart from annotations in certain cases, some of which are known to be inaccurate, they are not a reliable record of actual attendance and there can be no doubt that, unless some totally unknown document is unearthed, the names of all those actually present will never be known with absolute certainty.

It is important to appreciate that, although history has transformed the Ball held on 15 June into an event of major significance, it was actually a private affair, organised and paid for by the Richmonds, which was unrelated to any particular event or anniversary. Thus, the duchess had sole control over the invitations and, like any hostess, she did her best to include a mixture of guests who would ensure that her party went well. She invited a number of Dutch/Belgian aristocrats, at least some of whom had previously offered her hospitality, British civilians resident in and around Brussels, individuals of various nationalities, either resident in or passing through Brussels, diplomats, and officers of the British Army. It is also clear that she went to particular trouble to make it enjoyable for young people by inviting both junior army officers and people who would bring daughters of a suitable age. As in any such event, the size of the ballroom and supper-room set the limit on the total numbers that could be invited, which in this case was about 230. A further limit was placed by the distance of the guests from Brussels; even before the news arrived on the 15th that the French had crossed the frontier, the Anglo–Dutch army was on full alert so that commanders would not have allowed their officers to be more than a few hours' travel from their units.

The duchess was, however, under no obligation whatsoever to invite any particular individual or group, or to balance numbers between different groups, although, as she was a notorious snob, the majority of her guests were socially well connected. It would, however, be wrong to impute that, because some individual was not invited, he or she either had cause to consider themselves insulted or to feel belittled.

The Ball was a glittering and glamorous social occasion which, totally by chance, took place on the night that Napoleon's armies invaded Belgium. As a result, the party ended with many officers slipping away into the night to join their regiments, which were deploying for battle. Such historical significance was never foreseen at the time; the duchess's Ball was simply one of a succession of events whose purpose was nothing more than to enliven the Brussels social scene.

The Invitation Lists

The original manuscript invitation list – the 'Goodwood List' – is retained in Goodwood House; it is apparently in the duchess's own hand and is reproduced at Appendix A. In the late 1830s the then Lord Verulam asked the Duchess of Richmond for a copy of the list, which was duly sent, but what his purpose was has never been discovered and it was never published.[1] In the late 1880s Sir William Frazer, an amateur historian, asked Lady De Ros for a copy of the list; she was the former Lady Georgiana Lennox, one of the Duchess of Richmond's daughters and had been present at the Ball. Lady De Ros asked for and obtained a copy of the list from Lord Verulam; why she should not have requested a new copy of the Goodwood original is unclear. This was duly published in *Some Words on Wellington* by Sir William Frazer and again in 1893 in *A Sketch of the Life of Georgiana, Lady de Ros* by the Hon. Blanche Swinton, Lady de Ros's daughter. These two lists are identical and are referred to here by the name of the originator as the 'De Ros List'; it is reproduced at Appendix B. This list differs from the Goodwood List in certain respects, the names are in a different order and some annotations have been added, apparently by Lady De Ros. For example, to the names 'Marquis et Marquise d'Assche' is added '(from their house we saw the wounded brought in – Lord Uxbridge, Lord F. Somerset, &c.)'.

In 1915 a book was published in Belgium which included another version of the list. This was based on the De Ros list, but with the names regrouped and with corrections and annotations to many of the Belgian entries; this is named after its author as the 'Delhaize List' and is at Appendix C.

Next came the publication in 1936 of *A Mixed Bag* by C C R Murphy, which was essentially a series of essays and reminiscences by a British colonial officer, but which, for obscure reasons, included an essay on the Duchess of Richmond's Ball. Murphy had, however, been to Goodwood House and as a result he included a transcript of the Goodwood List, the only time that this has ever appeared in print. As this is identical to the Goodwood List itself, it is not repeated here.

The following list has been compiled by combining the information in the Goodwood, De Ros and Delhaize Lists; it also includes the fruits of additional research and corrects known errors.

Table II. INVITATIONS TO THE DUCHESS OF RICHMOND'S BALL
Part I All, less British Army

	Name/s	Remarks
Belgian/ Dutch	Duke Prosper-Louis d'Arenberg	Former officer in the French Army
	Duke Frederic-Auguste-Alexandre de Beaufort-Spontin, Duchess de Beaufort and Mademoiselles de Beaufort	Friends of the Richmonds
	Duke Charles Joseph and Duchesse d'Ursel	Friends of the Richmonds
	Prince Pierre d'Alcantara d'Arenberg	Former officer in the French Army; brother of Duke d'Arenberg
	Marquis and Marquess d'Assche	Friends of the Richmonds
	Count and Countess Mercy d'Argentau	Austrian minister to Bavaria
	Count and Countess de Grassiac	Governor of Southern Brabant
	Count Emile and Countess D'Oultremont	Accompanied by the Prince de Ligne, aged 10; see below
	Dowager-Countess D'Oultremont and Mademoiselles	Mother of Count Emile (above)
	Count and Countess Auguste Liedekerke-Beaufort and Mademoiselles	Countess was daughter of de la Tour Dupin (see below)
	Countess de Ruilly	
	Baron and Baroness van der Capellan	Secretary of state and governor of Belgian provinces

	Name/s	Remarks
	Baron and Baroness van der Linden D'Hoogvorst	Mayor of Brussels
	Mademoiselle and Mr C d'Hoogvorst	Possibly children of previous entry
	Madame Constant d'Hoogvorst	
	Baron de Herelt	
	Baron de Tuyll de Serooskerken	
French	General Count Charles-Eugene de Lalaing d'Audenarde and Countess de Lalaing	Second-in-command of Louis XVIII Garde du Corps
	Guillaume Jean Hyde	Civilian at court of Louis XVIII
	Count de la Rochefoucauld	Official at court of Louis XVIII at Ghent
Austrian	General Prince Auguste-Marie-Raymond, Duke d'Arenberg, Count de la Marck	General in the Austrian and Dutch armies
	General Count Heinrich Johann von Bellegarde	Austrian general
Diplomatic Corps	General Don Miguel Ricardo d'Alava	Spanish commissioner at Wellington's HQ
	Baron von Brockhausen	Prussian minister at The Hague
	General Count Pozzo di Borgo	Russian commissioner at Wellington's HQ
	Count and Countess de la Tour-Dupin	French minister of Louis XVIII at The Hague
	General Baron Vincent	Austrian commissioner at Wellington's HQ
	Colonel Jakob, Freiherr von Washington	Bavarian commissioner at Wellington's HQ
German Military	Duke Friedrich-Wilhelm of Brunswick-Wolfenbüttel	Sovereign duke and commander of Brunswick contingent

	Name/s	Remarks
	Colonel George-Guillaume-Auguste-Henri, Hereditary Prince of Nassau	Extra ADC to Wellington
	Major Georg, Baron Krauchenberg	3rd Hussars, KGL; ADC to Maj-Gen Dornberg
	Captain de Lübeck	ADC to Duke of Brunswick
Dutch/ Belgian Military	Major-General Prince Frederick of Orange	Younger brother of the Hereditary Prince; commander of a reserve division
	Colonel Baron d'Iroy	1st ADC/Prince Frederic of Orange
	Colonel L H T du Cayler	Dutch; ADC/Prince of Orange
	Colonel J A E Knijf	Dutch; ADC/Prince of Orange
English RN	Admiral Sir Sidney and Lady Smith, and the Miss Rumbolds	The Miss Rumbolds were Lady Smith's daughters from her previous marriage.
	Admiral Sir James Gambier	Lately in Ghent heading British delegation in peace talks with USA to end the War of 1812
	Rear-Admiral Sir Pulteney Malcolm, RN	Admiral commanding RN ships in the Scheldt river
	Commander the Hon. George Perceval, RN	
English Army – retired	General Sir Hew and Lady Jane Dalrymple-Hamilton	In Paris Sep 1814 to April/May 1815, then moved to Brussels
	General Francis Dundas	In Brussels on private business
English Civilians	Earl, Countess and Lady Elizabeth Conyngham	Lady Elizabeth was being wooed by Mr Legh MP
	Viscount Mount-Charles and the Hon. Mr Conyngham	Children of the above
	John Thelluson, second Baron Rendlesham	

	Name/s	Remarks
	Lord Henry George Apsley	Eldest son of third Earl Bathurst
	Lord and Lady George Seymour and Miss Seymour	Lord George Seymour of Wellingore, Lincolnshire
	Hon. John Capel, Lady Capel, and four Miss Capels	Father and two daughters attended
	Sir James Craufurd, Bt, Lady Craufurd and Miss Craufurd	Former British minister in Hamburg
	Sir William Johnston, Bt and Lady Johnston	Signed Will in Brussels on 16 May 1815; seventh baronet
	Mr, Mrs and Miss Lance and Mr Lance junior	Not identified; 'junior' suggests a child aged between 7 and 11
	Mr Charles Ord and the Miss Ords	Creevey's stepchildren
	Mr and Mrs Greathed	Of Uddens House near Wimborne, Dorset
	Mr Thomas Legh, MP	Of Lyme Hall, Cheshire
	Mr and Mrs Lloyd	Probably Hannibal Evans-Lloyd
	Dowager Countess Waldegrave	Her son, Lt-Col. John Waldegrave, was CO 54th Foot
	Countess Mountmorris and Lady Juliana Annesley	Mother and sister of Lady Frances Wedderburn-Webster; Earl Mountmorris was in Brussels but was ill
	Viscountess Hawarden	Wife of Cornwallis Maude, third Viscount Hawarden
	The Honourable Mrs Wellesley-Pole	Wife of Hon. William Wellesly-Pole; mother of Lady Fitzroy Somerset
	Lady Alvanley and Miss Ardens	Widow of first Lord Alvanley; Miss Ardens her daughters; Arden was Alvanley family name
	Lady Charlotte Greville	Her nephew was Lt A Greville, 1st Foot Guards – see below

	Name/s	Remarks
	Lady and Miss Sutton	Mother-in-law and sister-in-law of Lt-Col. Berkeley; she was the widow of Sir Thomas Sutton, MP
	Lady Susan Clinton	Wife of Lt-Gen. Sir Henry Clinton
	Lady William De Lancey	Magdalene (née Hall), wife of Colonel Sir William De Lancey
	Lady George Berkeley	Lucy (née Sutton), wife of Lt-Col. Sir George Berkeley
	Lady Fitzroy Somerset	Emily (née Wellesley), wife of Lord Fitzroy Somerset
	Lady Frances Wedderburn-Webster	Née Annesley; husband was in London
British Foreign Office	Sir Charles Stuart	British Ambassador at the Hague
	Hon. James Stuart	Foreign Office courier from London; not a near relative of Sir Charles
	Mr Clinton George Dawkins	Embassy staff in Brussels
	Mr George William Chad	Embassy staff in Brussels
	Mr Lionel Hervey	British representative at Ghent
	Mr John James	Sir Charles Stuart's Secretary of Embassy

Part II British Army

Name	Regiment	Appointment
Field Marshal the Duke of Wellington		Commander-in-chief Anglo–Netherlands Army
General the Hereditary Prince of Orange		Commander I Corps; General in British Army
Lt-Gen. Sir Henry Clinton		Commander 2nd Division
Lt-Gen. Lord Hill		Commander II Corps
Lt-Gen. Sir Thomas Picton		Commander 5th Division

Name	Regiment	Appointment
Lt-Gen. the Earl of Uxbridge		Commander Anglo–Dutch Cavalry
Maj.-Gen. Frederick Adam		Commander 3rd Infantry Brigade
Maj.-Gen. Sir Edward Barnes		Assistant Adjutant-General
Maj.-Gen. Sir John Byng		Commander 2nd (Guards) Brigade
Maj.-Gen. George Cooke		Commander 1st British Division
Maj.-Gen. Sir James Kempt		Commander 8th Infantry Brigade
Maj.-Gen. Peregrine Maitland		Commander 1st (Guards) Brigade
Maj.-Gen. Sir Denis Pack		Commander 9th Infantry Brigade
Maj.-Gen. Hon. Sir William Ponsonby		Commander 2nd Cavalry Brigade
Maj.-Gen. Lord Edward Somerset		Commander 1st Cavalry Brigade
Maj.-Gen. Sir Hussey Vivian		Commander 6th Cavalry Brigade
Col. Hon. Alexander Abercromby	2nd Foot Guards	Assistant Quartermaster General
Col. Sir Colin Campbell	2nd Foot Guards	Commandant at Wellington's HQ
Col. Sir William De Lancey	Permanent QMG	Deputy Quartermaster General
Col. Sir John Elley	Royal Horse Guards	Deputy Adjutant General
Col. Felton Hervey	14 Lt Dgns.	Assistant Quartermaster General
Col. Sir George Wood	Royal Artillery	Commander Royal Artillery
Lt-Col. Hon. Edward Acheson	2nd Foot Guards	Regimental Duty
Lt-Col. Delancey Barclay	1st Foot Guards	Assistant Adjutant General Cousin to Col. Sir William De Lancey
Lt-Col. Sir Andrew Barnard	95th Foot	Commanding Officer
Lt-Col. Sir George Berkeley	35th Foot	Assistant Adjutant General to Prince of Orange

Name	Regiment	Appointment
Lt-Col. Sir Henry Bradford	1st Foot Guards	Assistant Quartermaster General
Lt-Col. John Cameron	92nd Foot	Commanding Officer
Lt-Col. Charles F. Canning	3rd Foot Guards	ADC/Duke of Wellington
Lt-Col. Robert Henry Dick	42nd Foot	Second-in-Command
Lt-Col. John Fremantle	2nd Foot Guards	ADC/Duke of Wellington
Lt-Col. William Fuller	1 King's Dragoon Guards	Commanding Officer
Lt-Col. the Hon. Sir Alexander Gordon	3rd Foot Guards	ADC/Duke of Wellington
Lt-Col. Clement Hill	Royal Horse Guards	ADC to Gen. Hill
Lt-Col. Sir Robert Hill	Royal Horse Guards	Commanding Officer
Lt-Col. Sir Noel Hilll	1st Foot Guards	Deputy Adjutant General
Lt-Col. Lord Robert Manners	10 Light Dragoons	Regimental Duty
Lt-Col. Hon. Frederick Ponsonby	12 Light Dragoons	Commanding Officer
Lt-Col. The Earl of Portarlington	23 Light Dragoons	Commanding Officer
Lt-Col. Charles Rowan	52nd Foot	Second-in-Command
Lt-Col. Alexander, Lord Saltoun	1st Foot Guards	Regimental Duty
Lt-Col. Sir George Scovell	Half pay	Assistant Quartermaster General
Lt-Col. Lord Fitzroy Somerset	1st Foot Guards	Military Secretary/DofW
Lt-Col. Hon. James Stanhope	1st Foot Guards	Regimental Duty
Lt-Col. Ernst Otto, Baron von Tripp	60th Foot	ADC/Prince of Orange
Lt-Col. Robert Torrens	1st West India Regiment	Assistant Quartermaster General
Lt-Col. Alexander George Woodford	Coldstream Guards	Commanding Officer; brother of John (see next entry)

Name	Regiment	Appointment
Lt-Col. John George Woodford	1st Foot Guards	AQMG; brother of Alexander
Lt-Col. Henry Wyndham	2nd Foot Guards	Regimental Duty
Maj. Chatham Churchill	1st Foot Guards	ADC/Lord Hill
Maj. Hon. George Dawson	1st Dragoon Guards	Assistant Quartermaster General
Maj. Andrew Hamilton	4th West India Regiment	ADC/Barnes
Maj. Thomas Hunter Blair	91st Foot	BM/Adam
Maj. the Hon. Henry Percy	14 Lt Dragoons	Extra ADC/Duke of Wellington
Maj. the Hon. William Stuart	1st Foot Guards	Regimental Duty 3rd Major
Capt. Charles Allix	1st Foot Guards	Adjutant
Capt. Edward Bowater	3rd Foot Guards	Regimental Duty
Capt. George Bowles	2nd Foot Guards	Regimental Duty
Capt. the Hon. Orlando Bridgeman	1st Foot Guards	ADC/Hill
Capt. Francis Dawkins	1st Foot Guards	ADC/Clinton
Capt. Francis Disbrowe	1st Foot Guards	ADC/Cooke
Capt. Henry Dumaresq	9th Foot	ADC/Byng
Capt. James Elphinstone	7 Light Dragoons	Regimental Duty
Capt. James Fraser	7 Light Dragoons	ADC/Uxbridge
Capt. Charles Gore	Half pay	ADC/Kempt
Capt. James Gunthorpe	1st Foot Guards	BM/Maitland
Capt. John Gurwood	10 Hussars	ADC/Clinton
Capt. Robert Hesketh	3rd Foot Guards	Regimental Duty
Capt. Lord Arthur Hill	Half pay	ADC/DofW
Capt. Edward Keane	7 Light Dragoons	ADC/Vivian

Name	Regiment	Appointment
Capt. Digby Mackworth	7th Foot	ADC/Lord Hill
Capt. William Pakenham	RHA	Adjt RHA.
Capt. Hon. Francis Russell	Half pay	ADC/Prince of Orange
Capt. Horace Seymour	60th Foot	ADC/Uxbridge s/o Adml Lord Hugh Seymour; mother was Lady Anne Waldegrave
Capt. Arthur Shakespear	10th Light Dragoons	Regimental Duty
Capt. Charles Smyth	95th Foot	BM/Pack
Capt. Lord John Somerset	Half pay	ADC/PofO; his wife was daughter of Lord Annesley
Capt. William Verner	7 Light Dragoons	Regimental Duty
Capt. Thomas Wildman	7 Light Dragoons	ADC/Uxbridge
Capt. Charles Yorke	52nd Foot	ADC/Adam
Lt Francis Brooke	1st Kings Dragoons Guards	Regimental Duty
Lt Hon. George Cathcart	6 Dragoons	Extra ADC/Duke of Wellington
Lt Hon. Lionel Dawson	18th Light Dragoons	Brothers in 1KDG, 23rd Lt Dgns
Lt Hon. Hastings Forbes	3rd Foot Guards	Regimental Duty
Lt Charles Augustus Fitzroy	Royal Horse Guards	ADC/Vivian
Lt John Gordon	7 Light Dragoons	Regimental Duty
Lt James Robinson	32nd Foot	Regimental Duty
Lt Standish O'Grady	7 Light Dragoons	Regimental Duty
Lt Henry Somerset	18 Light Dragoons	ADC/Lord Edward Somerset

Name	Regiment	Appointment
Lt Henry Webster	9 Light Dragoons	ADC/Prince of Orange
Ensign David Baird	3rd Foot Guards	Regimental Duty
Ensign the Hon. T Seymour Bathurst	1st Foot Guards	Regimental Duty
Ensign the Hon. Ernest Edgcombe	1st Foot Guards	Regimental Duty
Ensign George Fludyer	1st Foot Guards	Regimental Duty
Ensign the Hon. James Forbes	Coldstream Guards	Regimental Duty; son of Gen. Lord Forbes; brother of Walter Forbes
Ensign the Hon. Walter Forbes	Coldstream Guards	Regimental Duty; brother of James Forbes
Ensign Algernon Greville	1st Foot Guards	Regimental Duty; nephew of Lady Charlotte Greville
Ensign James, Lord Hay	1st Foot Guards	ADC Maitland
Ensign the Hon. John Montagu	2nd Foot Guards	Regimental Duty; son of fourth Lord Rokeby; became fifth baron
Ensign the Hon. Henry Montagu	3rd Foot Guards	Regimental Duty; son of fourth Lord Rokeby
Ensign the Hon. Edward Stopford	3rd Foot Guards	ADC/Byng
Cornet William Huntley	1st Kings Dragoon Guards	Regimental Duty
Rev. Briscall	Chaplain	Chaplain at DofW HQ
Dr John Hume	Army medical staff	Wellington's personal doctor

Part III The Richmond Family

Name	Remarks
Duke of Richmond	
Duchess of Richmond	
Captain The Earl of March	Aged 24; ADC/Prince of Orange
Lieutenant Lord George Lennox	Aged 22; ADC/Duke of Wellington
Lady Georgiana Lennox	Aged 20
Lady Mary Lennox	Aged 25
Lady Sarah Lennox	Aged 23
Lady Jane Lennox	Aged 17
Lord William Pitt Lennox	Aged 16; ADC/Maitland
Spencer Madan	Boys' tutor

Not in the Invitation List but present

Such was the prestige of having been at the Ball that in the years following 1815 there were repeated claims that various additional people had been present. Firm evidence has been found for only six.

Major-General von Müffling Field Marshall Prince Blücher's liaison officer to the Duke of Wellington was Major-General Müffling, who was certainly the most important of the Allied officers attached to Wellington's HQ, and was both popular and respected in Brussels. All the other Allied liaison officers were on all the invitation lists – D'Alava (Spain), Pozzo di Borgo (Russia), Vincent (Austria) and Washington (Bavaria) – but not Müffling. This seems a curious oversight, but it is clear from his memoirs that he was dressed in full uniform and accompanied Wellington to the Ball, arriving at about midnight.[2]

Lieutenant Claude Alexander, 92nd Foot There is a jacket in the National Scottish Army Museum, Edinburgh, which was donated in the 1930s with the explanation that it had been worn at the Ball by Lieutenant Claude Alexander, Adjutant of the 92nd, an ancestor of the donor. Alexander's name is not on any Invitation List. It is unthinkable that Alexander should have 'gate-crashed', as not only did the Duchess know most of the officers of her father's regiment and particularly someone in a special position, such as the adjutant, but the Commanding Officer, Cameron of Fassiefern (who was present at the Ball) was the last man to permit rules, either military or social, to be flouted. But the regiment's pipers and dancers were due to perform at this prestigious occasion and it would have been perfectly proper – indeed, expected – of the adjutant that he should attend to ensure that all went well. Such attendance would have been 'on duty' and thus not requiring a separate invitation, which the Duchess would have well understood.

The Misses Perceval A donation to the Museum of Costume in Bath in 1969 comprises 'two ball-gowns worn by the Misses Perceval at the Eve-of-Waterloo Ball in Brussels – their brother being A.D.C. to Wellington.'[3] The dresses, shown at Plate 5, are definitely of the period, but there is no doubt that the Misses Perceval were not on any of the three known versions of the Invitation List, while none of Wellington's ADCs were named Perceval. But, Commander Hon. George Perceval, RN was on the invitation list (see Chapter X) and it is certainly possible that his sisters Helena and Caroline-Frances were in Brussels, probably staying with friends or relations (the Misses Arden were distant cousins).

Children It was a recognised practice at the time that parents could take children to balls such as this. Some may have had a specific written invitation, such as Mr Lance Junior, but others clearly did not. The **Prince de Ligne** was the 10-year-old son of the Countess d'Oultremont, and while his name appears with that of his mother in the Delhaize List, it is in neither the Goodwood nor the De Ros List. However, his name is mentioned by a number of those who were present and Cotton recounts an anecdote that the prince was seen sitting on the knee of the Duke of Brunswick. The present Prince de Ligne has confirmed to the author that his great-great-great grandfather was present.

The Dictionary of National Biography states that Lady Charlotte Greville's youngest son, **Henry Greville**, aged 15, was taken to the Ball by no less a person than the Duke of Wellington.[4] The Duke was well known for his excellent relations with children, so there seems to be no reason to doubt that Henry Greville was actually at the Ball and in his company, but, bearing in mind that the Duke and Müffling arrived at the Ball at about midnight, it seems more likely that the boy was already there.

Napoleonic Officers In the years following the war there were rumours that one or more officers from Napoleon's army travelled incognito throughout Belgium, spying out the land before the great attack. One such story went so far as to allege that a Colonel Labédoyère, one of Napoleon's aides-de-camp, entered the ballroom at rue de la Blanchisserie, but was misled by the revelry and dancing into reporting back to his master that the British were effete amateurs who could not possibly pose a serious threat to the professional and battle-hardened French forces.[5] There were many uniforms from a wide range of armies at the Ball and it would have been difficult to identify an interloper, but no definite proof has been found to substantiate this story.

Part V Summary

In summary, it appears that 228 people were invited, plus ten members of the Richmond household, making a total of 238.

	Nationality	Men	Ladies	Sons	Daughters**	Children
Civilians	Belgian	13	12	1	7	1
	British*	12	24	2	17	2
	French*	2	1			
Diplomats	Foreign	6	1			
	British	6				
Military	Austrian	1				
	Brunswick	2				
	French	1				
	Nassau	1				
	Netherlands	4				
	Prussian	1				
British	Army – serving***	104				
	Army – retired	2				
	KGL	1				
	RN – serving	2				
	RN – retired	2				
Richmond Family		2	1	3	4	
TOTALS		162	39	6	28	3
GRAND TOTAL		238				

Table IV Invitations – Summary

*   Includes Army/Navy officers, wives and children.

**   Where Invitation List states 'Misses/Mademoiselles' this has been taken as two, except for the Miss Rumbolds (three) and Miss Capels (four).

*** Includes the Hereditary Prince of Orange, who was a serving general in the British Army.

Attendance at the Ball

The Goodwood, De Ros, Delhaize Lists and the consolidated list given above all concern *invitations*. Captain Verner makes it clear that the Duchess gave him *written* invitations to deliver to the cavalry officers – 'she accordingly placed the letters or Cards in my hands.'[6] These he then passed by hand to the individuals concerned following a field-day at Grammont. It is impossible to set an accurate date on this but it would appear to have been at least a week before the 15th. The Duchess did not overlook very recent arrivals: it is known for certain, for example, that Rear-Admiral Sir Pulteney Malcolm did not arrive until 11 am on 14 June, but his name is on the Invitation List.[7]

Who actually attended is a different matter. As is normal in such situations, some of those who received invitations clearly declined well in advance. Lieutenant-Colonel Lord Fitzroy Somerset's wife, Emily, had given birth to their first child in late May 1815[8] and they were clearly otherwise engaged, while Lady Charlotte Capel was in the eighth month of her thirteenth pregnancy and stayed at home with her daughter Harriet, although her husband and two other daughters did attend.

Two newly married officers, Colonel Sir William De Lancey and Lieutenant-Colonel Lord Saltoun, turned down their invitations, both having been wrenched from their honeymoons. Others who were on the list are known to have been prevented from attending by the military developments on 15 June 1815. This included the commander 3rd Infantry Brigade, Major-General Adam, together with his ADC[9] (Captain Yorke), while the Prince of Orange's AQMG, Lieutenant-Colonel Sir George Berkeley, and one of his ADCs, Lieutenant Webster, were also absent, although the latter later delivered a message to the prince at the Ball about midnight. There were undoubtedly others.

There could also have been last-minute decisions not to attend. With the threat of the French armies just days, if not hours, away, some Belgian and English civilians may have left Brussels at short notice, whilst some Belgians may have remained in Brussels but deemed it unwise to attend such an English-oriented event at a time when their former occupiers seemed to be on the verge of regaining power.

If all these assumptions are correct it appears that as many as fifty of those on the lists may not have attended, but even if some of the assumptions are incorrect, it would still appear that total attendance probably did not exceed about 200–210.

NOTES

1   The present Lord Verulam has searched his family archives and cannot find any trace of the document sent to his ancestor; communication to this author.
2   The name of Major the Count de Sales, the Sardinian liaison officer, does not appear on any invitation list. He was certainly present in the Duke of Wellington's suite at Waterloo on 18 June, but it is not known whether he was in Brussels on 15 June. BLib Add Ms 34707. FO 328.
3   'The Waterloo Dresses,' Byrde and Saunders, Costume No. 34, 2000; p. 64.
4   *Dictionary of National Biography*, Entry for Greville, Henry William.
5   *L'histoire du Duc de Wellington*, General Brialmont, Brussels, 1856.
6   *Reminiscences of William Verner (1782–1871) 7th Hussars*.
7   '*Wednesday 14th*: At 11 am arrived at Bruxelles and waited upon His Grace the Duke of Wellington, consulted relative to my Instructions and the Service I am employed on to cooperate with the Allied Armies.' *The Journal of Rear-Admiral Pulteney Malcolm* (PRO ADM 50/87).
8   De Ros List is annotated 'Neither were present'. Also confirmed in Somerset's Account in *Waterloo Papers* pp. 6–7.
9   Adam and Yorke are marked as 'Not present' in the De Ros List.

CHAPTER VIII
Continental Guests

A total of forty-six invitations went to non-English guests who came from a variety of European countries and backgrounds.

DUTCH/BELGIAN

Frederick, Hereditary Prince of Orange As a prince of the blood royal, the Hereditary Prince was the senior guest, but as a serving general in the British Army he is included in Chapter XI.

William Frederick Charles, Prince of Orange The Hereditary Prince's younger brother, Prince William Frederick Charles (always known as Frederick), was born in 1797. Like his elder brother he spent most of his childhood in England, but was then commissioned into the Prussian Army in March 1813 and spent the remainder of the war as a staff officer with various Prussian headquarters. He took part in the advance across northern Europe into the Netherlands, accompanying von Bülow into the city of Brussels and thence onwards into France. He was recalled by his father and promoted to lieutenant-general in the Dutch service and appointed to command the 1st Division in the newly revived Dutch Army. On 4 April 1815 Prince Frederick was appointed commander of the Netherlands Field Army, but when his elder brother, the Hereditary Prince, handed over to the Duke of Wellington and became commander I Corps on 2 May, Prince Frederick was given command of the Netherlands Indian Brigade and the Netherlands 1st Division, which formed part of the 2nd Anglo–Netherlands Corps commanded by Lieutenant-General Lord Hill.

Prince and Duke Prosper-Louis d'Arenberg (b. 1785) The d'Arenbergs were a most distinguished family, whose title had been conferred by the Holy Roman Empire; all the children were either princes or princesses, but only the eldest son bore the title of duke. Three were invited to the Ball: the reigning Duke Prosper-Louis; his brother Prince Pierre d'Alcantara Charles (b. 1790), and his uncle, Prince Auguste Marie Raymond (b. 1753).

There were two curious links, neither of them happy, between the d'Arenberg family and that of their hostess, the Gordons.

Duke Prosper's father, Prince Louis-Engelbert (1750–1820) was the heir apparent to the dukedom, a handsome boy, full of promise and popular with his future subjects. Unfortunately, when he was just 15 years old he suffered a terrible accident while a member of a shooting party led by his father. In a moment of confusion, the boy was shot in the face at very close range by a British diplomat and, while the circumstances have never been adequately explained, it was said at the time that had the diplomat not fired then Duke Charles could well have done so, thus wounding his own son. This suggests that the boy may have got ahead of the firing line, either through foolhardiness or misunderstanding, but, whatever the reason, his face was seriously disfigured and, most serious of all, he lost the sight of both eyes. The person who caused this dreadful wound was the British ambassador, Sir William Gordon (1726–1798), whose family had interests in Jamaica and property in Somerset, but, as his name indicates, was a distant member of the same family as the Duchess of Richmond.

Louis-Engelbert inherited the dukedom from his father in 1778, married and had children, and proved to be a wise and enlightened ruler, but his disabilities were such that when his eldest son, Prince Prosper-Louis D'Arenberg (1786–1861), came of age in 1803, he chose to step down. The French occupation of the Austrian Netherlands in 1793 followed its usual brutal fashion and Louis-Engelbert's mother-in-law, Elizabeth Pauline, Countess de Lauragais, Duchesse de Brancas, was accused of sending letters to royalists and emigrés. She was found guilty and guillotined in Brussels on 7 February 1794. When he came to power, Napoleon confiscated the family's lands and deprived them of their ancient title, although, in partial compensation, he made Louis-Engelbert a count of the French Empire.

Having succeeded his father in 1803, Prince and Duke Prosper-Louis (1785–1861) joined the French Army and in 1806 was appointed commanding officer of the Régiment de Chevau-légers Belges, which was redesignated 27e Chasseurs à Cheval in 1808. The young man went on to secure his position a few months later when he married the Empress Josephine's niece, Stephanie Tascher de la Pagerie,[1] but the ill-fortune which seemed to dog this family returned in 1811. The duke was serving with the 27e Chasseurs in Spain when, on 28 October 1811, his unit was one of those taken completely by surprise in the British dawn attack which opened the Battle of Arroyo dos Molinos. As the Frenchmen emerged from their tents the pipers of the 92nd Foot, the Gordon Highlanders, with a due sense of irony, played 'Hey Johnny Cope, are ye waukin' yet' and in the confusion d'Arenberg was captured by a sword-wielding sergeant of the same regiment. Wellington was delighted by the capture of an officer linked by marriage to the emperor's family.

74

Yet more tragedies followed. In 1812 Louis-Engelbert's sister, Princess Pauline de Schwartzenburg, was in Paris for the celebrations of the marriage of Napoleon to Marie-Louise. During the celebrations the Austrian embassy caught fire and the unfortunate lady was burned to death. Then in 1814 another of Louis-Engelbert's sons, who was in Vienna for the Congress, was thrown by his horse and killed.

The third member of this family invited to the Ball was General Prince Auguste-Marie-Raymond, Duke d'Arenberg, Count de la Marck, a general in both the Austrian and Dutch armies.

The d'Arenbergs were among the leaders of Brussels society, but despite Louis-Engelbert's hunting accident, caused by a Gordon, and the capture of Prosper by the Gordon Highlanders, they appear to have attended the Ball.

Duke and Duchess de Beaufort and Mademoiselle Soon after their arrival in Brussels, Lady Caroline Capel wrote to her mother on 6 July 1814 that 'the two great Men of this Town are the Duke d'Arenberg . . . & the Duke de Beaufort. The latter you would like, He was the only Man of Rank & property in this country who made a firm stand against Bonaparte, who in consequence surrounded his most magnificent Chateau near this Town & burnt it to the ground . . .'[2]

Duke Frédéric-Auguste-Alexandre de Beaufort-Spontin (d.1817) had been appointed governor of the Austrian Netherlands by the Emperor of Austria as soon as the allies retook Brussels in February 1814 but he was quickly replaced, first by Baron de Horst, a Prussian and then by General Baron Vincent. Later in 1814 Prince William of Orange, the future King William, appointed the Duke de Beaufort president of his Privy Council. The duke's second wife, Ernestine, Countess de Starhemberg, was a daughter of Prince Louis-Joseph-Marie Starhemberg, who had lived in England during the Napoleonic Wars.

The Beauforts were good friends of the Capels. Lady Capel described her, slightly uncharitably, as '. . . a very amiable Ugly little Woman' and the two couples often met at both private dinner parties and at balls. The de Beauforts were also friends with the Richmonds and the two wives did as much as they could to foster good relations between the Belgian and Dutch communities and in early November 1814, for example, they were joint patrons of a large ball.

Duke Charles-Joseph and Duchess d'Ursel Charles-Joseph, fourth Duke d'Ursel was the son of Wolfgang-Guillaume, the third duke, who had played a brief role in the Brabançon Revolt of 1789. Charles-Joseph was appointed mayor of Brussels under Napoleon, remaining in office from 1809 until the job was taken over by Baron van der Linden d'Hooghvorst in 1814. Having been seen as the chief supporter of French rule he was arrested and exiled to Munster in Germany, but after only a month he was allowed to return home to become minister of the interior in the first provisional government. When the first proper government was established in late 1815, he became minister of public works. His wife, Josephine Ferrero-Fieschi, Princesse de Masserano, was a friend of the Duchess of Richmond.

Marquis and Marquise d'Assche Also in the top stratum of guests were Maximilien-Louis Count van der Noot, Marquis d'Assche (1764–1847) and his second wife, Adélaide-Marie-Népomucène-Ferdinande Agnès d'Yve (1792–1879), daughter of the Marquis d'Yve, Vicomte de Bavay. They had married in April 1812 at Brussels and the twenty-eight years difference in age was by no means unusual in those times. They got on well with the English colony, the marquise having been joint patron of a ball in late 1814 and she was described as, 'by her situation, spirit and high distinction, one of the leading ladies of high society in her age'.

They occupied a large residence on the corner of the rue Ducale, which was actually joined to the Palais Royal. Lord Uxbridge stayed there both before Waterloo and afterwards when he was recovering from his wounds and amputation. Tantalisingly, it is known that the marquise kept a journal which included descriptions of social life in Brussels (including the Ball) at this period, but it has been lost.[3] Like many of the ladies at the Ball, the marquise was pregnant, giving birth to a daughter on 1 September 1815. They were friends of the Richmonds, Lady Georgiana de Ros annotating their names in her invitation list with the comment: '. . . from their house we saw the wounded brought in – Lord Uxbridge, Lord F. Somerset, &c.'

Count and Countess d'Oultremont Charles-Ignace, Count d'Oultremont (d. 1802) married a very wealthy woman, Anne-Henriette du Neuf (1757–1830) and their eldest child, Emile (1787–1851), became Count d'Oultremont in 1802. Count Emile's first marriage was to his cousin, Marie-Françoise de Lierneux de Presles, who also came from a rich family, but she died soon afterwards and in late 1814 he married the recently widowed Princess Louise de Ligne (1785–1864). Thus, the pair attending the Ball were Emile, Count d'Oultremont and Countess Louise. The countess, generally reckoned to be the most beautiful woman present at the Ball, was accompanied by her 11-year-old son by her first marriage, Prince Eugene Lamoral de Ligne (1804–1880). He was the grandson of Field-Marshal Prince Charles Joseph de Ligne (1735–1814), whose vast estates were in Hainaut, but who spent most of his adult life either at the Austrian court or on campaign with the Austrian army – he was a field marshal in both the Austrian and Russian armies. The prince spent his final months in Vienna (he died in December 1814) and it was he who uttered the famous remark: *'Le Congrès danse mais ne marche pas.'* Prince Charles Joseph's two sons predeceased him, the elder in 1792, the second in a horse-riding accident in Vienna. The latter, Prince Louis Lamoral (1766–1813), married Comtesse Louise de Duras (1785–1864), and when his grandfather died in 1814, their son, Prince Eugene, became the head of the house of De Ligne at the tender age of 10.

Dowager-Countess d'Oultremont and Mademoiselles This was Count Emile's mother, Anne-Henriette d'Oultremont, the widow of Charles-Ignace. The 'Mademoiselles' were two (possibly more) of her daughters.

Count and Countess Mercy d'Argentau Count François de Mercy d'Argentau was at one time the Austrian ambassador to the Kingdom of Bavaria. When the new Kingdom of the Netherlands was established the count was appointed Grand Chamberlain to the King of the Netherlands and governor of the province of Southern Brabant. The family owned the Hôtel d'Argentau on the Place Royale in Brussels.

Baron and Baroness van der Capellan Following the departure of the French, Baron van der Capellan was appointed commissioner for the United Provinces in Brussels, i.e., the representative of William of Orange. He was then appointed the prince's representative at the Congress of Vienna, but travelled to Brussels following the return of Napoleon to France in early 1815. From 16 to 19 June 1815 he was responsible for issuing regular and reassuring bulletins on the progress of the war to the citizens of Brussels. At the end of 1815 he was sent as governor-general of the Dutch East Indies, a position he held until 1825.

Count and Countess Auguste de Liederkerque-Beaufort and Mademoiselles Count Auguste de Liederkerque-Beaufort (1789–1855) was a descendant of a cadet branch of the very important and ancient Liederkerque family. His wife Alix (usually known as Charlotte), whom he had married in 1813, was a daughter of the Count and Countess de la Tour Du Pin, who also attended the Ball. The 'Mademoiselles' were presumably the count's sisters.

Baron and Baroness D'Hoogvorst; Mademoiselle and Monsieur C D'Hoogvorst; Madame Constant D'Hoogvorst. Baron Joseph van der Linden d'Hoogvorst was appointed mayor of Brussels on 25 February 1814, following the entry of the Allies into the city on 1 February, a post he retained until 1817. Madame Constant d'Hoogvorst was his mother.[4]

Count and Countess De Grassiac; Countess De Ruilly; Baron de Herelt; Baron de Tuyll de Serooskerken. No information has been discovered.

FRENCH

General Count Charles-Eugene de Lalaing d'Audenarde and Countess de Lalaing. The Count de Lalaing d'Audenarde came from a Belgian family, but had served for many years in the French Army, where his appointments had included a captaincy in the 112e Ligne and command of the 3ème Cuirassiers. He commanded a brigade in 1812 and transferred to the service of Louis XVIII in 1814. On the return of Napoleon in 1815 he remained true to his oath to Louis XVIII and moved with the king to Ghent where he was appointed second-in-command of the *Garde du Corps*.

Count de la Rochefoucauld. The count, a descendant of a distinguished French family, was an official at the court of Louis XVIII at Ghent.

Count and Countess de la Tour-Dupin. The count was the French minister, representing Louis XVIII, at The Hague. Their daughter, Comtesse Auguste de Liederkerque-Beaufort, was also invited to the Ball.

Guillaume Jean Hyde de Neuville. The name 'Dr Hyde' appears in the Goodwood, De Ros and Delhaize Lists. There is no trace of a doctor of this name in either the Army List 1815 or the Waterloo Roll Call, but it is possible that this man may have been a British civilian doctor practising in Brussels. It is much more likely, however, that this was Guillaume Jean Hyde de Neuville (1776–1857).

Guillaume's grandfather, William Hyde, was a Scotsman who supported the Stuarts in the ill-fated '45 rebellion, then fled to France and settled there. His son, James Hyde, was brought up as a Frenchman and married a rich French woman; Guillaume was their son. Guillaume was a dedicated Royalist who led an extraordinarily adventurous life during the Revolution; he even, following the *coup d'état* of 18th Brumaire (9 November 1799), tried to persuade Napoleon to recall the Bourbons. One of his many enterprises was to endeavour to tunnel into the Abbey prison in order to release (the then) Commander Sidney Smith, RN, who was held there as a prisoner-of-war. Hyde failed but Smith escaped by a ruse and managed to reach England without further help from Hyde.

The young Frenchman then spent a period in hiding in Lyons under the name of 'Doctor Roland', until in 1806 Napoleon, by now emperor, suggested that he should emigrate to the United States. It was clearly dangerous to ignore such a specific suggestion and Hyde remained in the New World until 1814, when he returned to France and immediately became involved in various diplomatic negotiations on behalf of the restored Louis XVIII. He went to England where he met Sidney Smith, now a retired admiral, who showed him a map of the Mediterranean and pointed out the short distance between Napoleon's new home on Elba and the mainland. Hyde took this information back to Paris where Louis XVIII began to agitate, albeit without success, for the former emperor to be moved to a new and more remote prison.

When Louis XVIII fled to Ghent, Hyde joined him there and became involved in a variety of plans. Their main aim was for a Bourbon restoration, but Hyde's autobiography makes it very clear that the French court was actively involved in seeking to prevent a French military defeat by the Allies and, in Hyde's own words, '. . . seeking to spare [France] the shame of invasion.'[5]

Hyde made several trips to London carrying messages between the French king and the Duchess of Angoulême, a lady who, according to Napoleon, was 'the only *man* in the Bourbon family'. He was also known to the British ambassador, Sir Charles Stuart, who on 13 June 1815 wrote to London about Louis' plans to send men of influence to various French regions to foster pro-Bourbon support, in which:

> . . . a Mr Hyde is destined to endeavour to create a Movement in the vicinity of Havre, which it is hoped may give the Royalists a footing in that part of Normandy and perhaps enable them to gain possession of that town.[6]

There can be no doubt that Hyde would have been in contact with his old friend Sidney Smith in Brussels and that the latter would have introduced his French friend into English circles in the city. Hyde was completely bilingual and had an engaging personality, which made him a popular figure wherever he went. It thus appears very probable that Guillaume Jean Hyde was the man referred to as 'Dr Hyde' in the invitation lists, although, in the event, he would not have been able to attend as he left Ghent on the evening of 15 June carrying yet further messages to the duchesse, arriving in London late on the 18th.

AUSTRIAN

Field Marshal Friedrich Heinrich, Graf von Bellegarde (1760–1845)

Bellegarde's name was incorrectly spelt in the Goodwood and De Ros Lists as 'Belgade'. He was an Austrian general, whose family originally came from the Austrian Netherlands, but later settled in Savoy. He joined the Imperial Austrian Army in 1793 and rose rapidly, reaching the rank of general of cavalry in 1801 and field marshal in 1806. After a spell as governor of Galicia, he returned to the army, where he commanded the 1st Army Corps at the battles of Aspern-Essling (21–22 May 1809) and Wagram (5–6 July 1809). He then returned to the post of governor of Galicia until 1813 when he became governor-general of Lombardy and Venice. He was described as a thorough and effective administrator, and a sound military thinker, although more effective as a subordinate than in independent command.

Bellegarde was taken ill in early 1815 and told to take a rest by the Emperor of Austria. On 18 June 1816 he attended the first Waterloo anniversary dinner in Paris, as reported by Wellington's personal chaplain, Reverend Samuel Briscall, to his sister, '. . . you will recollect Bellegarde commanded the first Army that Bonaparte beat in Italy – he is a fine old Veteran and I sat at his right . . .'[7] To have attended that dinner he must have been present on the battlefield of Waterloo, which confirms his presence in Brussels, where he would have had numerous friends including Baron Vincent and the d'Arenbergs, through whom he would have met the Richmonds.

ALLIED REPRESENTATIVES

General Don Miguel Ricardo d'Alava (1770–1843). In June 1815 d'Alava combined the appointment of Spanish ambassador at The Hague with that of Spanish commissioner at Wellington's Anglo–Dutch headquarters, and as a noted *bon viveur* would have been the last man to fail to attend the Ball. Don Miguel Ricardo d'Alava was one of the great characters of the Napoleonic Wars, one of his most unusual distinctions being that he fought against Nelson at Trafalgar in 1805, where he was aboard the Spanish ship-of-the-line, *Principe de Asturias*, captained by his uncle, and ten years later he was at Wellington's side at Waterloo. He was one of Wellington's closest friends and a trusted confidant. Another Englishman who knew d'Alava well commented:

> Throughout the Peninsular War, during the time Wellington was Ambassador to Louis XVIII, at Brussels, during the Belgian campaign, and during the occupation of France by the Allied Armies, Alava was the constant guest of the 'Iron Duke'. Indeed, few men had greater influence with Wellington than this distinguished Spanish nobleman.[8]

D'Alava spoke a rather curious form of English, but his wide circle of English friends considered him to be a very amusing talker and raconteur. In later years Wellington gave him apartments in both London and Stratfield Saye, and about the only unfavourable comment anybody ever made about him was that he had 'bad teeth'.[9]

General Count Pozzo di Borgo. Carlo Andrea, Count Pozzo di Borgo (1764–1842) was another highly unusual character. He was born at Alata in Corsica and loathed the French revolutionaries, opposing the Jacobins when they tried to take power in Corsica and becoming a strong supporter of the British invasion of the island in 1794. Although still relatively young, he became the head of the British-sponsored civil government, so that when the French retook the island two years later he had no choice but to leave. He disliked the Buonaparte family and eventually gravitated to Russia where he joined the Imperial diplomatic service in 1804. He was one of the advocates of the Austro–Russian alliance in 1805, but when Tsar Alexander I and Napoleon concluded the Treaty of Tilsit in 1807 he left the service, only to be re-engaged in 1812 when Napoleon invaded Russia. Following Napoleon's first abdication in 1814, he was appointed Russian ambassador to France, where he gained many friends through his efforts to ameliorate the effects of the occupation on the French public, although Wellington was later to claim that Pozzo di Borgo was the recipient of many bribes.[10] With Napoleon's return he moved to The Netherlands where he was appointed Russian commissioner at Wellington's headquarters. He was unmarried at the time of the Duchess of Richmond's Ball, but in 1819 he married Maria Francesca Allessandri, by whom he had ten children.

General of Cavalry Karl, Baron Vincent (1757–1834). Karl Vincent was born in Florence of Lorranian parents and joined the Imperial Austrian Army at a young age. His early military service was with a famous Austrian cavalry regiment, Latour-Dragonen Nr.7, a predominantly Belgian unit which had been raised in 1790 by Count de Baillet-Latour and which remained faithful to its oath to the emperor, even during the Brabançon Revolt. Vincent continued to be promoted, at one time commanding his own regiment, the Cheveaux-Légères de Vincent, and in October 1797 he was one of the Austrian signatories to the Treaty of Campo Formio, which, among other provisions, transferred sovereignty of the Austrian Netherlands (i.e. Belgium) from the Hapsburgs to the French Republic.

As described earlier, the first man to be appointed governor of the Austrian Netherlands following the expulsion of the French was the Duke de Beaufort-Spontin, but he was quickly replaced, first by a Prussian, Baron de Horst, and then by Baron Vincent, who took office on 4 May 1814. Vincent held the post until August and was then appointed the emperor's ambassador to the court of Louis XVIII, first in Paris and then in Ghent, which he combined with being the official Austrian representative at Wellington's headquarters.

Colonel Jakob Washington (1778–1848). Because of his English-sounding name there has been some confusion about Jakob Washington. In the Goodwood and De Ros Lists he is named simply as 'Colonel Washington' and appears among the British officers, while in the Delhaize List he is named Dashington. In fact, he was an officer in the Army of the then independent kingdom of Bavaria and was King Ludwig I's commissioner at Wellington's headquarters, and thus directly equivalent to Generals d'Alava and Pozzo di Borgo.

The Washington family lived in the north of England from the 12th century and was divided into two main branches. In the 1650s one of the Sulgrave Manor branch emigrated to Virginia in 1657 to become the ancestor of George Washington, while another from the Hallhead Hall branch went to the Netherlands. The latter's descendant, James Washington, was born at The Hague in 1778 and fought against the French when they invaded, but was forced to flee to Bavaria where he joined the army under the name of Jakob Washington. He became the military adjutant to Crown Prince Ludwig (later King Ludwig I) and accompanied his master to the negotiations which led to the signing of the Treaty of Tilsit in 1807. He rose in rank to marshal of the court, in which capacity he accompanied the Crown Prince to the Congress of Vienna in 1814. When Napoleon's return to mainland France forced the break-up of the congress, Washington was despatched to Brussels as the Bavarian commissioner, where among other tasks he negotiated an agreement with Wellington concerning the employment of Bavarian troops in the coming campaign.[11]

Baron von Brockhausen. Karl Christian, Baron von Brockhausen was the Prussian ambassador at The Hague from March 1814 to February 1816.

BRUNSWICK

Friedrich Wilhelm, Duke of Brunswick-Wolfenbüttel. Friedrich Wilhelm, Duke of Brunswick (1771–1815) was the son of a distinguished general, the great-nephew of Frederick the Great and brother-in-law of England's Prince Regent. Described in Byron's *Childe Harold* as 'Brunswick's fated chieftain' he was present in Brussels in June 1815 as commander of an independent contingent of about divisional strength, which he had placed 'at the Prince Regent's disposition'.[12] His men were popularly known as 'the black Brunswickers', although it was only the hussar regiment and the guards battalion that wore full black with the death's-head cap-badge in mourning for the duke's father.[13]

The previous duke, Karl Wilhelm Ferdinand (1735–1806), served in the Seven Years War, under, first, the Duke of Cumberland and, secondly, his uncle Prince Ferdinand of Brunswick, and was present at the battles of Minden and Warburg. Following the end of the war, the prince visited England with his bride, Augusta, the daughter of the late Frederick, Prince of Wales (1707–51). Karl Wilhelm succeeded his father in 1780 and was a popular and effective ruler, but took up the sword again in 1792 as the

1. The Duchess of Richmond's Ball in Brussels on the evening of 15 June 1815. Lieutenant Webster (with sword) delivers his fateful message to the Duke of Wellington and the Prince of Orange, while some of the officers, realising what is afoot, are already saying farewell to their partners. By courtesy of the Trustees of the Goodwood Collection.

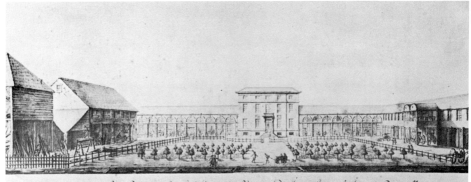

ue Perspective de La Fabrique de Voitures De Jean Simons le Jeune, à Bruxelles.

2. This large estate, formerly a carriage factory, was rented by the Richmond family in 1814. This view from the ramparts shows the main house (centre), to the right of which is the former carriage showroom where the Ball was held.

3. A Lieutenant and Captain of 2nd (Coldstream) Foot Guards in ball dress, his rank depicted by the single epaulette on the right shoulder.

4. An English aide-de-camp in evening dress. The single epaulette on his right shoulder indicates that he is a lieutenant in rank and ADC to an infantry general; if cavalry it would be on his left shoulder. Some officers went straight from the Ball and into battle at Quatre Bras dressed like this.

5. Two charming dresses, reputedly worn by the Misses Perceval at the Ball (see chapter VII). Undoubtedly contemporary with the Ball, they are made of brown silk gauze woven with vertical stripes. Virtually identical in design, each comprises a low-cut, high-waisted bodice with card brown gauze over-sleeves, and a full length skirt with three bias-cut flounces. By courtesy of the Museum of Costume, Bath.

6. The uniform of Lieutenant Claude Alexander, Adjutant, 92nd Foot (Gordon Highlanders). According to family tradition this was worn at the Ball, which seems highly likely, as described in Chapter VII. © and by courtesy of the National Museum of Scotland.

7. Lady Frances Wedderburn-Webster (1793-1837), seen here in 1812, was married to a foolish husband. She had numerous affairs, the most notorious being with the Duke of Wellington in May-June 1815 in Brussels, which resulted in a court case in England in 1816. By courtesy of the National Portrait Gallery, London.

8. Major-General Sir Edward Barnes (d. 1838) arrived in Brussels in September 1814. He was a dashing and wealthy bachelor, and became very popular in English social circles, but when he proposed to Maria Capel in February 1814 she rejected him instantly and firmly. By courtesy of the National Portrait Gallery, London.

9. The waltz delighted the younger generation in Brussels in 1814-15 and scandalized most of their parents. This picture, taken from a contemporary dancing-master's manual, shows the steps and it was the continuous physical contact, particularly the hands on each other's waists, that shocked generations used to more stately quadrille and English country dances.

10. Major features of the Ball were the sword dance and reels performed by sergeants of the Gordon Highlanders at the particular request of the Duchess of Richmond, whose father had raised the regiment.

11. Lieutenant-Colonel John Cameron of Fassiefern, Commanding Officer of the 92nd Foot, the Gordon Highlanders. One of the finest battalion commanders in Wellington's Army. He attended the Ball on 15 June, was wounded the following afternoon at Quatre Bras and died that evening.

12. Spencer Madan, a serious young man who was tutor to the Richmond children from September 1814 to January 1816. His letters give a detailed insight into life in the Richmond household, including his difficult relations with the Duchess and the many hair-raising misdeeds of her younger sons.
Courtesy CW Brocklebank, Esq.

13. *The Cricketers* by James West. Cricket was very popular with the British Army in Belgium in 1815 and the Duke of Richmond played regularly. The figure in military uniform is Ralph Izzard, uncle by marriage to Colonel Sir William De Lancey who died of wounds received at Waterloo. Private Collection.

commander of the combined Austrian and German army assembled to crush the French Revolution. Despite having some sympathy with the revolutionaries' demand for reform, he sheltered the Comte de Lille (the future King Louis XVIII) and led the advance into France. Interference from the King of Prussia led to Brunswick's resignation but he returned to service again in 1806 only to be severely wounded at the Battle of Auerstädt. He was carried with his retreating troops until he died on 10 November 1806.

Once his troops had overrun Brunswick, Napoleon absorbed the dukedom into the newly created Kingdom of Westphalia, so that the new duke, Friedrich Wilhelm, commenced his reign in exile in Austria, loathing the French in general and Napoleon in particular, and with the sworn intent of regaining his dukedom. He raised a corps of partisans which he led in a campaign against the French and at one stage was in control of his dukedom only to be forced out again following the Austrian defeat at Wagram. He took the remnants of his corps to the North Sea coast whence they escaped to England to continue the fight. Most of his troops served alongside the British in the Peninsula but others remained in England, until all were able to return to Brunswick in 1813–14.

On Napoleon's escape from Elba, Brunswick signed an agreement in Vienna on 18 April 1815 under which he agreed to serve under English command, and his men started to arrive in the Netherlands on 10 May with the final column arriving on 5 June. They were quartered around Vilvorde, north of Brussels, with Duke Friedrich's headquarters at Laecken. The total contingent was some 7,000 strong and formed a brigade, commanded by Duke Friedrich in person. Brunswick's presence at the Ball is verified in numerous accounts.

AIDES-DE-CAMP

Colonel Georg-Guillaume-Auguste-Henri, Hereditary Prince of Nassau. There is no doubt that a prince of Nassau was attached to Wellington's headquarters as an extra ADC, but there is some confusion about precisely who this was. According to Dalton's 'Waterloo Roll Call' he was the 'Hereditary Prince of Nassau-Usingen', son of Duke Bernard of Nassau.[14] According to the *Almanac de Gotha*, however, the Duke of Nassau-Usingen in 1815 was named Friedrich-Augustus, who died childless on 24 March 1816. Delhaize lists 'le duc héréditaire Adolphe de Nassau', but the only Prince Adolphe was born on 24 July 1817. To resolve this, a small historical excursion is necessary.

The Holy Roman Empire included a large number of minor Germanic states, which often changed their size and composition. Sometimes rulers died with multiple heirs, resulting in their fiefdom being split up, or without any heirs at all, which resulted in endless wrangling over who should succeed. On other occasions, dynastic marriages resulted in two states being combined. The inevitable outcome was to make their history confusing to outsiders.

The ruling family of the county of Nassau originated in the 12th century in the small town of Nassau on the Lahn river, their territory covering an area north and east of the Rhine (an area now subsumed in the modern-day *Länder* of Hesse and Rhineland-Palatinate). There were repeated re-orientations over the centuries, but the main branches were Nassau-Usingen, Nassau-Weilburg and Nassau-Dillenberg, each ruled by a count with the status of a prince of the Holy Roman Empire. One of the most significant changes came when Nassau-Dillenberg combined with the Dutch county of Orange in 1555, creating the house of Nassau-Orange, with the ruler gaining the additional title of Prince of Orange. This particular line eventually led to the current ruling houses of The Netherlands and Luxembourg, and it also produced King William III of England.

Napoleon's armies overran central Germany in 1806 and in August of that year he dissolved the Holy Roman Empire and replaced it with a number of new political entities, including the Confederation of the Rhine. One element of this new state was the Duchy of Nassau, which combined the smaller Nassauer territories into a single unit. Even then, Napoleon's tidy mind was defeated, since the locals insisted on two joint rulers, who were titled the Duke of Nassau and the Sovereign Prince (Grand Duke) of Nassau. Thus, Prince Friedrich-Augustus of Nassau-Usingen (d.1816) assumed the title of Duke of Nassau, while Prince Friedrich Wilhelm of Nassau-Weilburg (d.1816) became the Sovereign Prince (Grand Duke) of Nassau. This explains why, in his letter to the Duke of Wellington dated 10 June 1815 Grand Duke Friedrich of Nassau refers to 'le Duc de Nassau et moi' and 'le Duc mon cousin'.[15]

That letter concerned the organisation and subsidies for the Nassau contingent in the Anglo–Netherlands Army, which formed an independent brigade commanded by Major-General Baron von Krusé. Also included in that letter was a request for a Nassauer officer to be placed at army headquarters and this was Colonel Georg-Guillaume-Auguste-Henri, Hereditary Prince of Nassau (1792–1839), the son of Duke Friedrich-Wilhelm. His official appointment was as extra ADC to the duke and he was the officer invited to the Ball.[16]

Dutch ADCs The Hereditary Prince of Orange was very popular with the English community in Brussels and attended many social occasions there. Not surprisingly, his aides-de-camp frequently accompanied him to such events, making them well known to the English. Thus, the Duchess of Richmond's invitation list included the prince's principal ADC, Colonel L H T du Cayler, as well as Colonel J A E Knijff.

Frederick, Prince of Orange was also popular with the British and his principal ADC, Colonel Baron d'Iroy, was also invited to the Ball. D'Iroy was a friend of the Capels and highly thought of by Captain Digby Mackworth, who described him as having spent many years in England and speaking the language exceedingly well. (This officer's name was misspellt in the Goodwood List as 'd'Irvyre' and is omitted from the De Ros and Delhaize Lists.)

NOTES

1   There were no children of this marriage and they were divorced in 1816.
2   Capel Letters, p. 50.
3   There was an article 'La marquise d'Assche ou les Memoires perdus' by Carlo Bronne in the journal *Nouvelles Equisses Brussels 1946*, but this cannot be traced.
4   For unknown reasons, the Goodwood List shows 'Le Maire de Bruxelles' separately from 'Baron et Baroness d'Hoogvorst'; this is repeated in the De Ros List but the Delhaize List omits any mention of 'Le maire'. It is assumed that this was simply an error.
5   Hyde de Neuville, Vol. ii, p. 38.
6   Letter Stuart to Castlereagh dated 13 June 1815. PRO FO 27/117.
7   Briscall letters, NAM 2002–05–3. Letter dated Paris, 20 June 1816.
8   *My Recollections 1806–1873*, Vol. 2, Lord William Pitt Lennox, Hurst & Blacket,
9   Mrs Arbuthnot, Volume i, p. 409
10 20 Feb 1824. 'The Duke told me that Pozzo was the greatest rogue in Europe, that he was bribed by everybody & that, not having had a shilling in *1814*, he now has *50,000£*. I said that the Emperor of Russia wd send for him some day to Petersburg & squeeze it all out of him; but he said I might depend upon it that he never wd trust himself within the Emperor's grasp, that he was buying estates in Tuscany & that he wd make excuses upon the score of the climate' Mrs Arbuthnot, Volume i, p. 290.
11 Letter from Washington to Wellington in SD, Vol. X p. 265. Written in Brussels on 9 May and signed 'Washington. Colonel au service de S.M. le Roi de la Bavière.'
12 Wellington Dispatches, Vol. XII, pp. 290, 332.
13 The cap-badge for line infantry was the white horse of Brunswick and for Jaeger (rifle) units the usual hunting horn.
14 Dalton, 'Waterloo Roll Call', p. 10.
15 Supplementary Dispatches, Volume X, p. 451,
16 Prince Friedrich-Wilhelm died in January 1816 and was succeeded by Prince George. Then, when Prince Friedrich-Augustus also died in March 1816 without an heir, Prince George became the undisputed sole sovereign of the duchy.

CHAPTER IX
English Civilian Guests

The English civilian guests were largely people with titles or with strong social connections; people who in England would have been described as belonging to the 'Ten Thousand'.

Henry, Earl Conyngham and Family. The Conyngham family consisted of Henry, Earl Conyngham and his wife, Elizabeth, Countess Conyngham, together with their children, Viscount Mountcharles, the Hon. Albert Conyngham and Lady Elizabeth Conyngham. The family originated in Scotland but moved to Mount Charles in County Donegal, Ireland in 1611 and purchased the Slane estate in 1701. Henry, Earl Conyngham (1766–1832) was the eldest son of the second Baron Conyngham, and succeeded his father in 1787. He gave strong support to the Union in the Irish House of Lords for which he was created Viscount Conyngham of Mountcharles in the Irish peerage in 1789 and Earl Conyngham (still in the Irish peerage) in 1797.

He married Miss Elizabeth Denison, the daughter of a self-made Surrey merchant banker in 1794, and once the earl had established himself as a representative Irish peer in the House of Lords in London, they began an inexorable rise up the ladder of London society. In common with many society ladies of the time, the countess had a number of affairs, including one in the 1790s with Hon. John Ponsonby, reputedly the handsomest man of his time, while society gossip suggested that the father of her second son, the Hon. Albert Conyngham, was none other than the Prince of Wales. The countess was described as beautiful but portly, as well as shrewd and greedy, and was later to become the Prince Regent's acknowledged mistress.

Quite why they were in Brussels is not clear, since the earl and his wife were both close to the Prince Regent and are not known to have suffered financial problems, but they were clearly in no hurry to return to England as they spent the winter of 1815/16 in Italy. The Conynghams took three of their children to the Ball, their two sons plus Lady Elizabeth, who was reputedly being wooed (unsuccessfully) by Mr Legh, MP (see below). The second daughter, Lady Harriet, was not included in the Invitation List.

Earl Mountnorris and Family. Arthur Annesley, 1st Earl Mountnorris (1743–1816) and his family arrived in Brussels on 21 June 1814.[1] The earl was in very poor health and a personal doctor – a 'very clever medical man' according to Harriet Capel – was included in their entourage, but despite his ministrations the earl was regularly taken ill and died in Brussels in 1816. The earl was accompanied by his second wife, Countess Mountnorris (née Cavendish), and their two daughters, Lady Juliana Annesley and Lady Catherine Annesley, while their third daughter, Lady Frances Wedderburn-Webster, arrived with her husband a few months later.

The interests of her step-daughters were clearly close to Lady Mountnorris's heart. Lady Frances was already married and the countess married Lady Catherine off to Lord John Somerset in December, but she held out hopes for Lady Juliana right up to the Battle of Waterloo, Captain Digby Mackworth recording that on 6 June 1815:

> . . . I dined after the [cricket] match was over at General Maitland's, and met there a Lady Mountnorris and her daughter; the latter is rather good looking, but far from being in danger of setting the Thames on fire. Perhaps I injure them, but I cannot help thinking there is a little design formed against the heart of the handsome General. Lady M. is a noted old matchmaker, and the young Lady certainly appeared to set her cap at him in a very decided manner . . .

(Unbeknown to anyone but the two involved, however, General Maitland had his eyes on another lady and on this occasion the machinations of Lady Juliana and her mother came to naught[2].)

The earl was too ill to attend the Ball on 15 June and was not invited, while Mr James Wedderburn-Webster had returned to London in May and did not arrive back in Brussels until early August. Thus, the members of the family to be invited to the Ball were Countess Mountnorris and Lady Juliana, while Lady Somerset was invited with her husband and Lady Wedderburn-Webster without hers.

Lord Henry George Apsley. Aged 21, he was the eldest son of 3rd Earl Bathurst, who was married to the Duke of Richmond's youngest sister, the former Lady Georgiana Lennox. Apsley's younger brother, the Hon. Seymour Bathurst (1793–1834), was also in the Netherlands, serving with the 1st Foot Guards as an Ensign. Apsley was a suitor for his cousin, Lady Sarah Lennox, but it fell through 'for want of that odious thing called *Money*',[3] and she then went ahead and married Major-General Peregrine Maitland in August 1815. Apsley seems to have been a quiet and decent man, and it was he who had suggested his former Westminster school-fellow, Spencer Madan, as a potential tutor for the Richmond boys.[4]

John Thelluson, 2nd Baron Rendlesham (1785–1832). Lord Rendlesham's great-grandfather was a Genovese banker who moved to London to open the very successful bank of Necker & Thelluson, and his father had become the first Baron Rendlesham. The second Lord Rendlesham's first wife, Mary, daughter of Lieutenant-General Sir Samuel Dickins, died in August 1814 and why he should have been in Brussels in June 1815 is unclear, although the Duchess of Richmond, who was a heavy and not very successful gambler, would doubtless have been only too happy to impress a visiting banker. Rendlesham remained in Brussels until 27 June, when he carried a letter from Lady Georgiana Lennox to England.[5]

Lord and Lady George Seymour and Miss Seymour. The Capels note Lady George Seymour as being in Brussels in April 1815[6] and that Lord George Seymour returned to England at some time in March–April 1816.[7] This family cannot be identified with confidence, but the father may have been Lord George Seymour of Wellingore, Lincolnshire.

Hon. John Capel and Family. The Hon. John Thomas Capel (1769–1819), second son of the fourth Earl of Essex, married Lady Caroline Paget (1773–1847), daughter of the first Earl of Uxbridge in 1792. The Capels were devoted to each other – they had thirteen children between 1793 and 1815 – and were exceptionally well connected throughout the highest reaches of English society. Their life would have been easy and contented but for Capel's addiction to gambling and the enormous debts he incurred as a result. Thus, as soon as Napoleon's rule had been lifted, they went abroad to live more economically, arriving in Brussels in June 1814. They occupied a succession of houses, which had to be large to accommodate the large family and the number of servants which were essential to their status, but also cheap to suit their financial circumstances. The first house was in the Park and had a rent of only £100 per annum, ridiculously low by English standards, but even this proved too much and at the time of the Ball in June 1815 they were living in a villa outside Brussels, which was rent free. At the time of the Ball Lady Caroline was in the seventh month of her thirteenth pregnancy; so, while the Goodwood List states that 'Hon. John Capel, Lady Caroline Capel, and 4 Miss Capels' were invited, only the Hon. John Capel and two of his daughters, Georgiana (aged 20) and Maria (aged 18), actually attended while the other two daughters remained at home to look after their mother.[8]

Sir James and Lady Craufurd and Miss Jane Craufurd. This was almost certainly Sir James Craufurd, second Bt, the elder brother of Sir Charles Gregan-Craufurd and of Major-General Craufurd, famous throughout the British Army as 'Black Bob'. Sir James was formerly British minister in Hamburg (1800–3) and subsequently in Copenhagen. Lady Craufurd was the former Maria Theresa Gage, daughter of General the Hon. Thomas Gage, and they were accompanied by their daughter, Jane. The reason for the Craufurds' presence in Brussels has not been determined exactly; Sir James may have been on Foreign Office business, or they may simply have been on holiday. However, the most likely reason is that the Craufurds' two sons were stationed in Belgium. The eldest, Lieutenant Thomas Gage Craufurd, was in the 3rd Foot Guards, the other, Captain Alexander Charles Craufurd, was actually an officer in 2nd Ceylon Regiment, but was serving as a volunteer with the 12th Light Dragoons during the Waterloo campaign.[9]

Sir Hew and Lady Jane Dalrymple-Hamilton.[10] Sir Hew Dalrymple-Hamilton, 4th Bt, of North Berwick (1774–1834) and his wife, Lady Jane, went to Paris in September 1814, but were forced to leave when Napoleon returned. They arrived in Brussels on 4 June 1815 and were immediately welcomed by their friends in the British aristocracy. They spent the first night on the Hôtel de New York, but the following morning the Duchess of Richmond helped Lady Jane secure a month's lease on the Rints House in the Park. Sir Hew served for some years in the 1st Foot Guards and in 1803 was the lieutenant-colonel of the Ayrshire Militia. He was MP for Haddington (1795–1800), Ayrshire (1803–6) and Haddington Burghs (1820–6). His wife was the former Lady Jane Duncan (1779–1852), daughter of Admiral Lord Duncan, the victor at the Battle of Camperdown. They had one daughter, Henrietta, who was with them in Brussels, but does not appear on any of the invitation lists.

Sir William Johnston Bt and Lady Johnston. Sir William Johnston (1760–1844) seventh baronet, started adult life in the Honourable East India Company Army and saw active service fighting against the French on the Malabar coast. He was back in Scotland by 1783 when, at the age of 23, he married Mary, a lady then aged 57. She died childless in July 1802 and he remarried only six months later, his new wife being Maria (née Bacon), who bore him a number of children. Johnston raised the Prince of Wales's Own Fencibles in 1798 in response to the invasion scare; he commanded the regiment for four years, but it was disbanded in 1802. He represented New Windsor in the House of Commons from 1801 to 1806, but then hit financial difficulties. He lived in poverty in Edinburgh for several years, but then, like others in similarly straitened circumstances, took his family to the Continent in 1814. He was certainly in Brussels on 16 May 1815, as he signed his Will there on that day[11] and it seems logical that he and his wife were the couple named Johnston at the Ball. He remained in the Netherlands for the rest of his life, dying at the age of 84 at The Hague on 13 January 1844, the title passing to the eldest son of his second marriage.[12]

Anne, Lady Alvanley and the Miss Ardens. Richard Pepper Arden (1745–1804) was both a brilliant lawyer and a successful politician – at one time he was Attorney-General – as well as a friend of William Pitt. He was knighted in 1788 and raised to the peerage as Baron Alvanley of Alvanley in 1801. He died in 1804 and his widow, the former Anne Dorothea Wilbrahan-Bootle, outlived him by twenty-one years. His eldest son, Lord William Arden (1789–1849), joined the Coldstream Guards in 1804 at the tender age of 15 and served in the Peninsula from 1808. He then became one of the most prominent of the Regency 'bucks', being famous both for his dress and for his *bons mots*. He was also notorious for his extravagance and womanising, which rapidly depleted the family fortune. Indeed, Lady Caroline Capel wrote that Lord Alvanley had lost his sister's £10,000, thus preventing a match with a Mr Warrender after a two-year courtship.[13] Lady Alvanley and her two daughters were in Brussels by September 1814 and were still there at the time of the Ball, possibly, like so many others, seeking a 'more economical' place to live, but the selfish and profligate second Lord Alvanley appears never to have visited them.

Elizabeth Laura, Dowager Countess of Waldegrave (1760–1816). The Dowager Countess of Waldegrave was the daughter of the second Earl Waldegrave and married her cousin, the fourth earl, who died in 1789. She had four sons and one daughter, three of the four boys becoming the fifth, sixth and eighth earls, respectively. Two of the sons were drowned, the eldest, the fifth earl, aged 10, in the Thames in 1794, while her third son (the only one not to succeed to the title), Lieutenant Edward Waldegrave, RN, was drowned at sea in January 1809. The countess was almost certainly in Brussels to visit her second son, Lieutenant-Colonel John James, sixth Earl Waldegrave (1785–1835), who had taken command of the 54th Foot in 1812 and was still in command in 1815 (his regiment was part of the reserve at the Battle of Waterloo). Colonel Waldegrave had caused considerable scandal in the army as recorded by Captain Digby Mackworth:

> The 54th are commanded by Lord Waldegrave, who has greatly distressed his family by a very imprudent marriage. Many people think the marriage has not actually taken place, though he introduces the Lady everywhere as Lady Waldegrave. I know nothing of him but his appearance and manner are not those of a sensible man, and I am sure his conduct might make even a fool blush to be guilty of it.[14]

Another of the Dowager Lady Waldegrave's relatives was Captain Horace Seymour, 60th Foot, one of the Earl of Uxbridge's ADCs.

Viscountess Hawarden. Cornwallis Maude, first Viscount Hawarden died in 1803 and was survived by his wife, Anna Isabella (née Monck)

(1759–1851), who had borne him no fewer than twelve children. The eldest of the boys, Thomas Ralphe Maude, succeeded his father as second Viscount in 1803 but died unmarried only four years later. The second of the first Viscount's sons, also named Cornwallis Maude (1780–1856), then succeeded as third Viscount. He married Jane Bruce in July 1811 and it was this woman who, as Viscountess Hawarden, was invited to the Ball, but why she was without any other member of her family, and why she was in Brussels is not known.

Honourable Mrs Wellesley-Pole. Garret Wesley, first Earl of Mornington (1735–81) had four sons: Richard, later Marquess of Wellesley and then second Earl of Mornington; William, later third Earl of Mornington; Arthur, later first Duke of Wellington; and Henry, later first Baron Cowley. While the eldest brother spent a career in diplomacy and Arthur was involved in a military career, William devoted his life to a series of political appointments in England and Ireland. His first notable post was as First Secretary to the Admiralty (1807–9), but he then moved to Dublin as Chief Secretary for Ireland (1809–12) in succession to his brother Arthur who had gone off to fight in the Peninsula, and subsequently Chancellor of the Irish Exchequer (1811–12). The lord lieutenant during this period was the Duke of Richmond, and he and his wife knew the Richmonds well. Wellesley-Pole subsequently became Master of the Mint in 1814.

Wellesley-Pole married Katherine Elizabeth Forbes (1760–1851) in 1784. She was the daughter of Admiral the Hon. John Forbes and the couple had three children, one of whom was Emily, who had married Wellington's Military Secretary, Lieutenant-Colonel Lord Fitzroy Somerset, in 1814. She had her first child, a daughter, in Brussels in late May 1815, and there can be no doubt that the Hon. Mrs Wellesley-Pole was there to look after her daughter and grandchild.

Lady and Miss Sutton. Lady Sutton was the widow of Sir Thomas Sutton, first Bt, MP (1755–1813), and lived at Molesey in Surrey. She and her two daughters arrived in Brussels some time in early 1815 and were certainly there on 28 March, as Caroline Capel told her mother.[15] But of greater significance was the announcement of a marriage: 'Lately at Brussels, by special licence, Lt-Col. Sir G.H. Berkeley, to Miss Sutton, eldest daughter of Lady Sutton, of Molesey House, Surrey.'[16]

Lady Frances Wedderburn-Webster. Lady Frances Wedderburn-Webster was one of the daughters of Earl and Countess Mountnorris. Her husband, Mr James Wedderburn-Webster, was in London at the time of the Ball and Lady Frances attended either on her own or, more probably, with her family. More details about this lady are given in Appendix E.

Mr and Mrs Greathed. Edward Greathed of Uddens House, near Wimborne was a country landowner in Dorset. He married Mary Glyn in 1811 and in 1812 she gave birth to a son. They travelled to Brussels in 1814, where, among others, they were certainly known to the Capels.

Mr and Lady Charlotte Greville and Mr Greville junior. Charles Greville (1762–1832) was the grandson of the fifth Lord Brooke and his wife, Lady Charlotte Cavendish Bentinck (d.1862), the eldest daughter of William Henry, third Duke of Portland. They married in 1793 and had a number of children, of whom the eldest was Charles Cavendish Fulke Greville (1794–1865), the famous diarist; their other children were Henry William Greville (b.1801) and Harriet (b.1803).

The Grevilles spent several days in Brussels in July 1814 on their way to Spa and were so taken with the place and its society that they returned in September for a more extended stay. Lady Caroline Capel, however, was rather dismissive, commenting that: '. . . Lady Charlotte has adopted all the Foreign fashions & you cannot distinguish her from one of the most *outré* of the Natives . . .' As discussed in Chapter VII, the Grevilles' youngest son was also at the ball.

Mr, Mrs and Miss Lance and Mr Lance junior. It has not been possible to identify these four, but the term 'junior' suggests a boy aged between 7 and 14.

Mr Thomas Legh, MP. Colonel Thomas Peter Legh, MP (d.1797), fourth Baron of Newton in Lancashire, raised and paid for the 3rd Lancashire Light Dragoons, and was with his regiment in Edinburgh when he died in 1797. He left his large estates, including the family seat at Lyme Hall, Cheshire, to his eldest (natural) son, Thomas Legh (1793–1857), who was just 4 years old. Legh went up to Oxford in 1810 and afterwards travelled in Greece and Egypt, returning to England in November 1813. Having celebrated his 21st birthday in April 1814, he was elected MP for the family pocket borough, which he then represented until the abolition of such constituencies in 1832. He is known to have voted in the House of Commons on 8 May 1815, but then, desiring action in the forthcoming campaign against Napoleon, he went to Brussels. Once there, he attended the Ball where he is reputed to have flirted with Lady Elizabeth Conyngham.[17]

Mr and Mrs Lloyd. All three versions of the invitation list include 'Mr and Mrs Lloyd' and extensive research suggests that the most probable identity of this couple is Hannibal Evans Lloyd and his wife Anna, née Schwarzkopf. Hannibal Evans Lloyd (1771–1847) was the son of General Humphrey Evans Lloyd and a most unusual and highly gifted man. His father supported the Young Pretender in the '45, but was forgiven by the government to such an extent that he held a succession of commands in the British Army during the Seven Years War and negotiated the marriage of King George III's sister, Princess Augusta, to Duke Charles of Brunswick-Wolfenbüttel (their son was the Duke of Brunswick in Brussels who fought in the Waterloo campaign). Both Hannibal's parents died when he was young and he was then given a very rigorous and disciplined education by some near relatives. He lived in Hamburg in the early years of the 19th century where he perfected his command of the German language and married Fräulein Anna Schwarzkopf.

English residents of Hamburg were harshly treated by the French army of occupation and the Lloyd family eventually escaped and travelled to London, where his language skills and experience of life abroad quickly resulted in a job with the Foreign Office. Quite why he was in Brussels in 1815 is not known, but his employment by the Foreign Office and his previous acquaintance with Sir James Craufurd in Hamburg may have had some influence. Once there, his father's reputation and connections would have won him entrée to both the Duke of Brunswick and to the Richmond circle. Although it took place after the battle, Hannibal Lloyd used his presence in Brussels to assist Miss Charlotte Waldie in assembling and translating documentary material for her book *The Battle of Waterloo* by 'A Near Observer' which Lloyd then edited for her before it was published in London by John Booth.[18]

Mr Charles Ord and the Miss Ords. Charles Creevey was born in 1768 and, while his parents were poor, he received an excellent education, going up to Cambridge and being called to the bar in 1792, all of which gave rise to rumours, never substantiated, that he was the illegitimate son of Lord Molyneux of Croxteth. In 1802 Creevey married a well connected widow, Mrs Elizabeth Ord, whose first husband left her with two sons, three daughters and a considerable income. Creevey became an MP in 1802 and was pursuing a promising career when, in 1807, his party was ousted from power. The entire family moved to Brussels in 1814, partly because Mrs Creevey was in poor health and it was thought that the continent would be healthier and, secondly, because he was deep in debt and Brussels was cheaper. Neither Mr nor Mrs Creevey was invited to the Ball, but Mr Charles Ord (one of his two stepsons) and the Miss Ords (either two or three of his step-daughters) certainly were.

Army Officers' Wives. Four officers' wives were included on the invitation list, but, by coincidence, it would seem that none of them, nor their husbands, attended. Lady Susan Clinton's husband was at a divisional headquarters distant from Brussels, while Lady George Berkeley's husband was the AQMG at the Prince of Orange's headquarters and heavily involved in the developing situation on 15 June. Lady Fitzroy Somerset, who was not only Wellington's niece, but also the wife of his military secretary, Lieutenant-Colonel Lord Fitzroy Somerset, was living in Brussels but had given birth to her first child only three weeks previously, and did not attend. Finally, Lady William De Lancey had arrived in Brussels on 8 June but was not only recently married to the DQMG, Colonel Sir William De Lancey, but she had never been abroad before and was completely new to army ways and life. Thus, it was not surprising that she and her husband never intended to accept the invitation.

NOTES

1 Capel Letters, p. 47.
2 Maitland married the Duke of Richmond's daughter, Lady Sarah Lennox, in Paris in August 1815.
3 Capel Letters, p. 79.
4 *Spencer and Waterloo*, p. 9.
5 NAM 6305/122/2.
6 Capel Letters, p. 100.
7 Capel Letters, p. 158.
8 Capel Letters, p. 111.
9 I am indebted to Philip Haythornthwaite for drawing my attention to these relationships.
10 Information in this paragraph is based on the diary of Lady Jane Dalrymple-Hamilton, by kind permission of the present Sir Hew and Lady Dalrymple-Hamilton.
11 PRO PROB 11/2000 Quire 47 – folio 150.
12 *The Times*, 31 Jan. 1844, p. 8, col. B.
13 Capel Letters, p. 78.
14 The lady concerned was Anne King, who had accompanied the army in the Peninsula. Curiously, the wedding is recorded as having taken place on 30 October 1815; i.e. six months *after* Mackworth's diary entry.
15 Capel Letters, p. 97.
16 *Gentleman's Magazine*, April 1815, p. 370.
17 He is reported to have spent the day of the 18th on the battlefield of Waterloo; Creevey Papers, Vol. I, p. 233.
18 *Gentleman's Magazine*, Volume XXVIII, 1847, pp. 324–6.

CHAPTER X

English Officers of the Royal Navy, Diplomatic Corps and Retired Army

Included among the Duchess of Richmond's guests were four officers of the Royal Navy – two retired and two serving – two retired Army generals and five officials from the English embassy.

Vice-Admiral Sidney and Lady Smith, and Miss Rumbolds. Vice-Admiral William Sidney Smith (1764–1840) was an enterprising commander and a man of great zeal and undoubted courage, but with a fatal penchant for pomposity, self-aggrandisement and endless story-telling, which lost him many friends and probably cost him the most senior appointments in the Royal Navy. He always referred to himself as 'Sir Sidney' although his knighthood had been conferred by the King of Sweden and he did not receive the accolade from the English Crown until December 1815.

Smith entered the navy at the age of 13 and immediately went to North America, where he took part in many actions. He returned to England in 1784 and then went to France for two years as a private citizen, followed by a year in Morocco and six months in Sweden. With his normal brashness he appointed himself messenger between the King of Sweden and the King of England, but was treated with disdain when he arrived in Whitehall. He was in Turkey in 1794 when the war against France started and, meeting a number of British seamen in Smyrna, he purchased a boat and they all sailed to join the Mediterranean Fleet. Smith quickly established a reputation for talking too much and an overblown sense of his own importance; as a result, he was far less popular than his achievements warranted. In 1796 he was taken prisoner-of-war in France and held in Paris for two years, but then escaped and made his way back to England, where he was appointed to command *Tigre*, an 80-gun ship-of-the-line. Smith took her to the eastern Mediterranean where his determination and forceful leadership were responsible for Napoleon's first major defeat at Acre, which earned Smith well deserved praise in England and Turkey. Simultaneously, however, he assumed powers far beyond what was proper, upsetting both Lord St Vincent and Nelson,

while an extraordinary decision to negotiate and sign the Treaty of El
Arish with the French was not supported by Admiral Lord Keith, and the
campaign restarted. Nevertheless, Smith won promotion to rear-admiral
in 1805 and vice-admiral in 1810, but in 1814 his health broke down and
he returned to England and retirement.

In 1810 Smith married Caroline, Lady Rumbold (1760–1826), the widow
of a diplomat, Sir George Berriman Rumbold (d.1806), who had been
English consul-general in Hamburg in succession to Sir James Craufurd
(q.v.). Rumbold created a minor diplomatic incident when he dressed up
as a sergeant and tried to seduce some Danish soldiers, but there was an
even more serious incident when he was kidnapped by French agents and
accused of organising a network of spies. He died in 1807 leaving Lady
Rumbold with one son and three daughters.

Sir Sidney and family went to Paris in 1814 and thence to Brussels,
where he immediately settled into the English colony and visited units of
the British Army. Captain Digby Mackworth was not overawed by the
admiral, noting (9 June 1815) that

> Sir Sidney Smith . . . does us the honour of being our guest for a day
> or two. He appears to be a very pleasant man, fond of talking of his
> own exploits . . . and apparently altogether a man of more brilliancy
> than sound sense; more talent than judgment. When once he gets into
> the campaigns in Egypt, it is quite a hopeless case to attempt to get
> him out of them, but it must be confessed his histories and anecdotes
> are highly entertaining, to those who have not heard them too often
> before.

Wellington, upon whom Smith imposed himself on several occasions, was
even blunter:

> . . . of all the men whom I ever knew who have any reputation, the
> man who least deserves it is Sir Sidney Smith . . . At first out of
> deference to his name and general reputation I attended to him, but I
> soon found he was a mere vaporizer. I cannot believe that a man so
> silly in all other affairs can be a good naval officer.[1]

Thus, the family party attending the ball consisted of Sir Sidney, his wife
Lady Caroline, and his step-daughters, the Misses Caroline, Maria and
Emily Rumbold, none of them, sadly, in the first flush of youth, their ages
being 29, 27 and 25 respectively.

Rear-Admiral Sir Pulteney Malcolm (1768–1838). For the soldiers, the
most important naval guest at the Ball was Rear-Admiral Sir Pulteney
Malcolm who was in command of the Royal Navy squadron in the Scheldt

river. Malcolm was the third son of a Scottish sheep farmer and entered the Royal Navy as a midshipman at the age of 10, his first ship being a frigate, HMS *Sibylle*. He was commissioned lieutenant in 1783 and by the outbreak of the war against France in 1792 was first lieutenant of *Penelope*, in which he took part in many actions in the West Indies. He achieved the rank of post captain in 1794 when just 26 years old, an exceptionally early age considering that his family wielded no 'influence'. His first command was the frigate HMS *Fox*, which he took to the East Indies and where, in 1797, one of his tasks was to carry an unknown Army officer, Lieutenant-Colonel Arthur Wellesley, commanding officer of the 33rd Regiment, from the Cape of Good Hope to Calcutta. He continued his successes until the end of the first phase of the war in 1803 when his ship, HMS *Victorious*, was so severely damaged during a violent storm in the Bay of Biscay that he had to drive her ashore to save his crew, but his excellent seamanship ensured that this did nothing to harm his reputation.

In 1805, when commanding HMS *Donegal*, he accompanied Admiral Nelson in his chase to the West Indies in pursuit of the French fleet, but on their return to Spanish waters his ship was in such a bad shape that he put into Gibraltar for refit. He was still there when he heard that the combined Franco–Spanish fleet had sailed from Cadiz and by superhuman efforts he got *Donegal* to sea in a matter of hours; even so, he just missed being present at the Battle of Trafalgar, although he did come up with Collingwood in time to participate in the capture of several prizes.

In 1808 Malcolm, still commanding *Donegal*, commanded the ships which carried his old army friend, now Major-General Sir Arthur Wellesley, and his army from Cork to Portugal, where they were landed most successfully in Mondego Bay. That task completed, Malcolm continued his very active naval career, which included participating in the Action at Aix Roads under the command of Admiral Gambier in 1812.

In 1813 Malcolm was promoted rear-admiral, flying his flag in HMS *Royal Oak*. The war against the United States brought him yet more operations with the Army, including commanding the operational landing of the troops which would attack Washington and burn down the White House. He then returned to England in 1814 and was knighted in the honours list which marked the apparent end of the war. On the news of Napoleon's escape from Elba, however, he was immediately appointed to command the naval forces supporting the British and allied armies ashore in the Netherlands. His orders stated that:

> You will lose no time in acquainting the Commander-in-Chief of His Majesty's land forces [Wellington] of your arrival, and communicating with him on the subject of the service entrusted to your charge, repairing personally to the headquarters of the said Commander-in-Chief whenever it may be desirable for the purpose of your

communications with him, and you will use every exertion to render him and His Majesty's Allies all the aid, in naval co-operation, which may be in your power and which circumstances may require.[2]

Malcolm was soon in the Netherlands where in Ghent he bumped into some old friends. As Harry Smith, brigade-major to Major-General Lambert, was delighted to record on 12 June:

> While at Ghent I waited on Sir John Lambert every morning just after breakfast for orders. On one occasion we heard a voice thundering in the passage to him, 'Hallo there, where the devil's the door?' I went out, and to my astonishment saw our noble friend Admiral Malcolm. 'Why, where the devil has Lambert stowed himself? The house is as dark as a sheer hulk.' He was delighted to see us, and sang out, 'Come – bear a hand and get me some breakfast; no regular hours on shore as in the *Royal Oak*.'[3]

Admiral Sir James Gambier. Admiral Sir James Gambier (1756–1833) was a descendant of Huguenots (French protestants) who escaped from France at the time of the revocation of the Edict of Nantes (1685) to seek refuge in England. Then, like so many Huguenots, his family rose rapidly and when James was born his father was Lieutenant-Governor of the Bahamas. James entered the navy at a very early age being promoted to post-captain in 1778. He commanded *Defence* at the Glorious First of June (1 June 1798), his ship leading the British ships that broke through the French line. He was promoted rear-admiral in 1795 and vice-admiral in 1799. He spent a short time as Governor of Newfoundland in 1802–4, but then, having been promoted to admiral, he commanded the fleet at the bombardment of Copenhagen in 1807. The following year he took command of the Channel Fleet and in 1809 he commanded at the attack on the French shipping in Aix Roads, although he subsequently requested a court martial to clear his name, by which he was acquitted.

In 1814 he was one of the commissioners who met representatives of the United States at Ghent to negotiate an agreement to end the War of 1812. The resulting treaty was signed on 24 December 1814, following which Gambier went, first to Paris and thence to Brussels, where he was on 15 June 1815.

Commander Hon. George Perceval (1794–1874).[4] He was a younger son of the second Baron Arden and appears to have been distantly related to Lady Alvanley and the Miss Ardens, who featured elsewhere on the Duchess's invitation list. Known as the Hon. Mr Perceval, he joined the Royal Navy and was at Trafalgar as a midshipman aboard HMS *Orion*. Commissioned lieutenant in 1813, he served in North American waters aboard the frigate HMS *Tenedos*, and after some very lively actions against ships of the US Navy, he returned to England in early 1815. He was in Brussels in June 1815, apparently on a social visit with two of his sisters, and, by happy chance, was promoted to commander on 13 June, just before the Ball.[5]

General Francis Dundas. The Goodwood List includes the name 'Honourable General Dundas' but without any first names, which is repeated in the De Ros and Delhaize Lists. There were two generals named Dundas in the British Army in 1815, one of whom was the 80-year-old Sir David Dundas, who was unlikely to have been in Belgium at his age. The other was Francis Dundas, who was somewhat younger and was certainly in Belgium at this time as he subsequently wrote a report on the Battle of Waterloo.[6] He was not serving with the field army, and it is presumed that he was in Brussels on private business, although his subsequent account of the Battle of Waterloo makes it clear that he was present.

Sir Charles Stuart. The flight of King Louis XVIII to Ghent and the elevation of Prince William IV of Orange to King William I of the Netherlands required some adjustments by the Foreign Office. Sir Charles Stuart (1779–1845), who had been British ambassador in Paris, moved with his staff to the Netherlands, remaining ambassador to Louis XVIII but being stationed in Brussels rather than Ghent. Sir Charles was a grandson of the third Earl of Bute and the eldest son of General Sir Charles Stuart and had served as a diplomat in Spain and Portugal in 1808–10, where he got to know Wellington. Stuart was appointed to Paris in 1814 where Wellington was the British ambassador. He married Elizabeth, third daughter of the third Earl of Hardwicke, by whom he had two daughters. It would appear that none of his family was present in Brussels at the time of the Ball.

Creevey received a letter from his friend Henry Brougham MP in December 1814 telling him what to expect in the new ambassador:

> C. Stuart. . . is a plain man, of some prejudices, caring little for politics and of good practical sense. You will find none of his prejudices (which, after all, are little or nothing) at all of an aristocratic or disagreeable kind. He has no violent passions or acute feelings about him, and likes to go quietly on and enjoy himself in his way. He has read a great deal and seen much more, and done, for his standing, more business than any diplomatic man I ever heard of . . .[7]

Hon. James Stuart. He had only just arrived in Brussels bearing a Foreign Office letter, together with the Full Powers from the Prince Regent, authorising Sir Charles Stuart to negotiate and sign a new convention.[8] This was to cover the arrangements for the subsistence of the Allied armies once on French soil, and was to be negotiated with the representatives of the various Allied armies and with Louis XVIII. James Stuart may have been a relative of Sir Charles, but was certainly not his son, as the ambassador only had two daughters.

Clinton George Dawkins. He was a British diplomat under Sir Charles Stuart.

George William Chad (1784–1849). He was the second son of Sir George Chad, Bt, of Thursford Hall, Norfolk. He entered the Diplomatic Service in the early 1800s and went to Brussels in 1814 and was still there in June 1815. He wrote a book about these experiences,[9] but there are no other known published works, except for the posthumous publication of private records of his conversations with the Duke of Wellington.[10] He seems to have been a somewhat colourless character, although he corresponded with the Duke of Wellington over many years, continuing a friendship which started in Brussels.

Lionel Hervey. He was the British Foreign Office's representative to the court of Louis XVIII, for which purpose he was attached to Sir Charles Stuart's embassy '... to be near the person of His Most Christian Majesty ...'[11]

John James. He was the Secretary of Embassy to Sir Charles Stuart. Mention is made of him and his wife, Lady Emily James, in various contemporary accounts. Lady Emily gave birth to a child at Antwerp, but it died a few weeks later. When Lady De Lancey was at Antwerp (18–20 June 1815) she met Mr James and was told that he had lost his brother at Waterloo, and the only James to be killed was Ensign John James of the 30th Foot.[12] The Foreign Office issued instructions on 14 June that, in view of the Dutch king's decision to make his capital at The Hague, James was to leave the Embassy in Brussels and proceed to The Hague in the post of His Majesty's Minister Plenipotentiary to the Dutch Court.

NOTES

1 The Croker Papers, Vol. I, p. 348.
2 Letter Croker to Malcolm dated Admiralty Office, 7 June 1815.
3 Harry Smith, Chapter 24.
4 He appears in all the invitation lists as 'Hon. Mr Perceval' which is correct for his rank as lieutenant; but his promotion to commander was gazetted on 13 June 1815.

5   He succeeded his father as Baron Arden in 1840 and his cousin as the sixth Earl Egmont in 1841.
6   B.Lib Add 19,590 f.25.
7   Creevey Papers, p. 124; Letter Henry Brougham MP to Creevey, dated Southill, 28 Dec. 1814.
8   Foreign Office letter, June 13 1815. PRO FO 27/115.
9   *A Narrative of the Late Revolution in Holland*, John Murray, London, 1814.
10 *The Conversations of the First Duke of Wellington with George William Chad*; edited by the seventh Duke of Wellington; St Nicholas Press, Cambridge, 1956.
11 Foreign Office letter dated 24 April 1815. PRO FO 27/115.
12 *Lady De Lancey at Waterloo*, p. 111.

CHAPTER XI

The English Military Guests

The Duchess of Richmond's invitation list included 105 officers of the English Army and detailed analysis of these figures is at Appendix D. It is clear from all this that whichever category is examined, the proportions actually invited to the Ball were small, apart from the most senior of all, the commander-in-chief and his corps commanders, all of whom were invited and attended.

Army Commander-In-Chief

Field Marshal the Duke of Wellington Commander-in-Chief (1769–1852)

The commander-in-chief of the Anglo–Netherlands Army, Arthur Wellesley, was the third son of Garrett, first Earl of Mornington. He married the Hon. Catherine Pakenham in 1806, but although she had been with him for a short spell in Paris in 1814, she did not accompany him either to Vienna or to Brussels in 1815. Wellington arrived in Brussels on 4 April 1815 and lived there throughout the period up to the Battle of Waterloo, but with occasional absences to visit other headquarters or to attend military parades.

Corps Commanders

The Anglo–Netherlands Army was divided into three corps: I Corps – General Prince William of Orange; II Corps – Lieutenant-General Lord Hill; and the Cavalry – Lieutenant-General the Earl of Uxbridge. The reserve, positioned to the right rear of the battlefield, was under the direct command of the Duke of Wellington, but, if required, would probably have been commanded by Lieutenant-General the Duke of Richmond.

William Frederick George, Hereditary Prince of Orange (1792–1849)

The Hereditary Prince of Orange, who commanded I Corps of the army, was one of the major figures in Brussels society in the years 1814–15. The Nassau–Orange family had been hereditary *stadtholders* (heads-of-state) of the Dutch Republic since 1579 and his parents were Prince William

(1772–1837) and his wife Wilhelmina, daughter of Frederick-William II of Prussia. When the French overran the Netherlands in 1795, the family escaped first to Prussia and then to England where the young Prince William was brought up in an English environment with two tutors: one, an Englishman, for normal school subjects; and for military subjects, Lieutenant-Colonel de Constant Rebeque, who was an Old Etonian of Swiss origin! Still in exile, William was commissioned into the Prussian Army in 1809 and into the British Army in 1811 as a lieutenant-colonel. He was sent to the Peninsula as one of Wellington's ADCs and during his two years there he saw a great deal of action and was considered by all to be very brave, but little else, and certainly lacking in both military command experience and maturity (although it should be said that he was only 20 years old).

In 1813 he returned with his parents to the Netherlands, where he was promoted to major-general in the British Army and the following year he was promoted again, this time to general, to enable him to take command of the Anglo–Dutch garrison forces in succession to Lord Lynedoch. His one-time military tutor, de Constant Rebeque, now a major-general, was still with him, but his headquarters staff included a strong English element, including Major-General Sir Hudson Lowe as his Quartermaster-General, Major-General Edward Barnes as his Adjutant-General, and Lieutenant-Colonel Sir John Colborne as his Military Secretary.

The Hereditary Prince was a noted Anglophile and for a time it appeared that his relationship with England would become formalised, because on 13 December 1813 he became engaged to Princess Charlotte, the only daughter of the Prince Regent. Such a marriage would not only have linked England and the Netherlands, but in the longer term the Hereditary Prince would have become not only king of the Netherlands, but also king consort in England, while his wife would have been queen regnant of England and queen consort of the Netherlands. This was a most important dynastic marriage, with great political ramifications, and the detailed negotiations were necessarily protracted, but this, combined with the Hereditary Prince's absence in the Netherlands, allowed Charlotte to think again and to fall in love with Prince Frederick, nephew of the king of Prussia. All this resulted in her announcement on 16 June 1814 that she would not marry the Hereditary Prince and the engagement had to be formally terminated.

Despite this setback the young prince's fascination with all things English became so marked that the British government asked the Duke of Wellington, as the prince's former military commander, to bring him into line. Accordingly, the duke wrote on 12 December 1814 that while the prince's English education gave him that 'natural inclination', nevertheless, '. . . a Person in your high situation must get the better of his inclinations . . . for the sake of the higher Interests committed to his charge. [England would be glad to see] a marked preference in favour of your new subjects.'[1] This appears to have had some effect as he threw a large Ball in December at which, in contrast to his previous practice, the great majority of guests were Belgians, with just a handful of English present.

Lieutenant-General Lord Rowland Hill (1772–1842)

Hill commanded II Corps in the Waterloo campaign. The fourth child in a family of sixteen, he started his military service with the 53rd Foot in 1793 and was commanding the 90th Foot as a lieutenant-colonel two years later. He went to the Peninsula where he commanded the division which captured Colonel d'Arenberg at Arroyo dos Molinos. Hill was one of Wellington's most trusted subordinates, and was very popular with all ranks; indeed, Captain Digby Mackworth, one of his ADCs in the Waterloo campaign, confided to his journal that the general, when elevated to the peerage '. . . ought to have taken the title of Lord *Mountain* because he is a *great hill'*. His corps headquarters was at Grammont and as Mackworth definitely attended the Ball it seems highly probable that Hill did so as well.

Lieutenant-General Henry William Paget, second Earl of Uxbridge (1768–1854)

Uxbridge, the commander of the Anglo–Netherlands Cavalry Corps, came from an undistinguished family, which had progressed more by good luck than anything else. His father was Sir Henry Bayly, Bart (1744–1812), but on the death of a cousin Sir Henry obtained a royal licence in 1770 enabling him to assume the titles and bear arms as the ninth Baron Paget. Then, in 1780 Baron Paget inherited huge properties in England and Ireland, and four years later he was created first Earl of Uxbridge in Middlesex. Thus, having been born Henry Bayly and the heir to a baronetcy, the young man became first Henry Paget and then the heir to an earldom and a considerable fortune.

In 1793 his son, Henry Paget, used his father's money to raise a volunteer infantry regiment, the 80th Foot, which he commanded, but then found his metier as a cavalryman, and during the ill-fated Corunna expedition in 1808 he established a reputation as one of the most dashing British cavalry leaders.

His military career was, however, blighted for some years by a major social scandal when he eloped with Lady Charlotte Wellesley. Both were married at the time and both had children, but they obtained divorces and married each other. Despite inheriting his father's title in 1812, Paget, now second Earl of Uxbridge, was not employed in the Peninsula campaign, while his new wife was ostracised by 'polite' society. When the crisis over Napoleon's escape from Elba arose, however, Uxbridge was selected to command the cavalry and to be Wellington's designated successor should anything befall him. Fortunately, their military duty overrode any personal feelings and they got on reasonably well together during the short campaign. Uxbridge arrived in Brussels in early June without his wife, and, still considering himself something of a 'beau', attended the Ball together with his ADCs.

Divisional Commanders

There were five British infantry divisional commanders, of which three (Cooke, Clinton and Picton) were invited to the Ball. The other two, Colville and Cole, were not invited, the latter because he was on leave, having just got married.

Major-General George Cooke (1768–1837) Cooke was appointed an ensign in the 1st Foot Guards in 1784 and fought in the Low Countries in 1794 and 1799, being wounded in the latter. He was promoted to major-general in 1811 and went to the Peninsula, where he spent the first two years in the slightly unglamorous position of commander Cadiz garrison. He went with Graham to the Low Countries in 1813 and commanded one of the columns on the attack on Bergen-op-Zoom. Once hostilities ended, he remained in the British garrison and then became part of Wellington's army in 1815 as commander of the 1st (Guards) Division.

Lieutenant-General Sir Henry Clinton (1771–1829) Clinton was the second son of General Sir Henry Clinton, who had commanded the British forces in America during the War of Independence. His wife, Lady Susan, whom he married in 1799, was a daughter of Francis, Lord Elcho. Clinton arrived in Belgium in 1814, where he commanded the English troops under General the Hereditary Prince of Orange, and also tried to curb the latter's wilder plans. He remained to serve in the Waterloo campaign, commanding 2nd Division, but as his headquarters was a considerable distance from Brussels, it seems likely that neither he nor his wife attended the Ball. A further reason for not attending was that his relationship with Wellington had often been turbulent, not least because Clinton had twice disobeyed orders, never a wise thing to do where Wellington was concerned. One of his nephews, Captain Francis Dawkins, 1st Foot Guards, was his aide-de-camp.

Lieutenant-General Sir Thomas Picton (1758–1815) Picton, who commanded the 5th Division at Waterloo, was a very able general, but a foul-mouthed man and a very strict disciplinarian. He served in the 12th Foot from 1771 to 1779 but then spent twelve years on half-pay. Returning to active service in the West Indies in 1794, he remained there for ten years, managing to avoid the many ailments which struck down many

Englishmen in a notoriously unhealthy environment. He commanded 3rd Division in the Peninsula where he always led from the front; he was wounded in one of the assaults on Badajoz, and despite a short period on sick leave, remained with the division until the war ended. He was very reluctant to go to the Netherlands in 1815 as his relations with Wellington were not good and at 56 he felt that he deserved a rest. His reluctance was heightened by a premonition of death and he caused some alarm to a friend before he left England by lying down in an open grave and then remarking that it was just the right size.

According to his ADC, Captain Gronow, Picton arrived in Brussels on the afternoon of 15 June, so as his name appears in both the Goodwood and De Ros Lists, his invitation must have been issued at the very last minute. Not one of Picton's four ADCs were invited to the Ball, Picton's first meeting with Wellington took place on the morning of the 16th (indicating that they cannot have met at the Ball), and Gronow makes no mention of the Ball; it thus appears unlikely that Picton attended.[2]

Cavalry Brigade Commanders

There were seven cavalry brigades, five of them commanded by English officers, one by a Kings German Legion officer, and one by a Hanoverian. Of the five English commanders, three were invited to the Ball, of whom one did not attend; the two not invited were Major-Generals Sir John Vandeleur and Sir Colquhoun Grant.

Major-General Hon. Sir William Ponsonby (1772–1815) Sir William Ponsonby was the second son of a noted Irish Whig politician, William Brabazon Ponsonby, first Baron Ponsonby of Imokilly, County Cork. The younger William joined the army early and in 1803 was appointed to command the 5th Dragoon Guards. He later served in the Peninsula, where his brigade was not only successful but was also noted for its good discipline (not always a strong point among cavalry regiments) and completed the war without one soldier having been tried by General Court Martial. His wife was the Hon. Georgiana Fitzroy, daughter of the first Baron Southampton and cousin to Colonel Sir William De Lancey, Wellington's chief-of-staff. Lady Ponsonby had only just become pregnant at the time of her husband's death at the Battle of Waterloo and gave birth to a son in February 1816, who became the third Baron Ponsonby on the death of his uncle in 1839.

In the Waterloo campaign Ponsonby commanded the 2nd Cavalry Brigade, known as the 'Union Brigade' because it consisted of three regiments, one each from England, Scotland and Ireland – 1st Royal Dragoons, 2nd Royal North British Dragoons (Scots Greys) and 6th (Iniskilling) Dragoons, respectively.

Major-General Lord Edward Somerset (1776–1842) Lord Edward Somerset was the fourth son of Henry, fifth Duke of Beaufort and the brother of Lord Fitzroy Somerset, Wellington's military secretary. He was born in 1776 and was commissioned into the 10th Light Dragoons as a cornet in 1793 He was promoted captain in 1794 and spent his whole career with the cavalry except for a very brief spell with the 5th Foot. During the Peninsular War he commanded 4th Light Dragoons until promoted to command a cavalry brigade. He married Louisa, youngest daughter of the second Viscount Courtenay in 1805. At Waterloo he commanded the 1st British (Household) Cavalry Brigade, comprising four regiments: 1st Life Guards; 2nd Life Guards; Royal Horse Guards and 1st Dragoon Guards.

Major-General Sir Hussey Vivian (1775–1842) A Cornishman, Richard Hussey Vivian (always known as 'Hussey') was commissioned into a Devonshire regiment, 20th Foot, in 1793 and served in the Netherlands in the campaigns of 1795 and 1799. He then transferred to the cavalry, becoming commanding officer of the 7th Light Dragoons in December 1799, which was with Moore at Corunna (1809) and returned to the Peninsula to take part in the later battles, first as commanding officer but later as a brigade commander. He was severely wounded at the Battle of Toulouse. In the Waterloo campaign he commanded 6th Cavalry Brigade and definitely attended the Duchess of Richmond's Ball on 15 June.[3]

Infantry Brigade Commanders

Five of the nine British infantry brigade commanders in the Waterloo campaign were invited to the Ball. The four not invited were Major-Generals Halkett, Johnstone and Lambert, and Colonel Mitchell.

Major-General Frederick Adam (1781–1853) Frederick Adam was the youngest British major-general in the field at Waterloo and his career showed how judicious use of the purchase and exchange systems could result in rapid promotion. He was the fourth son of an Irish landowner and his father purchased him a commission in the 26th Foot in 1795, but he continued his education until he was 18, by which time he was on the books of the 27th Foot as a captain and went to war for the first time (Holland, 1799). Another exchange into the 9th Foot lasted just four months before he moved on to the 2nd Foot Guards, serving with them in Egypt in 1801. Further exchanges and promotions followed and in 1813 he went to the Peninsula as a brigade commander, but on the east coast, where he was one of the relatively few commanders to emerge with credit. He was promoted to major-general in 1814 and when the following year he commanded the 3rd British Infantry Brigade at Waterloo, he was just

34 years old and younger than all four of his battalion commanders. Adam was invited to the Ball but did not attend.

Major-General Sir John Byng (1772–1860) Byng was the youngest son of George Byng of Wrotham Park, Middlesex and the great-grandson of first Viscount Torrington. He was commissioned into the 33rd Foot in 1793 and served in the Flanders campaign under the young Lieutenant-Colonel Arthur Wellesley. He saw more active service with the 33rd in Ireland (1798) and then with the 60th in North America in 1800–2 before exchanging into 3rd Foot Guards in 1804. He took part in the Copenhagen and Walcheren expeditions and then went to the Peninsula, where he fought in all the later battles. He was granted the unusual honour of an augmentation to his family coat-of-arms of a hand grasping a colour to commemorate his achievement when, as brigade commander, he carried the regimental colour of the 31st Regiment during the final stages of an uphill attack and planted it on the summit. He married, first, a Miss McKenzie and, secondly, in 1809, Marianne James. He commanded 2nd (Guards) Brigade in the Waterloo campaign.

Major-General Sir James Kempt (1761–1854) The son of an English landowner, Kempt was commissioned into the 101st Foot in 1783 and had reached the rank of lieutenant-colonel by 1799. He served as aide-de-camp and then military secretary to General Abercromby in the Holland and Egyptian campaigns and then went to command 81st Foot. He was promoted major-general in 1812 and commanded a brigade in the Peninsula which he led in all the later battles up to the fall of Toulouse. In the Waterloo campaign he commanded the 8th Infantry Brigade.

Major-General Peregrine Maitland (1774–1854) Maitland, the son of Thomas Maitland of Shrubs Hall in the New Forest, was commissioned into 1st Foot Guards in 1792 and served in Flanders (1794) and later in the Peninsula, first under Moore and then under Wellesley. He was promoted major-general in 1814 and commanded the 1st (Guards) Brigade in the Waterloo campaign. His first marriage to the Hon. Louisa Crofton was tragically brief as she died in 1805 after just two years of marriage. In 1815 the young English ladies in the Netherlands considered such a 41-year-old widower with an established reputation to be a tremendous catch and several mothers encouraged their daughters to flirt with him. He fooled them all, however, because he eloped with and married Lady Sarah Lennox, the 23-year-old daughter of the Duke of Richmond, in Paris in October 1815. The romance must have begun in Brussels, but it seems to have gone entirely unnoticed by all the eagle-eyed Brussels gossips, not least her mother, who was livid that her daughter should have thrown herself away on a penniless and untitled officer.

Major-General Sir Denis Pack (1772–1823) Pack was the only son of the Anglican Dean of Ossory in Ireland and was commissioned into the 4th Dragoons in 1791. He saw service on the French coast in 1795 and ten years later took part in the ill-fated expedition to Buenos Aires. He commanded 71st Foot in the Peninsula in 1808 and in the Walcheren expedition in 1809, but refused promotion and a posting to Canada in order to return to the Peninsula in command of a Portuguese brigade. He was very brave and led from the front, but was renowned among his troops for his short temper. In the Waterloo campaign he commanded the 9th Infantry Brigade.

Personal Staff

The duke's personal staff consisted of a military secretary and a number of ADCs who are covered separately, below.

Lieutenant-Colonel Lord Fitzroy Somerset. Lord Fitzroy was the youngest son of Henry, fifth Duke of Beaufort, and one of four members of his family in the Waterloo army. He was with Wellington throughout the Peninsular War, being responsible for his personal office, dealing with all correspondence, and was the main channel for all from outside the headquarters who wished to deal with the commander-in-chief. In 1814 he married Lady Emily Wellesley-Pole, daughter of William Wellesley-Pole, Wellington's brother, whose wife was in Brussels and also invited to the Ball. Lady Emily had their first baby in Brussels in late May 1815, and although she and her husband were invited to the Ball, neither attended.

Quartermaster-General's Staff

In June 1815 the QMG's staff in the British element of Wellington's army comprised one Deputy QMG (colonel) and seventeen Assistant QMGs, who varied in rank from colonel to captain; seven of these were invited to the Ball, of which at least one did not attend. There were also twelve Deputy Assistant QMGs (majors/captains), none of whom were invited to the Ball. It should be noted that only a small number of these QMG officers were located at Wellington's headquarters, the majority being dispersed to corps and divisional headquarters.

Deputy Quartermaster-General

Wellington's first choice for QMG was the man who had served him so well in the Peninsula, Lieutenant-General Sir William Murray, but he was in Canada and did not return in time for the Waterloo campaign. As a result, Wellington called on Murray's deputy from Peninsular days,

Colonel Sir William De Lancey. De Lancey was of Huguenot descent, his family having settled in New York in 1685 and become very wealthy. All this was lost when the family supported the Crown during the War of Independence and William De Lancey was brought up in England. He spent his early military years in the infantry but then transferred to the Permanent Staff of the QMG Department (i.e. he was a professional staff officer). He was with Wellington throughout the Peninsular campaign, but when it ended, he was posted to Edinburgh where, after a lightning courtship, he married Magdalene Hall. They were on their honeymoon when the summons came and De Lancey arrived in Brussels in late May, followed by his wife in early June. Both were invited to the Ball but neither accepted.

Assistant Quartermaster-Generals

De Lancey had two principal subordinates, ranked as Assistant Quartermaster-Generals (AQMG): **Col. Hon. Alexander Abercromby (1784–1853)** and **Col. Felton Hervey**, both of whom were invited to the Ball. Abercromby was the son of General Sir Ralph Abercromby, who died in the attack on Aboukir Bay in 1801, as a result of which his widow was created a baroness in her own right. Alexander Abercromby commanded the 28th Foot in the Peninsula and later a brigade. Felton Hervey served in the 14th Light Dragoons in the Peninsula, where he lost an arm.

Five more AQMGs were invited: **Lieutenant-Colonel Sir Henry Hollis Bradford**, 1st Foot Guards, and **Lieutenant-Colonel Sir George Scovell** who was on half-pay at the time, but had been chief-of-communications in the Peninsula and was specifically recalled to duty by Wellington to carry out a similar task in May 1815.

Lieutenant-Colonel John George Woodford, 1st Foot Guards, was the Duchess of Richmond's cousin, as his mother, the former Lady Susan Gordon, was also the daughter of Cosmo-George, third Duke of Gordon.[4] His brother, commanding officer of the Coldstream Guards, was also invited to the Ball. Another AQMG, **Major Hon. George Dawson**, 1st Dragoon Guards, had two brothers present: his older brother, John, second Earl of Portarlington, and a younger brother, Hon. Lionel Dawson, who was serving with 18th Light Dragoons.

In 1815 **Lieutenant-Colonel Robert Torrens** (1780–1864) belonged to the 1st West India Regiment, but had, in fact, spent most of his service with the Royal Marines. A close relative of Major-General Sir Henry Torrens, the adjutant-general at the Horse Guards, Robert Torrens was a most unusual and highly gifted man. He had already published two lengthy novels,[5] but of much greater significance, he had also published the first of a series of influential treatises on economics, *An Essay on Money and Paper Currency* (1812). This work – at 312 pages it was something more than an essay – was written over the course of a long and cold winter on the island of Anhalt in the Kattegat, where Torrens was the garrison commander, and dealt with the balance of payments, legalisation of paper money and the cessation of trade with France, and established his reputation as one of the founders of modern economics. In Belgium, however, Torrens was engaged with De Lancey and others in writing out the 'routes' in the QMG's office on the evening of 15 June and is known still to have been there at 10pm; he may, therefore, not have attended the Ball.

Adjutant-General's Staff

The adjutant-general's staff was responsible for personnel matters, drill, discipline and prisoners-of-war. It had a total strength of twenty-four officers, many of them, as with the QMG staff, sent to corps and divisional headquarters, and, of these, five were invited to the Ball.

Adjutant-General

The AG was **Major-General Sir Edward Barnes**, whose family details are unknown, but may have been of Irish extraction. By 1794 he was a major in 99th Foot and as lieutenant-colonel in command 46th Foot he commanded a brigade at the capture of Martinique and Guadeloupe. He was on the staff in the Peninsular War and then commanded a brigade at the Battles of Vittoria, Pyrenees, Nivelle, Nive and Orthes, where he showed conspicuous bravery. He was appointed AG to the Prince of Orange in the Netherlands in September 1814 and retained the post under Wellington.

Barnes was popular with the military and civilians alike, and was highly thought of by both the Capel and Creevey families. He was exceptionally generous to the former, lending them army horses and baggage carts when they moved houses, Lady Caroline Capel telling her mother that Barnes '. . . is one of the most amiable & best creatures I have ever met with & doubly devoted to every individual of the Family from Capel to Adolphus – He is very rich & Most liberally minded . . .'[6]

Unfortunately, as described in Chapter V, when Barnes sought to make the relationship even closer, his proposal of marriage was firmly rejected by Maria Capel.

Deputy Adjutants-General

Barnes's principal assistant was **Colonel Sir John Elley** of the Royal Horse Guards, who had joined the army as a private soldier and then rose entirely on his own merits. Captain Harry Smith described him as '. . . a very tall, bony, and manly figure of a man, with grim-visaged war depicted in his countenance, with whiskers, moustaches, etc. like a French Pioneer'. Elley went through Customs at Dover where

> . . . his celebrated sword belted under his surtout . . . gave the coat-flap the appearance of having something large concealed under it. A lower order of Custom officer ran after him, rudely calling, 'I say, you officer, you! stop, stop, I say! What's that under your coat?' Sir John turned round, and drawing his weapon of defence in many a bloody fight, to the astonishment of the John Bulls, roared out through his moustache in a voice of thunder, 'That which I will run through your d—d guts, if you are impertinent to me!'[7]

Lieutenant-Colonel De Lancey Barclay, 1st Foot Guards, was the son of Susan De Lancey and Major Barclay, one of many Loyalist families to move to Canada after the American Revolution. He was Sir William De Lancey's second cousin.

Lieutenant-Colonel Sir George Berkeley, 35th Foot, was the eldest son of Admiral Sir George Berkeley. He served in the Peninsula, and as his parent regiment was the 35th Foot, he would certainly have been known to the Duke of Richmond, who had commanded the first battalion for some years at the turn of the century and was now colonel-in-chief of the regiment. During the third week of March 1815 he married a daughter of the late Sir Thomas Sutton, MP, for which his bride's mother and sister had been present. Sir George and Lady Berkeley and Lady and Miss Sutton were all invited to the Ball; Sir George was the AAG at the Prince of Orange's headquarters on 15 June and was almost certainly too busy to attend, but whether the others did or not cannot be established for certain.

Lieutenant-Colonel Sir Noel Hill, 1st Foot Guards, was the seventh son of Sir John Hill, Bart, and brother to Lieutenant-General Lord Hill. He served throughout the Peninsular campaign, for most of which he commanded the 1st Portuguese Infantry Regiment. He transferred to 1st Foot Guards in 1814 and was then appointed DAG at Wellington's headquarters.

Miscellaneous Appointments

As in any headquarters, there were a number of officers in what are best termed miscellaneous appointments. Nobody from the commissary-general's department or the staff of the deputy judge-advocate earned an invitation to the Ball, but three invitations were issued and, as far as is known, accepted.

Colonel Sir Colin Campbell, Coldstream Guards, was one of the most popular officers in the Army, but his job as headquarters commandant, especially to the Duke of Wellington, should not be thought a sinecure and required a great deal of forward planning and attention to detail. **Dr John Hume** was a deputy-inspector on the army medical staff, but had been Wellington's personal doctor since the Peninsular campaign; he was the only doctor to be invited to the Ball. The third of these men was **Reverend Samuel Briscall**. It would be stretching matters a bit to describe him as the duke's 'personal chaplain'. Nevertheless, he had joined the army headquarters during the Peninsular War where he earned the commander's approval for his well conducted but not overlong services. He held the same post in the Netherlands.

Brigade Majors

A brigade commander had three officers to assist him. One was an ADC, which was a personal appointment, selected by the commander, the second was a DAQMG, allocated by the QMG, and the third was correctly titled the 'major of brigade' (but always known as 'brigade major' (BM)). Despite the title, the post was frequently filled by a captain, but was a position of considerable prestige and the holder remained in post if the brigade commander changed. His responsibilities included the movement and deployment of the units of the brigade and the posting of picquets. There were thirteen British BMs in the Waterloo army; three were invited to the Ball, one of whom is known not to have attended.

Major Thomas Hunter Blair, 91st Foot[8] Thomas Hunter Blair, brigade major to Major-General Adam, was the grandson of Sir James Hunter Blair, Bart (1741–87) a Scottish banker and politician, who in his time was both an MP and Lord Provost of Edinburgh. Thomas was the younger brother of the third baronet and was in the army from an early age. He fought in the Peninsula and was captured at Talavera, following which he was held in France until the peace of 1814. His general (Adam) did not attend the Ball and it is probable that Hunter Blair did not do so either.

Captain James Gunthorpe, 1st Foot Guards Brigade Major to Major-General Peregrine Maitland, Gunthorpe was a member of a wealthy landowning family of Gunthorpe Hall near Fakenham in Norfolk.

Captain (Brevet-Major) Charles K Smyth, 95th Foot The BM to Major-General Sir Dennis Pack, 9th Infantry Brigade, Smyth's name was incorrectly listed in the Duchess of Richmond's invitations as 'Smith'. He was born in 1786, the son of the Rt Hon. John Smyth (1748–1811) of Heath Hall, near Wakefield, by his wife, Lady Georgiana Fitzroy. Georgiana was the eldest daughter of the third Duke of Grafton by his first wife, Anne Liddel, and she seems to have survived her parents' numerous affairs and subsequent acrimonious divorce with a fair degree of equanimity. Smyth was cousin to Captain Lord Charles Fitzroy, DAAG, and to Lieutenant Charles Fitzroy, ADC to Major-General Sir Hussey Vivian. He distinguished himself in the Peninsular War and was promoted brevet major in 1815. He was one of those who attended the Ball and who died from wounds received at Quatre Bras.

Aides-de-Camp

ADCs were something of a breed apart, being referred to as a general's 'family' and acting as his assistant in peacetime and as a courier in war. At a time when the only means of communication in battle was by word of mouth or handwritten message, this was a vital role, requiring quick understanding, excellent horsemanship, the ability to find one's way across the battlefield, and to deliver messages rapidly and accurately.

The army made a financial allowance for ADCs on the basis of: commander-in-chief – four; general – three; lieutenant-general – two and major-general – one. Some generals, however, chose to have more, meeting the additional expense out of their own pockets. The appointment was personal to the general and ended as soon as the general ceased to be in command. The army traditionally made fun of ADCs, one contemporary wag advising a potential ADC that his '... deportment [should] be haughty and insolent to your inferiors, humble and fawning to your superiors, solemn and distant to your equals'. But the glory and comforts were offset by danger; there were fifty-seven British ADCs at Quatre Bras and Waterloo – seven of them were killed and twelve wounded.

No fewer than twenty-nine ADCs were invited to the Ball, making them the largest single group of officers, although at least five of those failed to arrive due to the rapid development in the operational situation.

Wellington

Wellington had seven British ADCs – three guardsmen and four cavalrymen – six of whom were invited to the Ball, while the seventh, Lord George Lennox, attended as a member of the Richmond family.

These comprised three lieutenant-colonels from Guards regiments – **Canning** (3rd), **Fremantle** (2nd) and **Gordon** (3rd), and four cavalrymen – **Major the Hon. Henry Percy** (14th Light Dragoons), **Captain Lord Arthur Hill** (2nd Dragoons, but on half-pay at the time), and lieutenants **Lord George Lennox** (9th Light Dragoons) and the **Hon. George Cathcart** (6th Iniskilling Guards). Wellington's eighth ADC, also invited to the Ball, was the **Hereditary Prince of Nassau**, who was 'attached' as a courtesy to the Duke of Nassau.

Prince of Orange

The Prince of Orange had six English ADCs, of whom four were invited to the Ball, while the fifth, **Captain the Earl of March**, attended as a member of the Richmond family. The senior ADC, **Lieutenant-Colonel Otto Ernst, Baron Trip van Zoutlandt**, was Dutch by birth but had gone to England when the French overran his country, where he was commissioned into the 10th Light Dragoons in 1800. He then filled a variety of ADC posts with senior British officers until 1814 when, by now in the 60th Rifles, he was appointed senior ADC to the Prince of Orange. He was well known in English circles in Brussels and formed an ill-fated attachment with Lady Harriet Capel, which came to her father's notice in May 1815 resulting in a duel in which the Duke of Richmond acted as Capel's second – see Chapter V. Trip's name appears in the Goodwood, De Ros and Delhaize Lists, but it seems highly unlikely that he would have attended a function where he would have met the Duke of Richmond, Capel and even, possibly, Harriet, as well.

The other British ADCs invited to the Ball were **Captain Lord John Somerset**, Lord Fitzroy Somerset's brother, who had married Lady Catherine Annesley in December 1814, **Captain the Hon. Francis Russell**, on half-pay, and **Lieutenant Henry Webster**, 9th Light Dragoons. The latter did not attend as a guest, but arrived at the Ball late in the evening in order to deliver a message to the Prince of Orange.

Uxbridge

Uxbridge had four ADCs, the senior of whom, Major Thornhill, 7th Hussars, was not invited. The other three were both invited and attended: **Captain James Fraser** and **Captain Thomas Wildman**, both of the 7th Hussars, and **Captain Horace Seymour**, 60th Foot. Wildman was immensely rich, purchasing the Byron home at Newstead Abbey for £95,000, while Seymour was famed for his impressive size and great physical strength; the latter's aunt, Lady Waldegrave, was staying in Brussels and also attended the Ball. Uxbridge and all four of his ADCs were wounded on 15 June.

Hill

Hill had four ADCs, of whom the senior, Major Egerton, 34th Foot, was not invited. The others, who were invited, were **Major Chatham Churchill**, 1st Foot Guards; **Captain Hon. Orlando Bridgeman**, 1st Foot Guards; and **Captain Digby Mackworth**, 7th Foot.

Clinton

As a lieutenant-general, Clinton was entitled to three ADCs, but had only two: **Captain Dawkins**, 1st Foot Guards; and **Captain Gurwood**, 10th Hussars. It is doubtful that Clinton and Dawkins attended, but Gurwood almost certainly did, as he was involved in helping the Duchess of Richmond make the arrangements for the Ball.

Cooke

Commanding the 1st (Guards) Division, Cooke was accompanied to the Ball by one of his two ADCs, **Captain George Disbrowe**, 1st Foot Guards. Disbrowe's main claim to fame was that he was descended from a noted Roundhead soldier who had married one of Oliver Cromwell's sisters.

Barnes

Although a staff officer, the Adjutant-General, Major-General Barnes, was entitled to one ADC. In his case this was **Major Andrew Hamilton** of the 4th West India Regiment. During the months before Waterloo, Hamilton was courting Miss Anne Ord and kept her step-father, Thomas Creevey, well up-to-date with information from inside the headquarters.

Brigades

Eight brigade commanders were invited to the Ball; in six cases their ADCs were also invited, but Ponsonby's and Pack's were not. In no case was an ADC invited if his brigade commander had not already also been invited. Major-General Adam's ADC, **Captain Yorke**, was invited to the Ball but, like his general, he did not attend.

Lord Edward Somerset

Like a number of generals, Lord Edward Somerset employed a relation as his ADC; in this case, his nephew **Lieutenant Henry Somerset**, 18th Hussars (1794–1862). Henry Somerset was the eldest son of Lord Charles Somerset and his wife, one of fourteen daughters of the second Viscount Courtenay.

Vivian

Captain Edward Keane was one of many officers of the 7th Hussars invited to the Ball. He was the son of Sir John Keane, first Bart. The second ADC was **Lieutenant Charles Fitzroy**, Royal Horse Guards, the eldest son of Lord Charles Fitzroy, one of the thirteen children of the third Duke of Grafton's second marriage. Lieutenant Fitzroy had served with Blücher's Prussian Army in 1813–14 from Leipzig to the fall of Paris. He subsequently married Lady Mary Lennox (1790–1847), eldest daughter of the fourth Duke of Richmond,

Maitland

Maitland's ADC was **Ensign James, Lord Hay** (1797–1815) of the 1st Foot Guards, the eldest son of the sixteenth Earl of Errol. He was a popular young man, Lady Caroline Capel writing in February 1815 that 'Lord Hay son of Lord Errol is a new recruit [to her family circle] & a most agreeable one, he is very poor I hear, is very good-looking I know & particularly Gentleman-like . . .'[9] Many mourned his death on the afternoon following the Ball, when he was shot and killed instantly at Quatre Bras by a French cavalry skirmisher; he was a month short of his 19th birthday when he died.

Byng

Byng had two ADCs at this time, both of whom were invited to the Ball. The official ADC was **Captain Dumaresq**, 9th Foot, a native of Jersey, who was present at no fewer than thirteen battles during the Peninsular War. He served as a volunteer with the engineers at the sieges of Burgos and Badajoz, and again at the assaults on Salamanca, where he received the terms of capitulation from the officer commanding and delivered it to the general of the forces, Lord Wellington. Byng's additional ADC was **Lieutenant the Hon. Edward Stopford**, 3rd Foot Guards, second son of the third Earl of Courtown.

Kempt

Captain the Hon. Charles Gore (1793–1869), son of Arthur Gore, second Earl of Arran, was commissioned into the 6th Foot, but exchanged into the 43rd Foot in 1811 in the Peninsula. After some experience with the regiment, he served as ADC to Major-General Sir Andrew Barnard at Salamanca (22 July 1812), but then became ADC to Major-General Sir James Kempt for the Battle of Vittoria (21 June 1813). He then stayed with Kempt for the remainder of the Peninsular War, accompanied him to North America in 1814 and was with him during the Waterloo campaign.

Dornberg

Major-General Dornberg, an officer in the British Army's King's German Legion (KGL), commanded the 3rd Cavalry Brigade in the Waterloo campaign. Dornberg himself was not invited to the Ball, but **Major Georg, Baron Krauchenberg** was. Krauchenberg was an officer in the KGL's 3rd Hussar Regiment and was well known in Brussels circles, appearing in Lady Caroline Capel's list of 'agreeable' young men, where she described him as '. . . a very good Man & an excellent soldier, & ready to die *for any of Us*.'[10] This was the only case in the Invitation List where an ADC was invited, but not the general whom he served.

THE REGIMENTS

The British fighting elements of Wellington's army (including the reserves) comprised twenty-five infantry battalions and sixteen cavalry regiments, and officers from eight battalions and seven regiments were included in the invitation list to the Ball.

Royal Horse Guards

The sole officer from the Royal Horse Guards was the commanding officer, **Sir Clement Hill**, the brother of Lieutenant-General Lord Hill.

1st (King's) Dragoon Guards

Of the three who were invited, **Lieutenant-Colonel William Fuller**, the commanding officer and **Lieutenant Francis Brooke** were among the seven KDG officers to be killed on 18 June. The third, **Cornet William Huntley**, was among those who survived.

7th (Queen's Own) Light Dragoons (Hussars)

The 7th Hussars were stationed around the town of Grammont and two of the officers are known to have travelled together to attend the Ball: **Captain William Verner** and **Lieutenant Standish O'Grady**.[11] These two had already stayed with the Richmonds a few weeks earlier, as Verner had been one of the duke's ADCs when the latter was lord lieutenant of Ireland. The other two officers on the Invitation List were **Captain James Elphinstone** and **Lieutenant John Gordon**.

10th (Prince of Wales's Own Royal) Light Dragoons (Hussars)

Two officers were invited: **Lieutenant-Colonel Robert Manners**, the second-in-command, and **Captain Arthur Shakespear**. Manners was the third son of the fourth Duke of Rutland and his mother, Lady Mary Somerset, the daughter of the third Duke of Beaufort. Thus, Manners was cousin to Lieutenant-Colonel Lord Fitzroy Somerset and Captain Lord John Somerset. Like Verner, Shakespear also left a written record stating that he attended the Ball.[12]

12th Light Dragoons

Lieutenant-Colonel the Hon. Frederick Ponsonby (1783–1841), the commanding officer, was the only member of his regiment to be invited to the Ball. He was the second son of the third Earl of Bessborough. Ponsonby suffered no fewer than seven wounds at Waterloo and, despite being known to have lost a great deal of blood, was then bled again by the doctors in Brussels and nursed by his sister, the somewhat erratic Lady Caroline Lamb.[13] But, despite the attentions of doctors and his nurse, he managed to survive.

18th Light Dragoons (Hussars)

The only officer in the 18th Hussars to be invited to the Ball, **Lt the Hon. Lionel Dawson**, had one brother in the 23rd Light Dragoons (Lieutenant-Colonel Earl of Portarlington; see below), while another, Major the Hon. George Dawson was on the staff as an AQMG. Lionel Dawson's role during the battle was the unglamorous one of supervising the regiment's baggage train.

23rd Light Dragoons

Lieutenant-Colonel John Dawson, second Earl of Portarlington, the only officer of the 23rd Dragoons to attend the Ball, became a tragic figure. He had distinguished himself in the Peninsula and did so again on 17 June during the withdrawal from Quatre Bras to Waterloo. But that night he was taken so ill that he was evacuated to Brussels and as a consequence was not present during the early part of the battle on 18 June. On recovering a little in Brussels and realising that a battle was in progress, Portarlington rushed back to the field and, unable to find his own regiment in the confusion, took part in several charges as an extra sabre in the 18th Hussars. Portarlington was mortified at being absent from his regiment on such an occasion and resigned. His courage was never doubted, the Prince Regent treated him with great sympathy, his officers bought him a very handsome farewell gift and other friends tried to help, but he never recovered from what he perceived to be a disgrace and died in poverty in 1845.[14]

1st Foot Guards

The 2nd and 3rd Battalions of the 1st Foot Guards had sixty-seven officers employed at regimental duty (with a further eighteen in appointments as staff officers or ADCs). Of those sixty-seven, eight were invited to the Ball, one of whom certainly did not attend. Not surprisingly, the Guards officers invited by the Duchess of Richmond were well connected.

Major the Hon. William Stuart, the third major, was a son of the tenth Baron Blantyre, **Captain the Hon. James Stanhope** was the third son of the third Earl Stanhope, and **Ensign the Hon. T Seymour Bathurst** was the third son of the third Earl Bathurst and of Georgiana Lennox, one of the Duke of Richmond's three sisters. **Ensign the Hon. Ernest Edgcombe** was the eldest son of the third Earl Edgcombe, while **Ensign George Fludyer** was the eldest son of George Fludyer and his wife, Lady Mary Fane, daughter of the ninth Earl of Westmoreland. **Ensign Algernon Greville** was the son of Captain W Fulke Greville, RN, and thus a member of the Warwick family, as well as being a nephew of Lady Charlotte Greville. The only one without aristocratic connections was **Captain Charles Allix**, the adjutant, who was descended from Pierre Allix (1641–1717), a French Protestant divine, who had been compelled to seek refuge in London in 1685, following the revocation of the Edict of Nantes. Like so many Huguenot families (for example, the De Lanceys), Allix's descendants prospered and Charles's father was a landowner at Swaffham House in Cambridgeshire. **Lieutenant-Colonel Alexander, Lord Saltoun** was invited to the Ball but did not attend. As described in Chapter V, his heart was elsewhere.

2nd Battalion, 2nd (Coldstream) Foot Guards

Seven of the twenty-eight Coldstream officers were invited to the Ball. These included the commanding officer, **Lieutenant-Colonel Alexander Woodford**, the elder brother of Colonel John Woodford (see above) and thus also a cousin to the Duchess of Richmond. **Captain George Bowles**, the second son of William Bowles of Heale House in Wiltshire, was definitely at the Ball and left a valuable account of various incidents there. If the reserve had been formed it would have been commanded by the Duke of Richmond, and Bowles would have been his ADC.[15] Also invited were **Captain Hon. Edward Acheson**, the second son of the first Viscount Gosford, **Captain Henry Wyndham**, the natural son of the third Earl Egremont, and three ensigns: two brothers, the **Hon. James** and the **Hon. Walter Forbes**, sons of General Lord Forbes; and the **Hon. John Montagu**, eldest son and heir of the fourth Lord Rokeby.

3rd Foot Guards

There were thirty-three officers of the 3rd Foot Guards at regimental duty, of whom five were invited to the Ball. Two of these came from aristocratic families: **Lieutenant the Hon. Hastings Forbes** was the third son of the sixth Earl of Granard, while **Ensign the Hon. Henry Montagu**, the youngest and most junior officer in the regiment, was the second son of the fourth Lord Rokeby (and eventually became the sixth Baron Rokeby). **Captain Edward Bowater** was the son of Admiral Bowater. **Captain Robert Hesketh** was the son of Robert Hesketh, a country landowner.

Ensign David Baird was the nephew of General Sir David Baird, Bt, succeeding to his uncle's baronetcy in 1829.

32nd Foot

Lieutenant James Robinson was the only officer from his regiment to be invited to the Ball, but no records survive other than his dates of service and mention of being wounded at Waterloo.[16] There is nothing at all on his family, but he must have been well connected for the duchess, a noted snob, to have invited him. It is possible, but not proven, that he was related to the Baron Robinson of Grantham.

42nd Foot

When he attended the Ball on 15 June **Lieutenant-Colonel Robert Henry Dick** was second-in-command of the 42nd Foot, but took command on the afternoon of 16 June when his commanding officer, Lieutenant-Colonel Sir Robert Macara, was killed at Quatre Bras.

52nd Foot

Lieutenant-Colonel Sir John Colborne was military secretary to the Hereditary Prince of Orange from mid-1814 until May 1815 when he returned to command his regiment, 52nd Foot, in the forthcoming campaign. He was one of the finest and most respected commanding officers in Wellington's army and would have been well known to the Duke of Richmond, not least because the latter's eldest son, Captain the Earl of March, was one of his officers (albeit detached to serve as an ADC). Colborne's name does not appear on the invitation list, but it is unthinkable that he would have been passed over; thus, it is far more likely that he was asked if he would like to be invited and refused, suggesting that his second-in-command, **Lieutenant-Colonel Charles Rowan**, be invited instead. Rowan was an Irishman from County Antrim and had served with the regiment and on the staff in the Peninsula.

92nd Foot

Lieutenant-Colonel John Cameron of Fassiefern took command of 1/92nd Foot in March 1809, his first task being to take his men on the disastrous Walcheren expedition, following which he had to nurse them all back to health. The battalion next went to Portugal arriving in October 1810 (at which time Lieutenant Claude Alexander was already the adjutant) being deployed into the Lines of Torres Vedras. Cameron was very firm but also extremely fair, and paid very keen attention to the welfare of his highlanders. The 92nd took part in the extraordinary night attack at Arroyo dos Molinos (28 October 1811) in the course of which they captured Colonel Prince d'Arenberg (see page 74). The battalion continued its fighting through to southern France in April 1814, and then sailed for Ireland, arriving on 26 July.

Normal peacetime garrison life ensued until April 1815 when Napoleon's escape from Elba resulted in the 92nd being rushed to the Netherlands, arriving at Ostend on 10 May. They then moved by barge and on foot to Brussels, which was reached on 28 May. Perhaps it was the delights of a foreign capital city which caused Cameron, whose battalion order book was littered with minor rebukes for his officers, to issue a dry reminder on 11 June that 'Officers will find it through life a useful maxim to be rather an hour too soon than one minute too late'.

On the 15th came the Duchess of Richmond's Ball at which the 92nd provided a team of four sergeants and Pipe-Major Alexander Cameron, who performed a reel and a sword dance for the guests.[17] But while the pipes were playing the battalion was assembling for battle and marched out of Brussels early on the 16th. On reaching Quatre Bras they were thrown straight into fierce hand-to-hand combat in the course of which Cameron was shot. He was taken back to Waterloo village where he died that night. He had been in constant command of the battalion for six years and three months and was one of that small band of commanding officers upon whose courage, leadership and tactical excellence the success of Wellington's army depended.

95th Foot (Riflemen)

The 95th was present in Wellington's army in considerable strength and included the 1st and 2nd battalions complete, plus two companies of the 3rd battalion, a total of sixty-five officers (not including those in staff appointments). Despite this, the only officer to be invited to the Ball was **Lieutenant-Colonel Sir Andrew Barnard**, commanding officer of the first battalion.

Royal Artillery and Royal Engineers

The Royal Regiment of Artillery (RA), Royal Horse Artillery (RHA) and Corps of Royal Engineers (RE) were organised, administered and paid for by the Board of Ordnance at Woolwich, but were placed under army command in operational theatres. There were ninety RA/RHA officers in Wellington's army and eleven REs, of which two and none respectively were invited to the Ball. The two artillerymen to be invited were the Commander Royal Artillery, **Colonel Sir George Wood**, and his adjutant, **Captain William Pakenham RHA**.

NOTES

1   Elizabeth Longford, *Wellington*, quoting from the Hague Royal Archives.
2   *Reminiscences of Captain Gronow*.
3   'At night we all went to the Duchess of Richmond's Ball', Siborne, Waterloo Letters, p. 151.
4   Lady Susan was the second wife of Colonel John Woodford and the widow of the ninth Earl of Westmoreland.
5   The novels were *Coelibia choosing a Husband*, 2 vols, London, 1809, and *The Victim of Intolerance or the hermit of Killarney*, 3 vols, London 1814.
6   Capel Letters, p. 86.
7   Harry Smith, *Autobiography*, Chapter 28.
8   The correct surname is 'Hunter Blair' but is not hyphenated.
9   Capel Letters, p. 85.
10 Capel Letters, p. 86.
11 *Reminiscences of William Verner* (1782–1871) 7th Hussars.
12 *Journal* of Captain Arthur Shakespear, courtesy of Lady Anne Dalrymple-Hamilton.
13 Susan Mornington, *Lady Caroline Lamb*, pp. 146–9.
14 Portarlington was not alone in being taken ill and sent back to Brussels on the night of 17 June. The same happened to Lieutenant John Cowell of the 2nd Foot Guards; unlike Portarlington he did not reach Waterloo on the 18th, but still received the medal.
15 *A Series of Letters of The First Earl of Malmesbury, His Family and Friends*, 1745–1820, ed. Earl of Malmesbury, R Bentley, London, 1852. Vol. II, p. 455.
16 PRO: WO 25/722 shows that he was born in 1792, took up his first appointment as ensign in 1807 and purchased promotion to lieutenant in 1810. He married in 1825 and had two children. He left the Army, still a lieutenant in 1823 and spent a further six years on half-pay. The National Army Museum, Waterloo Roll Call and the modern Regimental museums have no more information.
17 Lady Louisa Tighe (formerly Lady Louisa Lennox) wrote in a letter dated 13 January 1889: 'I well remember the Gordon Highlanders dancing reels at the ball; my mother thought it would interest the foreigners to see them, which it did.' Gardyne, *The Life of a Regiment*, p. 349.

CHAPTER XII

The Location of the Ball

A curious feature of this famous occasion is that the actual location of the Ball – on the face of it a simple matter – has been the subject of prolonged, contradictory and sometimes acrimonious debate. The early end to the Ball and the subsequent Battles of Quatre Bras and Waterloo, followed by the exodus from Brussels as the Allies advanced on Paris were, of course, totally unexpected. As a result, the Ball quickly slipped into the background.

Tours of the Waterloo battlefield commenced within days of the battle and there was soon a small but thriving tourist industry, in which the guides concentrated on the battlefield itself and the village of Waterloo, but, if asked, would say that the Ball was held in the Hôtel de Ville in the Grande Place. Quite how they came to this conclusion is not clear, since many Bruxellois would have known the truth, but it may have been because it was such a splendid and imposing building, and it is certainly true that some balls, particularly those hosted by the Mayor of Brussels, did take place there.

Lord Byron visited Brussels in 1816 and his poem, 'Childe Harold', depicted the Ball in a romantic and dramatic light. Many people reading that poem found the lines:

> 'Within a window'd niche of that high hall
> Sate Brunswick's fated chieftain . . .'

and concluded that he could only be referring to the Hôtel de Ville. Close reading of 'Childe Harold', however, reveals that the poet never actually offers any positive identification of the location of the Ball and there is no reason to believe that 'high hall' and 'window'd niche' were anything other than poetic licence. After all, his description of how 'a thousand hearts beat happily' is also a gross exaggeration of the numbers actually attending the Ball.

During the remainder of the 19th century, three other potential locations were put forward: two sites in the rue de la Blanchisserie – the stables and the coach-house – and the Maison du Roi. The Maison du Roi theory surfaced in the *Illustrated London News* in the mid-19th century, and was again discussed in that journal on 16 June 1923. The magazine's main argument in the latter article was that when it was first suggested, nobody had opposed it, but the whole idea simply lacks credibility, as the Duchess of Richmond would not have used the king's palace. That leaves the last two, and there can, in fact, be no doubt that the Ball was held in the Richmonds' residence in the rue de la Blanchisserie; most convincing of all, every Lennox family record says that that was where it was held, the only point at issue being precisely where.

The Richmonds had three requirements for their residence. First, it had to be commensurate with their ducal dignity. Secondly, it had to accommodate a family of some fifteen persons and a large number of servants, together with the associated impedimenta, such as coaches and horses. And finally, its price had to match their straitened circumstances; in other words, it had to be affordable. The selected house was a three-storey residence of some size, with a large garden, located in the lower (and less fashionable) end of the town. This whole formed a rectangular plot extending from the old ramparts at the foot of the garden to the rue de la Blanchisserie, and bordered on one side by the rue Marais and on the other by a footpath, running roughly parallel to the rue Marais and which separated the estate from a working laundry.[1]

The street fronting the Richmond residence was originally named rue de la Fontaine, as it ran past the site of a small spring. In the 17th century, however, a laundry business was established on the site; as a result the street became known as rue de la Blanchisserie de la Fontaine, which was soon shortened to rue de la Blanchisserie. It was for this reason, that the Duke of Wellington always referred, jokingly, to the Richmonds' residence as 'the Wash-house'.

Adjacent to the laundry was a modest estate, which was acquired in the 1790s by Jean Simons, a very successful coachbuilder married to an actress, Julie Candeille. Simons' coaches were used by a very distinguished clientele, including the Emperor Napoleon I. Simons built a grand, three-storied residence for his family, flanked by two barn-like, two-storied wings, which accommodated most of his business. Viewed from the ramparts, the wing to the right of the villa housed the company offices, the workshop and a large, open coach-house in which his products were stored and displayed to potential clients. This wing was distinct from the main building, but connected to it by an annexe, enabling family members to move between the house and the business premises without exposing themselves to the weather. There were numerous other buildings on the estate, the only three significant to this story being the stables, a long, low structure on the opposite side of the courtyard to the main house, and unconnected with it in any way,[2] a gate-house, accommodating the concierge, and a small, self-contained residence, possibly a dower-house, in the garden.

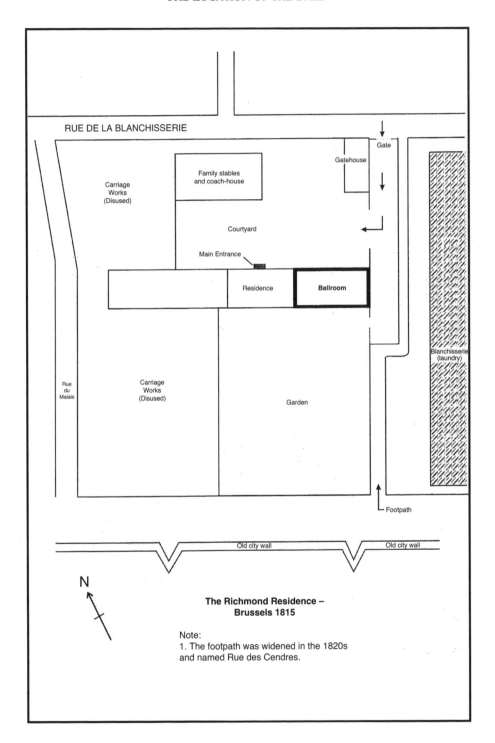

RUE DE LA BLANCHISSERIE

Gate

Gatehouse

Family stables
and coach-house

Carriage
Works
(Disused)

Courtyard

Main Entrance

Residence

Ballroom

Blanchisserie
(laundry)

Rue
du
Malais

Carriage
Works
(Disused)

Garden

Footpath

Old city wall

Old city wall

N

**The Richmond Residence –
Brussels 1815**

Note:
1. The footpath was widened in the 1820s
and named Rue des Cendres.

The coach-building business and the residence were inherited by the eldest son, Michel-Jean Simons in 1810, who already had his own business as a supplier of stationery to the army. In continuance of the family tradition, he too had married an actress, one Anne-Françoise-Elisabeth Lange, who performed on the Parisian stage, but she was so extravagant that she dragged her unfortunate husband into considerable debt. As a result, he was forced to rent out his estate, fully furnished, and his first tenant, who took up residence in September 1814, was the Duke of Richmond.

The coach showroom was standing empty, so it was converted by the Richmonds into a school- and playroom for the younger children, as confirmed by Lady Georgiana de Ros, the Richmonds' third daughter:

> In 1814 we went to live at Brussels, in a house in the Rue de la Blanchisserie, with a large garden extending to the ramparts ... My mother's now famous ball took place in a large room on the ground floor, on the left of the entrance, connected with the rest of the house by an anteroom. It had been used by the coachbuilder, from whom the house was hired, to put carriages in, but it was papered before we came there; and I recollect the paper – a trellis pattern with roses. My sisters used the room as a schoolroom, and we used to play battledore and shuttlecock there on a wet day.[3]

Lady de Ros lived until her 96th year and remained alert to the last, so as this was written when she was in her 60s and recalling events when she was 19, it seems very unlikely that she would be mistaken. It should be added that her views were supported to the hilt by her brother, Lord William Lennox and her sister, Lady Louisa Tighe, who had been 15 and 11 at the time. There was an element of confusion, however; the plan included in Lady de Ros's book, which had been drawn by Lord William Lennox and corroborated by his two sisters, was incorrect in one respect, in that it showed the ballroom to be an integral part of the villa, whereas, as explained above, it was actually part of a separate building, albeit linked to the main house by an annexe.

An additional factor was introduced by Lieutenant Webster, who arrived at about 11pm to deliver a message to the Hereditary Prince. Webster is quite clear that the building where the Ball was held had two storeys, with a seated supper being served on the ground floor and the dancing taking place on the first floor. He says: 'On my telling the Suisse I had despatches of moment for the Prince, he asked me if I would wait five minutes; "for," said he, "the Duchess has just given orders for the band to go upstairs, and the party are now about to rise."' Webster duly waited and then, '. . . saw the Duchess of Richmond taking the Prince of Orange's arm, and Lady Charlotte Greville the Duke's, on their way to the ball-room. The moment they had reached the foot of the stairs I hastened to the Prince's side . . .' A few minutes later, '. . . As soon as the last couple had mounted the *première étage,* the Duke of Wellington descended, and espying me, beckoned me to him . . .'[4]

Two people added to the confusion. The first was Sir William Fraser, Bt, described by *The Times* as a 'well-known collector of great men's relics and an interesting and pleasant writer',[5] who published a slim volume in 1889[6] recounting a visit to Brussels during which he had gone to some pains to locate the specific room in which the Ball had been held. He agreed that the Ball took place in the residence in rue de la Blanchisserie, but he chose as the actual spot a long, narrow, two-storey building, which has since been proved to have been the coach-house and stables for the family in the villa (as opposed to the business premises) and was on the opposite side of the courtyard from the main house and not connected to it in any way. Sir William clung tenaciously to this theory, wrote several books on the subject, and originated a lengthy exchange of letters in both *The Times* and the information exchange publication known as *Notes and Queries.*

The problem was exacerbated by the fact that by the 1880s most of the buildings and the street layout had changed. This process had started in the early 1820s when the left wing of the villa was knocked down, together with the gateman's cottage, and a new road driven through from the junction of the footpath and rue de la Blanchisserie, across the left half of the courtyard, over the site of the ballroom and then through the gardens and the ramparts to join up with a street beyond. This new street was named rue des Cendres. As the entrance to the Simons villa was on the new street the house was renumbered No. 7 rue des Cendres, while the old stables became No. 42 rue de la Blanchisserie. The villa was subsequently incorporated into a new hospital building, while the stables became a small brewery.

Thomas Hardy then entered the controversy with his mammoth work *The Dynasts.* This includes a scene at the Ball, to which is appended a footnote:

> This famous ball has become so embedded in the history of the Hundred Days as to be an integral part of it. Yet in spite of the efforts that have been made to locate the room which saw the memorable gathering (by the present writer more than thirty years back, among other enthusiasts) a dispassionate judgment must deny that its site has as yet been proven. Even Sir W. Fraser is not convincing. The event happened less than a century ago, but the spot is almost as phantasmal in its elusive mystery as towered Camelot, the palace of Priam, or the hill of Calvary.[7]

Sir William and his supporters were, of course, entitled to their views, and Thomas Hardy to his indecision, but the weight of evidence, supported by the Lennox family and Belgian experts, is against them. Even *The Times* of 14 June 1915, the centenary of the Ball, despite the fact that the world had much else to worry about at the time, addressed the issue, bringing all its weight to bear on the side of Lady de Ros's solution.

NOTES

1   Some time after 1815 a new street, the rue de Cendres, was driven from the rue de la Blanchisserie and on through the garden of the Simons property and then through the ramparts of the old city wall. It ran parallel to the footpath and involved the demolition of part of the Simons property.
2   The stables was later converted into a residence and occupied by a family named Van Ginderachter.
3   *Reminiscences of Lady de Ros*, pp. 122–3.
4   J C Young, *A Memoir of C M Young*, Vol. ii, pp. 98–102.
5   *The Times* Monday 14 June 1915.
6   Fraser, Sir William Augustus Bart, *Words on Wellington: The Duke, Waterloo, the Ball*, J C Nimmo, London, 1889.
7   Hardy, Thomas, *The Dynasts. a drama of the Napoleonic wars, in three parts, nineteen acts, & one hundred and thirty scenes*, Macmillan, New York, London, 1904, p. 45.

CHAPTER XIII
The Ball
Morning, 15 June 1815

During the days prior to 15 June rumours were constantly circulating around Brussels concerning French concentrations and their moves towards the frontier. Similar rumours described supposed Allied countermoves. As usual in such circumstances, many proved to be false and the civilians never really knew what to believe. Lieutenant-Colonel Sir George Scovell's groom, Edward Heeley, wrote on the 14th that there was a general feeling that hostilities would commence about 25 June, as a result of which soldiers were to be seen sharpening their swords and purchasing cloth to make into bandages; otherwise, all continued as tranquilly as before.[1] A similar attitude prevailed in the higher echelons of society where there was a matching feeling that nothing would now happen until all the Allied armies, acting in concert, advanced into France at the beginning of July. As a result, the morning of the 15th seemed to all in Brussels to be the start of another sunny and peaceful day, and war seemed almost as far away as ever. Indeed, it was etched forever in Lady De Lancey's memory: '. . . Thursday 15th June forenoon was the happiest time of my life.'

There was an investiture that morning when, among others, Lieutenant-Colonel John Cameron of Fassifern, Commanding Officer of the 92nd Foot, received his richly deserved insignia as a Commander of the Order of the Bath. In the lower town, the final preparations for the Ball were being made at the Richmond residence, supervised by the Richmonds' household staff, assisted by Captain Gurwood of the 10th Hussars.[2]

At military headquarters, Wellington had already made all the necessary plans to deploy his army should Napoleon invade, but he now needed clear and unequivocal indications of the French main thrust before issuing the orders for the actual deployment. He was under no illusion about the importance of his decision; he was, in fact, in a similar position to Admiral Jellicoe, commander-in-chief of the British Grand Fleet exactly a hundred years later, who, in Churchill's words, 'was the only man who could lose the war in an afternoon'.

133

Afternoon

Wellington received some indications of French activity during the morning of the 15th but none of it was sufficiently firm or on such a scale that it warranted a decision to deploy. So, as always, the duke kept calm and carried on with routine work. At 1pm he wrote to Lieutenant-General Clinton on the question of renumbering the infantry divisions to fit in with the system used in the Peninsula, proposing that Clinton's 2nd Division become the 6th, while Colville's 4th would become the 2nd,[3] a matter of minimal consequence in the grand scheme of things, but the sort of trivia which preoccupies British generals from time to time. He then turned his attention to a lengthy letter to the Emperor of Russia on the overall military situation. That he should have been writing on such subjects clearly indicates that he did not feel under any particular pressure from events.

Others, too, were taking things calmly. Lord Fitzroy Somerset was with his wife and infant daughter, the De Lanceys were relaxing in their apartment, and when Lord Hill called at the Richmonds' house in the early afternoon, Lady Georgiana Lennox observed that he was very relaxed and '. . . disclaimed any knowledge of a move'.[4]

Two new arrivals, Miss Charlotte Waldie and her sister, got to Brussels in the early afternoon and went straight to the Park, which they found,

> . . . crowded with officers, in every variety of military uniform, with elegant women, and with lively parties and gay groups of British and Belgic people, loitering, walking, talking, and sitting under the trees! There could be not be a more animated, a more holiday scene; every thing looked gay and festive, and every thing spoke of hope, confidence and busy expectation.[5]

A number of separate dinner parties were held in Brussels that afternoon, hosted by, among others Wellington, d'Alava and Uxbridge. The young Prince of Orange had been touring his outposts but came to Brussels to join Wellington for dinner at three o'clock, when he briefed the duke on the latest developments as he knew them.[6] But, at some time before 5pm they were interrupted by the Prussian liaison officer, Major-General von Müffling, who had just received a message from General von Zieten.[7] They discussed the situation, and Wellington told Müffling that although he had received no news of French advances on his own front, particularly from Mons, he would, nevertheless, put all his units at readiness to move.

Wellington's military secretary, Lord Fitzroy Somerset, was still at home when he received the news and immediately hurried to head-quarters, where, at about 5pm, he found Wellington walking in the Park, issuing a stream of orders to the officers around him. As promised to Müffling, the duke was instructing that everything was to be made ready for a rapid move, but he was waiting for more precise information on Napoleon's movements and objectives before ordering actual movement to start.[8] The troops most immediately to hand were Picton's 5th Division, which had arrived in Brussels only that morning, together with the Duke of Brunswick's contingent and the Nassauers, and these he put at immediate readiness to march.[9]

According to her diary, Lady Dalrymple-Hamilton and her husband went for a gentle after-dinner walk on the ramparts and then returned home to find two French friends, Count de Chabot and Count Maynard, waiting for them.[10] They discussed the latest developments over a cup of tea and Chabot remarked that he would not be surprised if Bonaparte commenced his advance that very day, since it was the anniversary of two of his most successful battles – Marengo[11] in 1800 and Friedland[12] in 1807 – and as the emperor was known to be superstitious he could consider this a fortunate omen.[13] The next visitor was Lord Apsley, who arrived between 5 and 6pm to tell them that Wellington had received credible intelligence that the French had been at Charleroi the previous night and that it seemed probable that the British troops would march the following morning – a prime example of how rapidly news travelled around Brussels. Meanwhile, Apsley added, Wellington had announced his intention to go to the Ball and was passing the word around that he hoped other officers would do the same.

Colonel De Lancey had gone to dinner with General d'Alava, leaving his wife alone, but shortly after he had departed an ADC arrived at his house with an urgent message. Magdalene redirected him to the Spanish general's residence and only a few minutes later she saw her husband ride past in the opposite direction, heading for the duke's house, which was only a short distance away.[14] This was almost certainly the message sent by Lieutenant-Colonel Berkeley, the assistant quartermaster-general at the Prince of Orange's headquarters at Braine-le-Comte,[15] as described by Lord Fitzroy Somerset:

> About five o'clock in the afternoon the Duke of Wellington while at dinner received from the Prince of Orange, who was at Braine le Compte, a report sent to His Royal Highness from his advanced posts (probably from Mons or L'Eveque), informing him that the French had attacked the Prussians' advanced posts on the Sambre. The Duke immediately directed the Quarter Master General (Colonel DeLancey), to send orders for the troops to assemble at the headquarters of their respective divisions and to be in readiness to march at the shortest notice.[16]

The duke could have stopped the Ball at any time during the afternoon or early evening of the 15th – a single sentence would have sufficed. But, by mid-afternoon, when he knew that the French were definitely advancing, he also knew that a number of commanders, senior staff officers and ADCs would already be making their way to Brussels for the Ball and that to have cancelled it could well have caused some confusion.

Also in the duke's mind was that there were a number of Belgians who were known to be ready to welcome the return of Napoleon and French rule. According to Lady De Ros, '. . . there was a great supper prepared at Brussels on the 18th for Napoleon, by some strong Bonapartists of the name of Tresigny'. According to others, Napoleon had his first decrees ready for issue from the Palace of Laeken on 18 June and already had a list of Belgians prepared to collaborate with him. Indeed, this concern over the reaction of the Bruxellois and, in particular, the pro-Napoleonic elements, would concern Wellington well into the night, as will be seen.

Evening

By the late afternoon people in Brussels could hear the sound of gunfire to the south, which gave encouragement to those hoping for a return to French rule and heightened the concerns of those who did not. As the shadows lengthened the preparations for the Ball were finalised and virtually all the guests from outside Brussels had arrived in the city. Among the latter were two young cavalry officers, Captain Verner and Lieutenant O'Grady, who

> . . . proceeded to Brussels in Cabriolet. We went in our usual uniform taking with us our Evening dress for the Ball. We put up at an Hotel (de Suède) in the lower town, which was at no great distance from the Duke of Richmond's residence, and having dined and dressed we proceeded to the Ball.

Meanwhile, Wellington's headquarters staff were hard at work producing and sending out the 'routes', which told the waiting units where to march to and what roads to follow on the way. Lieutenant Basil Jackson of the Royal Staff Corps

> . . . was walking in the park when a soldier of the Guards, attached to the Quartermaster-General's office, summoned me to attend Sir William De Lancey. He had received orders to concentrate the Army towards the frontier, which had until then remained quiet in cantonments. I was employed, along with others, for about two hours

in writing out 'routes' for the several divisions, foreign as well as British, which were despatched by orderly Hussars of 3rd Regiment of the German Legion . . .[17]

At about 9pm Colonel De Lancey took a short break and returned to his apartment to inform his wife that she was to be ready to go Antwerp at six o'clock the following morning. He told her that he would be writing all night and asked her to have plenty of strong green tea ready to keep him going. Prior to this, the unfortunate Magdalene had led a quiet life in Scotland and England, with wealthy parents who sheltered her from almost every hardship. Now, after just seven days in Brussels, she found herself in the very midst of a military system she could barely have understood and, not surprisingly, was somewhat confused.

In the QMG's office, staff officers were hard at work copying out the 'routes' for the divisions and brigades, preparing the orders for the couriers and then briefing them. These officers had been joined by Major De Lacy Evans, who had just arrived in the city, and who, as a trained QMG staff officer, also lent a hand.[18]

The position was (as usual) neatly summed up by Captain Digby Mackworth, whose diary for the following day noted:

> . . . The greater part of our staff went yesterday evening to a ball given by the Duchess of Richmond, which was of course attended by 'Everybody' at Bruxelles. We had heard during the day that the French had begun to advance and we knew that Bonaparte had joined them; still it was thought that, as the Prussian army was nearer to them than we were, we should have quite sufficient notice of their approach to make the necessary preparations to give them a warm and hearty reception.

The Ball

The Ball started at about 10 o'clock, with the guests arriving in coaches, carriages and cabriolets, all of which soon cluttered up the streets around the Richmonds' house. The Lennox family were all present, including the boys' tutor, the Prince of Orange was wearing his British Army general's scarlet jacket with blue facings, while the Duke of Brunswick was in his jet-black uniform, and all the lady guests were in their finest dresses. But, there was an underlying tension and most present, and particularly those in the Army, were acutely aware that the Duke of Wellington, the star of every party he attended, had not yet arrived.

The duke was, in fact, otherwise engaged. He is known to have written two brief letters. The first was to the Duke de Berri, timed at 9.30pm, which informed him that the enemy was advancing and requesting the duke to concentrate his small force at Alost.[19] The second was to the Duke de Feltre suggesting that he should make preparatory arrangements for the French court to leave Ghent; this was timed at 10pm.[20] The quartermaster-general's staff were also still hard at work and a series of supplementary movement orders were completed at about 10 o'clock and despatched by couriers to the field headquarters.[21]

Just after 10pm Wellington, De Lancey and Somerset were discussing the situation when the latter remarked: 'No doubt we shall be able to manage these fellows', to which the duke replied that there was '. . . little doubt of that, provided he did not make a false movement.' He then reiterated his instructions to De Lancey that the troops must not be ordered to march until further information had been received.[22]

The Prussian liaison officer, Müffling, was in his quarters preparing a message to Blücher, but with the names of the rendezvous left blank, so that he could fill them in as soon as he received the word from Wellington. He had also posted a courier-chaise immediately outside his front door, so that everything was ready to go with the least delay. The Prussian waited until just before midnight when Wellington hurried in to tell him that a message had just been received from General Dornberg, as a result of which he had decided on Nivelles and Quatre-Bras as his concentration points. Müffling quickly completed his message and despatched it and then, as he and the duke discussed the situation, De Lancey arrived to find Wellington '. . . standing looking over a map with a Prussian general, who was in full-dress uniform with orders . . .'[23]

Bugles and drum began to sound the 'assembly' in Brussels at about 10.30pm and the 1st/95th, for example, were formed up in quarter-distance columns by 11.00pm, whereupon, with no further orders forthcoming, they piled arms and, as good soldiers always do, went to sleep, using their haversacks as pillows.[24]

Their discussion completed, the duke remarked that everyone in Brussels had heard the sound of distant cannon-fire just before dusk, so he proposed that he and Müffling should go to the Ball, then snatch some sleep before leaving at 5am to join the troops in the field. With that, De Lancey returned to his apartment and his wife, while Wellington and Müffling went to the rue de la Blanchisserie.[25]

The duke's long-awaited arrival at 'the Wash-house' was noted by all and as he entered the ballroom Lady Georgiana Lennox immediately quit her partner to rush up to him. Were the rumours of the French advance correct, she asked, to which he replied bluntly, 'Yes, they are true; we are off tomorrow.' From a distance Wellington looked cheerful and relaxed, but Lady Dalrymple-Hamilton, who spent some time sitting with him on a sofa, noted that, although outwardly gay and cheerful, he had an expression of care and anxiety. Indeed, although he spoke to her politely enough, he seemed preoccupied, and would frequently stop in the middle of a sentence to give instructions to nearby officers, particularly the Prince of Orange and the Duke of Brunswick.

The Duchess of Richmond had gone to great lengths to arrange a memorable evening and one of the entertainments was a display of Highland Dancing by four sergeants of the 92nd Foot, accompanied by pipers. Sergeant Robertson of the 92nd Foot recorded at the time:

> Colonel Cameron ... was present at a splendid ball given by the Duchess of Richmond, daughter of the 7th Duke of Gordon, who was brother to the Marquess of Huntly. She had invited some sergeants of the 92nd to show the company, especially the Belgians, the Highland Reel and sword dance, which they did . . .[26]

This link between the duchess and the regiment was unusually strong because not only had she played a part in its birth, but she had also, whilst in Ireland during her husband's lord lieutenancy, maintained close links with the second battalion which was also stationed in Ireland. A later chronicler of the regiment contacted two of the Richmond daughters in the 1890s for confirmation of the event. Lady Georgiana De Ros told him that she had not personally seen it as she was, at the time, helping her brother, the Earl of March, to pack prior to departing for Braine-le-Comte (this suggests that the display took place after rather than before supper). However the other sister, Lady Louisa Tighe, wrote:

> I well remember the Gordon Highlanders dancing reels at the ball; my mother thought it would interest the foreigners to see them, which it did ... there was quite a crowd to look at the Scotch dancers.[27]

On such an important occasion the dancers were accompanied by the legendary pipe-major Alexander Cameron, a redoubtable figure, who had played his pipes at many a battle against the French, most famously at Fuentes d'Oñoro (3 May 1811). There a bullet penetrated the bag causing 'a piteous and unwarlike skirl', whereupon, incensed by the damage to a beloved set of pipes and humiliated by the unmusical end to his playing, the pipe-major grabbed a musket, fired it at the offending enemy sniper, drew his sword and rushed into the fight shouting (in Gaelic) 'We'll give them a different type of music.'[28]

Meanwhile, Lieutenant Henry Webster, one of the ADCs to the Prince of Orange, had been held back at the latter's headquarters at Braine-le-Comte for an important message, which was eventually handed to him at about 10pm. Webster then galloped the whole way, changing horses once, and with the added benefit of bright moonlight, reached Brussels after covering the ten miles in little over an hour. He went straight to the rue de la Blanchisserie, where the crowd of carriages was such that he had to abandon his horse and complete his journey on foot. The gate-porter asked him to wait five minutes as the company was about to rise from supper and the sudden arrival of a mud-spattered courier might cause alarm among the ladies. Webster saw sense in this and peeped through the doors, where he saw the Duchess of Richmond on the Prince of Orange's arm, and Lady Charlotte Greville on the duke's, on their way back to the ball-room. At the first opportunity he hastened to the Prince of Orange and handed him the despatch, which the prince immediately passed unread to the duke, who simply placed it in a coat pocket. Webster then waited out of sight in the hall, but as soon as the last couple had passed Wellington, having obviously read the message, returned and told him in a low voice to summon the prince's carriage for him to return to his headquarters at Braine-le-Comte.

Inside the ballroom, the Duke of Brunswick was sitting on a chair, dangling the 10-year-old Prince de Ligne on his knee, but as soon as he heard that the French were advancing, he leapt to his feet, dropping the unfortunate child onto the floor. Brunswick then left to join his troops, but found time to speak to Lady Georgiana Lennox and to assure her that his Brunswickers would be sure to distinguish themselves, as she had done them the honour of accompanying the Duke of Wellington to their review several weeks earlier.

Elsewhere, Lady Jane Lennox was having the time of her life – as would any pretty 17-year-old surrounded by dashing young men in gorgeous uniforms. She recalled:

> Well I remember the rising from that supper-table, and all that followed immediately after it. I know I was in a state of wild delight; the scene itself was so stirring, and the company so brilliant, I recollect, on reaching the ballroom after supper, I was scanning over my tablets, which were filled from top to bottom with the names of the partners to whom I was engaged; when, on raising my eyes, I became aware of a great preponderance of ladies in the room. White muslins and tarlatans[29] abounded; but the gallant uniforms had sensibly diminished.

Indeed, the word had been passed around and the officers were making their way quietly out of the ballroom, so that the remaining dancers came to a halt and the orchestra stopped in mid-bar. The unfortunate Duchess of Richmond stood at the exit, imploring the departing officers to 'wait one little hour more' and 'not spoil her ball'. But they were implacable and picked their way past her, went to their carriages or horses, mounted and departed into the night, still in all their finery, but exulting that their long, tiresome days of idleness were at last at an end.[30]

There were some tender farewells, but when Lady Georgiana Lennox was saying farewell to James, Lord Hay, a dashing young ensign in the 1st Foot Guards, she found him to be so excited at the prospect of impending action and of the honours he was about to earn that it had an opposite effect on her and she felt 'quite provoked'.

It was at this juncture that Verner and O'Grady arrived, but as they entered they met Lord George Lennox, an old friend of Verner's, who told them that news had arrived of a Prussian defeat and that all officers had been told to return to their units forthwith. The two young cavalry officers could not resist the temptation to enter the ballroom for a quick look and found it in a state of confusion, with Lord Uxbridge personally chivvying his cavalry officers to hurry back to their units. Realising that there was no opportunity for even one dance, the two young men returned to their hotel, changed back into their day uniforms and set off on the return journey, reaching their regiment at about 6am, where they were just in time to mount their horses and join their troops before the order to move off was given.

In the hush following this exodus, those remaining became aware of noises from outside – drums rolling and bugles sounding, calling the troops in Brussels to assemble on parade. They also heard the tramping of infantry as companies marched to join up into battalions, and then battalions into brigades, the neighing of horses and the clatter of their hooves as the cavalry assembled, and the rumble of artillery caissons and supply wagons over the cobblestones. This cacophony of sound added up to only one thing – the army was deploying for war.

Inside, one last scene was being played out as Wellington asked the Duke of Richmond in a whisper whether he had a map. Richmond took him into a small room and while Wellington closed the door, took out a map and spread it on a bed. Wellington said, 'Napoleon has *humbugged* me by God, he has gained twenty-four hours march on me', to which the Duke of Richmond asked him what he intended to do. 'I have ordered the army to concentrate at Quatre-Bras,' Wellington replied, 'but we shall not stop him there, and, if so, I must fight him *here*,' placing his thumbnail on the position at Waterloo. He then wished the Duke of Richmond 'adieu' and left the house by a side door.[31] Colonel De Lancey was still hard at work and at 2am he went round to the duke's house to clear up a few questions but was told by a servant that Wellington was already asleep.[32]

The civilian guests made their way home through streets alive with soldiers. Mr Creevey was waiting up for his son and daughters to come home, which they did at about 2.30, accompanied by Major Hamilton, and they gave him the news that the Prussians had been driven out of Charleroi and that the British Army was now deploying to meet the advancing French. Lady Dalrymple-Hamilton and her husband likewise left the Ball just after two and made their way past the troops.

Many people in the city found it impossible to go to bed, waiting to see the troops depart. About four o'clock the orders were given and they started to move off, the English and Scotsmen of Picton's division, the Brunswickers and the Nassauers, all setting out along the high road to Charleroi, which would take them through the Forêt de Soignes and the village of Waterloo and on to Quatre Bras. The De Lanceys stood together at a window, watching them march through a city gate '... and saw the whole army go out. Regiment after regiment passed through and melted away in the mist of the morning.'[33]

The dramatic conclusion to the Duchess of Richmond's Ball marked the end of two years of almost constant partying in Brussels. The tired civilians wended their way homewards, ready for a night's sleep, but for the officers, as they raced through the darkness to reach their units before they set off for war, the evening had scarcely begun.

NOTES

1   Edward Heeley, *Journal*, p. 105.
2   '... for I was then at H.Q., but I was too much occupied with the organization of the ball at the Duke of Richmond's to recollect much about what else was to take place that night ...' BL Add Ms 34706 f460.
3   WD, pp. 469–70.
4   Lady De Ros, p. 122.
5   Waldie, p. 26.
6   WSD, Vol. X. p. 524.
7   'Als am 15ten Juni der General von Zieten vor Charleroy angegriffen und dadurch der Krieg eröffnet war, sendete er einen Offizier an mich ab, der um 3 Uhr in Brüssels eintraf.' (On 15 June General von Zieten was attacked before Charleroi, signifying the start of the war, and he sent an officer to me who entered Brussels at 3am.) Müffling, *Aus Meinem Leben*, p. 228.
8   Somerset, op. cit., p. 7.
9   Lord Fitzroy Somerset's *Account of the Events from 15–18 June 1815*, Waterloo Papers, p. 7.
10 Count de Chabot was married to Lady Isabella, daughter of William, second Duke of Leinster.
11 At Marengo in Italy (14 June 1800) Napoleon totally defeated the Austrians; it also gave him the political influence to return to Paris to confirm his position as leader of France.
12 At Friedland in East Prussia (14 June 1807), a total victory over the Russians.
13 Lady Dalrymple-Hamilton's account.
14 David Miller, *Lady De Lancey at Waterloo*, p. 106.
15 WSD, Vol. X, p. 480.
16 Lord Fitzroy Somerset's *Account*; Waterloo papers, p. 7. There appears to be an error in this report, in that the Prince of Orange was already with Wellington and the message came from his headquarters rather than from the prince himself. There is also a minor discrepancy in the timings, with Lady De Lancey saying that her husband left to go to d'Alava's house at about 6pm, while Somerset says that the message was received at about five o'clock.

17   A Staff Officer (Basil Jackson), 'Recollections of Waterloo', *Colburn's United Service Magazine*, 1847 Part III, p. 3.
18   Gurwood added a footnote to the so-called 'De Lancey Memorandum' stating that Colonel De Lacy Evans was with Colonel De Lancey when the routes were issued and despatched on the evening of 15 June. Gurwood, *Dispatches*, 1852 edition, pp. 142–3.
19   *Dispatches*, Volume XII, p. 473.
20   *Dispatches*, Volume XII, pp. 473–4.
21   *Dispatches*, Volume XII, pp. 474–5.
22   Somerset, op. cit.
23   Müffling states that the duke came to see him in his room at about midnight. ('Gegen Mitternacht trat der Herzog von Wellington in mein Zimmer') – *Aus Meinem Leben*, p 229. Lady De Lancey says that her husband went to Wellington's house where he found the duke half-dressed and preparing for the Ball, while talking to a Prussian general – obviously, Müffling. (*Lady De Lancey at Waterloo*, p. 107). As Müffling was present at the meeting and Lady De Lancey was not, I have accepted the former's version of events.
24   Letter from Regimental Archives, The Royal Green Jackets, 19 September 2003.
25   Based on 'Die hier befindlichen zahlreichen Freunde Napoleons (da man gegen Abend vor den Thoren von Brüssel das Kanonenfeuer deutlich hören konnte) machen lange Hälse, die Gutgesinnten müssen beruhigt werden, lassen Sie uns daher noch auf den Ball zur Herzogin von Richmond gehen, von wo wir darauf um 5 Uhr von hier nach Quatre-Bras zu den versammelten Truppen abreiten. So geschah es; der herzog zeigte sich auf dem Ball (wo die Honoratioren von ganz Brüssel versammelt waren) sehr heiter, blieb bis 3 Uhr, und um 5 Uhr waren wir zur Pferde.' (The numerous friends of Napoleon in this city (who this evening could clearly hear the sound of cannon fire outside the gates of Brussels) are all agog, the loyal citizens must be calmed down, so let us both go to the Duchess of Richmond's Ball and remain until three [o'clock]; at five we were mounted on our horses.) Müffling, *Aus Meinem Leben*, p. 230.
26   *Journal* of Sergeant D Robertson, late 92nd Foot, p. 153.
27   *The Life of a Regiment. The History of the Gordon Highlanders*, by Lt-Col. C Greenhill Gardyne. David Douglas, Edinburgh, 1901, Volume 1 1794–1816, p. 349.
28   Gardyne, op. cit., p. 210.
29   Tarlatan was a thin, but stiffly starched, open-weave muslin used to make ladies' dresses.
30   Digby Mackworth, op. cit.
31   This conversation between Wellington and the Duke of Richmond in the latter's dressing-room was repeated by the Duke of Richmond to Captain Bowles, just two minutes after it had taken place. Had Richmond taken command of the reserves, as planned, Bowles would have been his ADC. *A Series of Letters of the First Earl of Malmesbury, His Family and Friends; 1745–1820*, ed. Earl of Malmesbury, R Bentley, London, 1852. Vol. II, p. 455. The story is corroborated by Lady De Ros, op. cit., p. 133.
32   *Lady De Lancey at Waterloo*, p. 107.
33   Ibid., p. 170.

CHAPTER XIV

Envoi

Many wild claims have been made about the Ball. Lady Caroline Lamb, who arrived in Brussels some weeks after the event to nurse her wounded brother, wrote that 'The D(uche)ss of Richmond's Ball has been much censured. There never was such a Ball – so fine and so sad. All the young men who appeared there shot dead a few days after.'[1] As with so many of this young woman's remarks, this was a considerable exaggeration, although it reflects one view current in Brussels at the time. But, as shown in Appendix D, only eleven of those invited to the Ball were killed between 16 and 18 June, of whom only four were junior officers.

Another widely held impression was reflected in the Capel letters: '. . . The Duchess of Richmond gave a sort of Farewell Ball on the 15th – at which all the Military in and about Bruxelles were present . . .'[2] In reality, only 103 military in total were invited, of whom a significant proportion were from headquarters and units well outside Brussels, while many of those stationed in Brussels were not invited. In fact, ninety-four officers out of a total of 1,064 in the field army were invited, of which fifty-six (out of 166) were from the various headquarters, fifteen from the cavalry and twenty-five from the infantry. These were, by any standard, very small proportions.

Some observers have suggested that the duchess should have balanced her guest list to give a fairer proportion to each element of society in Belgium and in the Anglo–Netherlands Army. Thus, Delhaize refers to Major Krauchenberg, *'représentait le général Dornberg et toute la Légion allemande'* (represented General Dornberg and the whole of the [King's] German Legion). Again, there is no question of anyone being 'represented'; Major Krauchenberg was well known in English circles in Brussels and was invited as an individual. Indeed, even within the English Army, of sixteen cavalry regiments, nobody was invited from seven, nor anybody from eighteen of the twenty-six infantry battalions. The Duke of Richmond was colonel-in-chief of the 35th (Sussex) Foot and had served as commanding officer for seven years, but the only officer of the 35th to be invited was Lieutenant-Colonel Sir George Berkeley, and he was serving on the staff.[3]

As regards the English military, again the predominant factors seem to have been that they were either known to the duchess or the duke, or that they were well-connected – preferably both. It must also be remembered that the duke was a very sociable man and, as a soldier himself, had a natural inclination for military friendships. Thus, during his year in Brussels he had mixed with both cavalry and infantry officers not only at social gatherings, but also at the various horse races and, in particular, cricket matches, and in the latter as an enthusiastic participant rather than a spectator.

Belgian and Dutch civilian guests numbered thirty-four people from sixteen families, which was undoubtedly a small proportion of the aristocratic residents in and around the city. However, most of those on the invitation list, such as the Beaufort, d'Arenberg, d'Assche, d'Ursel and d'Oultremont families, are known to have given the Richmonds hospitality at dinners, balls or hunting parties. Possibly the only guest invited in his official, as opposed to personal, capacity was Baron van der Linden d'Hoogvoorst, who appears in the invitation list not by name but by his office as 'Le Maire de Bruxelles'. There have been suggestions that the duchess deliberately did not invite Belgians known to be pro-French, but she probably left them off her list more because she did not like them or did not owe them any hospitality, rather than because they favoured Napoleon above the Allies. Similarly, the English civilian guests represented only a small proportion of the expatriate families in the city.

There were many French supporters of Louis XVIII in Brussels or nearby in Ghent, but only two were invited, presumably having been personal contacts. Similarly, only four German and four Dutch army officers were invited, but all eight were well known to the Richmonds.

The conclusion must be that this was a private party, thrown by the Duchess of Richmond and her husband, neither of whom occupied any official position in the city. Naturally, the duchess wanted it to be a glittering affair which would do credit to her social status, but with very few exceptions those invited were people whom she had known well in Ireland, England or Scotland, or had got to know in Belgium.

This was by no means the first large ball that the Duchess had given and had it taken place on 14 June, it would have merited, at most, a minor footnote in the histories of the Hundred Days. On the other hand, had it been scheduled for the 16th it would, like Wellington's party planned for the 21st, never have taken place. But it was fated to be held on the night that Wellington's army deployed for war and to combine the magic of a glittering assembly waltzing into the small hours with the drama of arriving messengers and anxious conferences, and all ending with the pathos of the final farewells, as the soldiers went off to war. There was the dignity of the Duke of Brunswick promising Lady Georgiana Lennox that his army would uphold its honour and the innocent bravado of Lord Hay, boasting of the glory that soon would be his, but both were fated to die before nightfall.

The Ball on 15 June 1815 was a social event without parallel in military history, but by accident rather than design. It combined elegance and sophistication with a sense of impending doom, and gaiety with tragedy. Above all, it ensured that the name of Charlotte, Duchess of Richmond will live on in the history books.

NOTES

1 *Lady Caroline Lamb*, Susan Mornington, p. 148.
2 Capel Letters, p. 111.
3 The 35th had changed its county affiliation from Dorset to Sussex in 1805.

APPENDIX A
The Goodwood List

Introductory Notes
1. *Source: Mrs Rosemary Baird, Keeper of the Goodwood Collection.*
2. *This is an exact transcription of the list held at Goodwood House, except that some corrections have been made by the author of this book to the spelling, where there is irrefutable proof of who was meant and the correct spelling.*
3. *In some cases, several names appear on the same line. This has been retained in this list.*
4. *Some names in the original are followed by one or more letters 'O', but without any indication of what this might signify. This is examined below.*
5. *The original writer of the list makes much use of the prefix 'Honourable', suggesting a usage different from that of today.*
6. *A total of thirty-eight entries in this list are suffixed with one or more letters 'O', but without any further explanation as to the meaning; these were not repeated in the De Ros List. One possible explanation is that the person marked 'O' had not attended, either by declining the invitation prior to the Ball or by deciding on the day not to attend. Thus, Major-General Adam and Colonel Sir William and Lady De Lancey are all known not to have attended and their names are marked with 'O'. On the other hand, Lieutenant-Colonel Lord Saltoun of the 1st Foot Guards is known to have stayed away, but his name is not marked with an 'O', while Captain Yorke is marked as 'not present' by Lady De Ros but is not marked with an 'O' in the Goodwood List. Hence, while the letter 'O' clearly meant something to the writer, there is no conclusive explanation of what was meant.*

Ball June 15 1815

His R H Prince of Orange
His R H Duke of Brunswick
Duke of Wellington
Duc et Duchesse de Beaufort et Mademoiselles
Duc et Duchesse d'Ursel
Marquis et Marquise d'Assche
Comtesse de Lalaing

Comte et Comtesse d'Oultremont   0
Comtesse douariere et les mademoiselles d'Oultremont
Comte et Comtesse Liedekerke Beaufort et Mademoiselles
Comte et Comtesse Majeste Liedekerke   0
Comte et Comtesse Latourdupin
Comtesse de Ruilly   0
Baron et Baronesse d'Hoogvoorst   0
Mademoiselle et Monsieur d'Hoogvoorst   000
Madame Constant d'Hoogvoorst   0
Comte et Comtesse de Mercy d'Argenteau
Lady Charlotte Greville
Mr, Lady Caroline & 4 Miss Capels   00
Sir H & Lady Susan Clinton   0
Lady Frances Webster
Countess Mountmorris & Lady Annesley
Lord and Lady John Somerset   00
Lady Alvanley and the Miss Ardens
Sir J Lady & Miss Craufurd
Lord and Lady Fitzroy Somerset   00
Honourable Mrs Pole
Sir George and Lady Berkeley   00
Lady and Miss Sutton   00
Lady George and Miss Seymour
Mr, Mrs and Miss Lance and Mr Lance junior
Mr and the Miss Ords
Mr and Mrs Greathed
Sir Sidney Lady Smith and Miss Rumbolds
Sir Wm and Lady Johnstone
Earl and Countess Conyngham
Lady Elizth Conyngham
Mr and Mrs Lloyd
Viscountess Hawarden
Sir H and Lady D Hamilton
Countess of Waldegrave
Sir William and Lady Delancey   00
Monsieur and Madame Vanderkapellan
Comte et Comtesse de Granne
Sir Charles Stuart   0
Mr Stuart   Mr Dawkins   Mr Chad
Baron Brockkausen
Baron Vincent
General Pozzo de Borgo &c
Col Washington
General Allava

Prince of Nassau
Earl of Uxbridge
Earl of Portarlington
Sir John Byng
Sir John Elley
Sir James Gambier
Sir George Scovell
Sir George Wood
General Cook   0
General Maitland   0
Sir Henry Bradford
Colonel Woodford
Colonel J Woodford   0
Colonel Rowan 52   0
Colonel Hill   0
Sir R Hill   0 Sir Noel Hill   0
Mr James
Mr Hume   Dr Hyde
Major Branckenberg   0
Major Gunthorpe   0
Major Churchill
Major Hamilton
Colonel Wyndham   0
Col Canning

HRH Prince Frederick of Orange
Baron d'Irvyre   0
Lord Edward Somerset
Sir William Ponsonby
Prince Auguste   Prince Pierre
Duc d'Arenberg   0
Comte de Bellegarde
Comte de la Rochefoucault   0
Lord Hill   0
Lord Charles Fitzroy   Captain Mackworth
Sir Hussey Vivian   Captain Fitzroy
Major Harris   Captain Keane   0
Captain Wildman 7th   Captain Frazer
Captain Elphinstone 7   Captain Verner 7
Lord Robert Manners   0
Lord Rendlesham
Sir Andrew Barnard
Sir Dennis Racke
Sir James Kempt   0

General Adam   0
General d'Oudenarde   0
Sir Pulteney Malcolm
Sir Thomas Picton
Honourable Colonel Stanhope
Honourable Colonel Abercromby   0
Honourable Colonel Ponsonby
Sir Edward Barnes
Colonel Bounter
Colonel Fuller
Sir Colin Campbell   Honourable Sir Alex Gordon
Colonel Freemantle   Colonel Hervey
Lord Arthur Hill   Reverend Mr Brisicollo
Honourable Major Percy   H. Mr Cathcart
Honourable Colonel Acheson
Colonel Dick 42
Colonel Cameron 92nd
Lord Hay   0
Captain Webster   Colonel Tripp
H. Mr Bussell
Colonel Durngler (?)
Captain Somerset ADC
Captain Yorke ADC
Captain Gore ADC
Major Hunter Blair   0
Mr Brooke R D Guard
Mr Huntley   Ditto
Captain Packenham R. Artillery   0
Mr Lionel Hervey
Mr Leigh   Honourable Mr Percival
H. Mr Horace Seymour ADC
Colonel Knife   0
Captain de Lubeck ADC
Mr Shakespeare 10th
Mr O'Grady 7th
Honourable Mr Bridgeman
Mr Smith 95th
Honourable General Dundas
Honourable Mr Stopford
Captain Dumaresc ADC
Captain Dawkins ADC
Captain Disbrowe ADC
Honourable Mr John Gordon
Honourable Major Dawson

Captain Bowles
Captain Hesketh
Honourable Mr Edgecombe
Honourable S Bathurst
Colonel Torrens
Mr Hudyer
Captain Gurwood 10th
2. Mr Montagus
Mr A Greville
Honourable Mr Dawson 18th L. Dragoons
Colonel Barclay   0
Honourable Hastings Forbes
Honourable the Mr Forbess
Captain Alex Mr Baird
Mr Robinson 32nd
Lord Saltoun
Honourable Colonel Stewart
Lord Apsley
Le Maire de Bruxelles
Baron de Herdt

NOTES:

Only one Comte de Liederkerke-Beaufort is known to have existed and the entries on lines 10 and 11 appear to have been an unintentional duplication.
Baron d'Hoogvoorst (line 14) was the mayor of Brussels. The entry *Le Maire de Bruxelles* (penultimate line) appears, therefore, to be another unintentional duplication.

APPENDIX B

The De Ros List

Introductory Notes:
1. *Sources.*
   a. *This list was supplied to Sir William Frazer by Lady De Ros in the late 1880s, who had obtained it from Lord Verulam. It was first published in Fraser's* Words on Wellington, *pages 260–6.*
   b. *The identical list was then published in* Reminiscences of Lady de Ros, *pp. 124–32.*
   c. *Since these two lists are identical only one is given here, which is designated the 'De Ros List'.*
2. *The order of the names, their spelling and the ranks (or their absence) given here is exactly as in the original.*
3. *The supplementary comments in brackets appear to have been added by Lady De Ros; for example, 'from their house we saw the wounded brought in'.*

The following is the List of Invitations to the Duchess of Richmond's Ball at Brussels, June 15, 1815:

H.R.H. the Prince of Orange.
H.R.H. Prince Frederic of Orange.
H.R.H. the Duke of Brunswick.
Prince of Nassau.
Duc d'Arenberg.
Prince Auguste d'Arenberg.
Prince Pierre d'Arenberg.
Le Maire de Bruxelles.
Duc et Duchesse de Beaufort et Mademoiselle.
Duc et Duchesse d'Ursel.
Marquis et Marquise d'Assche (from their house we saw the wounded brought in – Lord Uxbridge, Lord F. Somerset, &c.).
Comte et Comtesse d'Oultremont.
Comtesse-Douairiére d'Oultremont et les Mesdemoiselles.
Comte et Comtesse Liedekerke Beaufort.
Comte et Comtesse Auguste Liedekerke et Mademoiselle.

Comte et Comtesse Latour Lupin.
Comte et Comtesse Mercy d'Argenteau.
Comte et Comtesse de Grasiac.
Comtesse de Luiny.
Comtesse de Ruilly.
Baron et Baronne d'Hooghvoorst.
Mademoiselle d'Hooghvoorst et Monsieur C. d'Hooghvoorst.
Madame Constant d'Hooghvoorst.
Monsieur et Madame Vander Capellan.
Baron de Herelt.
Baron de Tuybe.
Baron Brockhausen.
General Baron Vincent (wounded at Waterloo).
General Pozzo di Borgo.
General Alava.
Comte de Belgade.
Comte de la Rochefoucauld.
Gen. D'Oudenarde.
Col. Knife (?), A.D.C.
Col. Ducayla.
Major Ronnchenberg, A.D.C.
Col. Tripp, A.D.C.
Capt. de Lubeck, A.D.C. to H.R.H. the Duke of Brunswick.
Earl and Countess of Conyngham, and Lady Elizabeth Conyngham.
   Viscount Mount Charles and Hon. Mr. Conyngham (afterwards 2nd
   Marquess Conyngham).
Countess Mount Norris and Lady Juliana Annesley.
Countess-Dowager of Waldegrave.
Duke of Wellington.
Lord and Lady Fitzroy Somerset (neither were present; Lord Fitzroy lost
   his arm at Waterloo).
Lord and Lady John Somerset.
Mr and Lady Frances Webster.
Mr and Lady Caroline Capel and Miss Capel.
Lord and Lady George Seymour and Miss Seymour.
Mr. and Lady Charlotte Greville.
Viscountess Hawarden.
Sir Henry and Lady Susan Clinton (he was Lt-Gen. and G. C. B., and
   commanded a Division).
Lady Alvanley and the Miss Ardens.
Sir James, Lady, and Miss Craufurd.
Sir George Berkeley, K.C.B., and Lady Berkeley.
Lady and Miss Sutton.
Sir Sidney and Lady Smith, and Miss Rumbolds.

Sir William and Lady Johnstone.
Sir Hew and Lady Dalrymple.
Sir William. and Lady Delancy.
Hon. Mrs Pole (afterwards Lady Maryborough).
Mr., Mrs., and Miss Lance, and Mr. Lance, jun.
Mr. and the Miss Ords.
Mr. and Mrs. Greathed.
Mr. and Mrs. Lloyd.
Hon. Sir Charles Stuart, G.C.B. (Minister at Bruxelles) and Mr. Stuart.
Earl of Uxbridge (commanded the Cavalry; lost his leg at Waterloo).
Earl of Portarlington.
Earl of March, A.D.C. to H.R.H. the Prince of Orange.
Gen. Lord Edward Somerset (commanded a Brigade of Cavalry; wounded at Waterloo).
Lord Charles FitzRoy.
Lord Robert Manners.
Lt-Gen. Lord Hill (commanding the 2nd Corps).
Lord Rendlesham.
Lord Hay, A.D.C. (killed at Quatre-Bras).
Lord Saltoun.
Lord Apsley (afterwards Earl Bathurst).
Hon. Col. Stanhope (Guards).
Hon. Col. Abercromby (Guards; wounded).
Hon. Col. Ponsonby (afterwards Sir Frederick Ponsonby, K.C.B.; severely wounded).
Hon. Col. Acheson (Guards).
Hon. Col. Stewart.
Hon. Mr. 0. Bridgeman, A.D.C. to Lord Hill.
Hon. Mr. Percival.
Hon. Mr. Stopford.
Hon. Mr. John Gordon.
Hon. Mr. Edgecombe.
Hon. Mr. Seymour Bathurst, A.D.C. to Gen. Maitland.
Hon. Mr. Forbes.
Hon. Mr. Hastings Forbes.
Hon. Major Dawson.
Hon. Mr. Dawson, 18th Light Dragoons.
Maj.-Gen. Sir Hussey Vivian (commanded a Brigade of Cavalry).
Mr. Horace Seymour, A.D.C. (afterwards Sir Horace Seymour, K.C.B.).
Col. Hervey, A.D.C. (afterwards Sir Felton Hervey, Bart.).
Col. Fremantle, A.D.C.
Lord George Lennox, A.D.C.
Lord Arthur Hill, A.D.C. (afterwards Gen. Lord Sandys).

Hon. Major Percy, A.D.C. (son of 1st Earl of Beverley. He brought home three Eagles and despatches).

Hon. G. Cathcart, A.D.C. (afterwards Sir George Cathcart killed at Inkerman, 1854).

Hon. Sir Alexander Gordon, A.D.C. (died of his wounds at Waterloo).

Sir Colin Campbell, K.C.B., A.D.C.

Sir John Byng, G.C.B. (created Earl of Strafford; commanded 2nd Brigade of Guards).

Lt.-Gen. Sir John Elley, K.C.B.

Sir George Scovell, K.C.B. (Major commanding Staff Corps of Cavalry).

Sir George Wood, Col. R. A.

Sir Henry Bradford.

Sir Robert Hill, Kt } (brothers of Lord Hill).
Sir Noel Hill, K.C.B.

Sir William Ponsonby, K.C.B. (brother of Lord Ponsonby; commanded a Brigade of Cavalry; killed at Waterloo).

Sir Andrew Barnard (afterwards Governor of Chelsea Hospital).

Sir Denis Pack, Maj.-Gen., G.C.B. (commanded a Brigade)

Sir James Kemp, Maj.-Gen., G.C.B. (commanded a Brigade).

Sir Pulteney Malcolm.

Sir Thomas Picton, Lt Gen. (commanded 5th Division; killed at Waterloo).

Maj.-Gen. Sir Edward Barnes, Adjt-Gen. (wounded at Waterloo).

Sir James Gambier.

Hon. General Dundas.

Lt.-Gen. Cooke (commanded 1st Division).

Maj.-Gen. Maitland (afterwards Sir Peregrine, G.C.B; commanded 1st Brigade of Guards).

Maj.-Gen. Adam (not present; commanded a Brigade; afterwards Sir Frederick Adam, K.C.B.).

Col. Washington.

Col. Woodford (afterwards F.M. G.C.B., Governor of Chelsea).

Col. Rowan, 52nd (afterwards Sir Charles Rowan, Chief Commissioner of Police).

Col. Wyndham (afterwards Gen. Sir Henry Wyndham).

Col. Cumming, 18th Light Dragoons.

Col. Bowater (afterwards Gen. Sir Edward Bowater)

Col. Torrens (afterwards Adjt-Gen. in India).

Col. Fuller.

Col. Dick, 42nd (killed at Sobraon, 1846).

Col. Cameron. 92nd (killed at Quatre-Bras).

Col. Barclay, A.D.C. to the Duke of York.

Col. Hill (?) (Col. Clement Hill, brother to Lord Hill).

Major Gunthorpe, A.D.C. to Gen. Maitland.
Sir Alexander Woodford.
Major Churchill, A.D.C. to Lord Hill and Q.M.G. (killed in India).
Major Hamilton, A.D.C. to Gen. Sir E. Barnes.
Major Harris, Brigade Major to Sir Hussey Vivian (lost an arm).
Major Hunter Blair (wounded).
Capt. Mackworth, A.D.C. to Lord Hill.
Capt. Keane, A.D.C. to Sir Hussey Vivian.
Capt. FitzRoy.
Capt. Wildman, 7th Hussars, A.D.C. to Lord Uxbridge.
Capt. Fraser, 7th Hussars (afterwards Sir James Fraser, Bart.).
Capt. Verner, 7th Hussars.
Capt. Elphinstone, 7th Hussars (taken prisoner June 17).
Capt. Webster.
Capt. Somerset, A D.C. to Gen. Lord Edward Somerset.
Capt. Yorke, A.D.C. to Gen. Adam (afterwards Sir Charles Yorke; not
    present).
Capt. Gore, A.D.C. to Sir James Kempt.
Capt. Pakenham, R.A.
Capt. Dumaresq, A.D.C. to Gen. Sir John Byng (died of wounds).
Capt. Dawkins, A.D.C.
Capt. Disbrowe, A.D.C. to Gen. Sir G. Cook.
Capt. Bowles, Coldstream Guards (afterwards Gen. Sir George Bowles,
    Lieutenant of the Tower).
Capt. Hesketh, Grenadier Guards.
Capt Gurwood (afterwards Col. Gurwood).
Capt. Allix, Grenadier Guards.
Mr. Russell, A. D. C.
Mr. Brooke, 12th Dragoon Guards.
Mr. Huntley, 12th Dragoon Guards.
Mr. Lionel Hervey (in diplomacy).
Mr. Leigh.
Mr. Shakespear, 18th.
Mr. O'Grady, 7th Hussars (afterwards Lord Guillamore).
Mr. Smith, 95th. Brigadier-Major to Sir Denis Packe (killed at
    Waterloo).
Mr. Fludyer, Scots Fusilier Guards.
2 Mr. Montagus (John, and Henry, late Lord Rokeby, G.C.R).
Mr. A. Greville.
Mr. Baird.
Mr. Robinson, 32nd.
Mr. James.
Mr. Chad.
Mr. Dawkins.

Dr. Hyde.
Mr. Hume.
Rev. Mr. Brixall.

NOTE:

There appear to have been the same unintentional duplication as in the Goodwood List (Appendix A).

APPENDIX C
The Delhaize List

Introductory Notes :

1. *Source:* « Études Relatives a la Campagne de 1815 en Belgique publiées a l'occasion du Centenaire de Waterloo; *J Delhaize and W Aerts, De Boek, Brussels, 1915, pages 328–31.*

2. *Delhaize based his list on the De Ros List, but has omitted most of those known not to have actually attended. However, he does include others who are known not to have attended: for example, Sir William and Lady De Lancey and Mr Webster. He has also added some comments.*

3. *Delhaize has regrouped the names into three general groups:*
   a. *Belgian aristocracy.*
   b. *English aristocracy.*
   c. *Military.*

Voici la liste des invités: les altesses d'abord

le prince Guillaume d'Orange (blessé le 18 juin) et le prince Frédéric des Pays-Bas; le duc Frédéric-Guillaume de Brunswick (tué le 16), le duc héréditaire Adolphe de Nassau, colonel et aide de camp de Wellington; les trois ducs d'Arenberg: Prosper-Louis, ancien colonel du 27e chasseurs francais, Auguste-Marie-Raymond comte de la Marck, l'ami de Mirabeau, général dans les armées autrichienne et néerlandaise, et Pierre, ancien officier d'ordonnance de Napoléon.

Puis les personnages officiels et l'aristocratie bruxelloise: le baron van der Linden d'Hoogvoorst, maire de Bruxelles;

le baron van der Capellen, secrétaire d'é'tat, gouverneur des provinces belges, et la baronne;

le duc el la duchesse de Beaufort et Mlle;

le duc et la duchesse d'Ursel;

le marquis et la marquise d'Assche;

le comte et la comtesse d'Oultremont et le prince de Ligne;

la comtesse douairière d'Oultremont et Mlles;

le comte et la comtesse de Liedekerke-Beaufort;

le comte et la comtesse de Mercy-Argenteau;

le baron el la baronne d'Hoogvoorst;
Mlle d'Hoogvoorst et M. C. d'Hoogvoorst;
Mme Constant d'Hoogvoorst;

Quelques noms historiques: le général baron Vincent, le général comte Pozzo di Borgo, le général don Ricardos y Alava, représentant respectivement l'Autriche, la Russie et l'Espagne à l'état-major de l'armée de Pays-Bas; le comte de Latour-Dupin, ministre de Louis XVIII à La Haye, ancien préfet de la Dyle en 1813, et la comtesse; Charles-Eugène comte de Lalaing d'Audenarde, général, commandant en second les Gardes du Corps du Roi;[1] le baron de Brockhausen, ministre de Prusse à La Haye; l'amiral Sidney Smith, célèbre avant Waterloo; et le commodore Pulteney Malcolm, célèbre depuis.

Quelques membres de l'aristocratie anglaise:
comte et comtesse de Conyngham et lady Elisabeth;
vicomte Mount-Charles;
hon. Mr. Conyngham. (depuis 2e marquis de Conyngham);
comtesse Mount-Norris et lady Juliana Annesley;
comtesse douairière de Waldegrave;
lord et lady John Somerset;
Mr et lady Frances Webster;
Mr et lady Caroline Capel et miss Capel;
lady Smith et miss Rumbolds (femme et fille de l'amiral);
lord et lady George Seymour et miss Seymour;
Mr et lady Charlotte Greville;
vicomtesse Hawarden;
lady Alvanley et miss Ardens;
sir James, lady et miss Craufurd;
lady et miss Sutton;
sir William et lady Johnstone;
sir Hew et lady Dalrymple;
hon. Mrs Pole (depuis lady Maryborough);
hon. sir Charles Stuart, ministre a Bruxelles;
lord Rendlesham;
lord Apsley (depuis comte Bathurst);
sir James Gambier;
Mr et Mrs Lance, miss Lance et Mr Lance jun.; Mr & Mrs Ords; Mr & Mrs Greathed; Mr & Mrs Lloyd; Mr Stuart; hon. Mr Percival; hon. John Gordon; Mr Lionel Hervey; Mr Leigh; Mr Chad; Mr Dawkins; Dr Hyde et Mr Hume.

Des officiers sans emploi à l'armée des Pays-Bas: l'honorable général Dundas; le colonel Barclay, aide de camp du duc d'York; le colonel Dashington; les capitaines Fitzroy et Pakenham;

Diverses notabilités: le comte et la comtesse de Grasiac (?); la comtesse de Luiny (?); la comtesse de Ruilly (?); le baron de Herelt; le baron de Tuyll de Serooskerken; le comte de Bellegarde (?)²; le comte de la Rochefoucauld;

Enfin l'armée anglo-néerlandaise:

les princes d'Orange, déja nommés; le duc de Wellington; le duc de Brunswick et les généraux Hill, Barnes, Uxbridge (blessé le 18), Cooke, Clinton,³ Picton (tué le 18), Maitland, Byng, Kempt (blessé le 18), Pack (blessé le 18), Somerset, Ponsonby (tué le 18) et Vivian avec leurs aides de camp:

Pour le prince Guillaume d'Orange, les colonels néerlandais de Knijff et Ducaylar, les Anglais Tripp (lieut-col. du 60e), le capitaine hon. F. Russel;

Pour Wellington, le duc de Nassau déjà cité, l'honorable sir Alexandre Gordon, lieutenant-colonel au 3e régiment des Gardes, tué le 18, l'honorable H. Percy, lieutenant-colonel au 14e dragons-légers, chargé de porter la nouvelle de la victoire de Waterloo au régent d'Angleterre; l'honorable G. Cathcart, lieutenant au 6e dragons-gardes, tué quarante ans plus tard à Inkerman, ou i1 était général, et lord Arthur Hill (depuis lord Sandys), capitaine.

Lord Hill était accompané de son frère et premier aide de camp, Clement Hill, lieutenant- colonel dans les Horse-Guards, blessé le 18, du major C. H. Churchill du 1er Gardes, tué plus tard dans les Indes, du capitaine Mackworth des Royal Fusiliers et du capitaine Bridgeman du 1er Gardes, blessé le 18 juin.

L'état-major d'Uxbridge comprenait les capitaines Wildman et Fraser du 7e hussards, et le major Seymour du Royal American. (tous blessés).

Aides de camp), de Barnes, le major A. Hamilton du 4e West India Regiment, blessé;

de Cooke, G. Desbrowe, lieutenant et capitaine au 1er Gardes

de Clinton, F. Dawkins, du même régiment, ainsi que les deux aides de camp Gunthorpe et lord James Hay (tué le 16) de Maitland;

de Byng, le capitaine Dumaresq du 9e d'infanterie (blessé le 18)

de Kempt, le capitaine Ch. Gore;

de Pack, le capitaine C. Smith du 93e tué

de Somerset, son parent H. Somerset, lieutenant au 18e hussards

de Vivian, les capitaines T.-N. Harris (blessé le 18) et E. Keane, du 7e hussards;

Représentaient l'état-major: sir William Delancey,⁴ colonel député-quartier maître général, tué le 18; sir John Elley, lieutenant-colonel des Gardes à cheval (blessé); lord Ch. Fittzroy, lieutenant et capitaine au 1er Gardes; l'honorable A Abercromby, capitaine et lieutenant-colonel aux Coldstream-Guards (blessé le 18); l'honorable G-L. Dawson, major au 1er dragons-gardes (blessé); Felton-Hervey, colonel du 14e dragons-légers; sir

Colin Campbell, colonel des Coldstream Guards, l'une des figures militaires les plus populaires du Royaume-Uni; sir George Scowell, lieutenant-colonel; sir Henry Bradford (blessé) et sir Noel Hill (frère du général) tous deux capitaines et lieutenants-colonels au 1er Gardes; le lieutenantcolonel R. Torrens du 1er West India Regiment et le révérend Sam Briscall, chapelain de l'armée.

Les chefs de corps et commandants en second invités étaient le commandant en chef de l'Artillerie, sir George Wood, colonel; Stuart du 1er Gardes (blessé); Woodford des Coldstreams; C. Rowan, major du 52e d'infanterie (blessé); R-H. Dick, des Royal Highlanders, lieutenant-colonel (blessé le 16), qui fut tué à Sobraon en 1846; Cameron du 92e, tué le 16; Barnard, du 95e, blessé; Fuller des Dragons Gardes, tué le 18; lord Robert Manners, lieutenant-colonel au 10e hussards; Ponsonby du 12e dragons-légers (blessé le 18), le comte de Portarlington du 23e dragons-légers et sir Robert Chambers Hill, un frère encore du général, lieutenant-colonel des Horse-Guards, blessé le 18.

Citons enfin quelques officiers de rang moindre:

Du 1er Gardes, lord Saltoun, Stanhope, Seymour Bathurst, Fludyer (blessé), Edgecumbe, Alger, Greville.

Des Coldstreams: Acheson, Forbes, Bowles (plus tard sir George Bowles lieutenant de la Tour de Londres); John Montague (blessé); Wyndham (blessé);

Du 3e Gardes Hastings Forbes (tué); Bowater (blessé) Hesketh (blessé) Stopford, Henry Montague (plus tard lord Rokeby) Baird et James

J. Robinson, lieutenant au 32e régiment (blessé); Brooke et Huntley du 1er dragons-gardes; Dawson du 18e hussards; Shakespear, capitaine au 10e hussards; Standish O'Grady; Elphinstone (blessé et fait prisonnier le 17) et Werner (blessé) du 7e hussards.

Le capitaine aide de camp Krauchenberg, représentait le général Dornberg et toute la Légion allemande.

NOTES

1   Le comte de Lalaing (1779–1859) né à Paris de parents belges, fut capitaine au 112e de ligne puis écuyer de l'impératrice Joséphine, officier de la Légion d'honneur, colonel du 3e cuirassiers en 1811 et général de brigade en 1812. Rallié aux Bourbons, il suivit le roi à Gand, commanda les Gardes du Corps sous le duc de Mouchy, devint lieutenant général en 1823, puis en 1852, sénateur et grand officier de la Légion d'honneur.

2   Dans la liste, donnée par lady de Ros, quelques noms sont sans doute mal orthographiés. Il en est deux ou trois que nous reproduisons sous toutes réserves. Ils sont accostés d'un point d'interrogation.

3   Avec lady Susan Clinton.

4   Avec lady Delancey.

APPENDIX D

Statistics

There are many myths about the Ball, many of them revolving around just what proportion of the Army or its leaders was invited. In order to dispel at least some of these, it is necessary to analyse the figures in some detail and the following tables show that, however the figures are broken down, the numbers were actually a very small proportion of the whole.

Table V: Commanders and Staffs

This table shows that fifty-nine out of 164 commanders and their staffs were invited, i.e., thirty-six percent. Two out of five divisional headquarters and four out of nine brigade headquarters were not represented at all.

Formation	Commander	Officers	
		Strength	Invited
Army HQ	Wellington	83	23
Cavalry	Uxbridge	5	4
I Corps	Prince of Orange	7	2
II Corps	Hill	6	5
1 Cavalry Brigade	Somerset	2	2
2 Cavalry Brigade	Ponsonby	4	1
4 Cavalry Brigade	Vandeleur	3	0
5 Cavalry Brigade	Grant	4	0
6 Cavalry Brigade	Vivian	4	3
1 British Infantry Division	Cooke	3	2
2 British Infantry Division	Clinton	3	3
4 British Infantry Division	Colville	4	0
5 British Infantry Division	Picton	5	1
6 British Infantry Division	Cole	3	0
1 British Infantry Brigade	Maitland	3	3
2 British Infantry Brigade	Byng	3	3
3 British Infantry Brigade	Adam	4	3

Formation	Commande	Officers	
		Strength	Invited
4 British Infantry Brigade	Mitchell	2	0
5 British Infantry Brigade	Halkett	4	0
6 British Infantry Brigade	Johnstone	3	0
8 British Infantry Brigade	Kempt	3	2
9 British Infantry Brigade	Pack	3	2
10 British Infantry Brigade	Lambert	3	0
TOTALS		164	59

1. This table covers British formations only and excludes KGL, Hanoverian, Brunswick and Dutch divisions and brigades; e.g, HQ 3rd Division, 2nd Brigade KGL, etc. It includes foreign officers holding British commissions, e.g., Hereditary Prince of Orange and Baron von Tripp.
2. ADCs are shown at their relevant HQs and are NOT counted in their regimental strengths.
3. AG and QMG officers are grouped together at Army HQ, but many were detached to corps and divisional HQs.
4. The authorised establishment of a brigade HQ was the commander, ADC and Major of Brigade (Brigade Major).

Table VI: Field Units

This table shows all the British field units in Wellington's army, their officer strength on 15 June and the numbers invited. In all, thirty-eight out of 1,303 officers were invited (2.9 percent).

There was a total of sixteen cavalry regiments (not all at full strength) and no officers were invited from nine of them. Even of those receiving invitations, the largest number from a single unit was only four (7 Hussars), so that in no case was a cavalry regiment seriously short of officers due to invitations to the Ball.

Of the thirty infantry battalions, twenty-one were not represented at all in the invitation list and the largest group came from 2/1 and 3/1 Foot Guards, with a total of nine out of sixty-six officers (fourteen percent).

STATISTICS

Brigade	Regiment	Officers		Remarks
		Strength	Invited	
1 Cavalry Brigade	1 Life Guards	10	0	2 sqns only
	2 Life Guards	13	0	2 sqns only
	Royal Horse Guards	14	1	
	1 Kings Dragoon Guards	25	3	
2 Cavalry Brigade	1 Royal Dragoons	21	0	
	2 (Royal North British) Dragoons	23	0	
	6 (Iniskilling) Dragoons	18	0	
3 Cavalry Brigade	23 Light Dragoons	23	1	
4 Cavalry Brigade	11 Light Dragoons	24	0	
	12 Dragoons	21	1	
	16 Light Dragoons	26	0	
5 Cavalry Brigade	7 Hussars	20	4	
	15 Hussars	22	0	
6 Cavalry Brigade	10 Royal Hussars	20	2	
	18 Hussars	18	1	
7 Cavalry Brigade	13 Light Dragoons	24	0	
1 British Infantry Brigade	2/1 and 3/1 Foot Guards	66	9	See note
2 British Infantry Brigade	2/2 Foot Guards	27	6	
	2/3 Foot Guards	33	5	
3 British Infantry Brigade	1/52 Foot	53	1	
	71 Foot	45	0	
	2/95 Rifles	30	0	
	3/95 Rifles	8	0	2 companies only
4 British Infantry Brigade	3/14 Foot	34	0	
	1/23 Foot	35	0	
	51st Light Infantry	35	0	
5 British Infantry Brigade	2/30 Foot	38	0	
	33 Foot	36	0	
	2/69 Foot	29	0	
	73 Foot	26	0	
6 British Infantry Brigade	2/35 Foot	32	0	
	54 Foot	36	0	
	2/59 Foot	30	0	
	1/91 Foot	37	0	

Brigade	Regiment	Officers		Remarks
		Strength	Invited	
8 British	28 Foot	34	0	
Infantry	32 Foot	38	1	
Brigade	79 Foot	41	0	
	1/95 Rifles	26	1	
9 British	3/1 Foot	37	0	
Infantry	42 Foot	31	1	
Brigade	2/44 Foot	25	0	
	1/92 Foot	38	1	
10 British	1/4 Foot	24	0	Just back
Infantry				from USA
Brigade	1/27 Foot	19	0	
	1/40 Foot	38	0	
		1303	38	

1. It has not proved possible to split the officers of 1st Foot Guards between the two battalions present.

Table VII: Headquarters Staff

The headquarters staff was divided into two main branches: Adjutant-General and Quartermaster-General, but many of these officers were deployed to Corps and Divisonal Headquarters and since it is impossible to locate all of these precisely, they are all included in one figure. Most of the invitations to these officers were to those serving in or near Brussels on 15 June. The proportion receiving invitations in the first place is small, but, even so, a number of these who were engaged in preparing and issuing movement orders (routes) on the evening of 15 June are known not to have attended the Ball.

Branch	Officers	
	Total Strength	Invited
Adjutant-General	24	7
Quartermaster-General	30	6
Deputy Judge-Advocate	1	0
Headquarters Commandant	1	1
Army Chaplains	6	1
	62	15

Table VIII: Miscellaneous Corps

There were three bodies answerable direct to Army headquarters. Only one doctor was invited (and that was Wellington's personal physician) and none at all from either the Royal Staff Corps or the Royal Waggon Train, both of which were directed by the Quartermaster-General's department.

Branch	Officers	
	Total Strength	Invited
Army Medical Staff	17	1
Royal Staff Corps	5	0
Royal Waggon Train	12	0
	34	1

Table IX: Corps of the Department of the Master-General of the Ordnance

The Master-General of the Ordnance was a very senior officer, independent of the Army, whose vast department was based at Woolwich. He was responsible for the provision of all weapons for the Army, and also provided the Royal Artillery and Royal Engineers, together with his own medical department and drivers for the Royal Artillery.

Branch	Officers	
	Total Strength	Invited
Corps of Royal Engineers	11	0
Royal Regiment of Artillery	90	2
Corps of Royal Artillery Drivers	10	0
Ordnance Medical Department	17	0
	128	2

Table X: Military Casualties

There are many myths concerning casualties, including that the field of Quatre Bras was littered with the bodies of officers still in their Ball uniform, and that most of those attending the Ball were killed either at Quatre Bras or Waterloo. This table shows that a total of eleven of those invited to the Ball died in the following three days, three at Quatre Bras and eight at Waterloo, with two more dying of wounds received at Waterloo after ten days and eighteen months, respectively. A total of thirty-six received wounds of varying degress of severity.

		Name	Regiment	Appointment
Killed	Quatre Bras	Duke Friedrich-Wilhelm of Brunswick-Wolfenbuttel		Commander Brunswick contingent
		Lt-Col John Cameron	92nd Foot	Regimental Duty Commanding officer
		Ensign James, Lord Hay	1st Foot Guards	ADC/ Maitland
Killed	Waterloo	Lt-Gen Sir Thomas Picton		Commander 5th Division
		Maj-Gen Sir William Ponsonby		Commander 2nd Cavalry Brigade
		Lt-Col. Charles Canning	3rd Foot Guards	ADC/ DofW
		Lt-Col. William Fuller	1KDG	Regimental Duty Commanding officer
		Lt-Col. Hon. Sir Alexander Gordon	3rd Foot Guards	ADC/DofW
		Capt Charles Smyth	95th Foot	ADC/Pack
		Lt Francis Brooke	1st KDG	Regimental Duty
		Lt Hon. Hastings Forbes	3rd Foot Guards	Regimental Duty
Died of wounds	Waterloo	Colonel Sir William De Lancey	Permanent QMG	Deputy QMG Died 26 June1815
		Lt-Col Sir Henry Hollis Bradford	1st Foot Guards	Assistant QMG Died December 1816
Wounded	Waterloo	Prince William of Orange		Commander II Corps
		Lt-Gen The Earl of Uxbridge		Commander Cavalry
		Maj-Gen Frederick Adam		Commander 3rd Inf Brigade
		Maj-Gen Sir Edward Barnes		Assistant Adjutant-General
		Maj-Gen Sir George Cooke		Commander 1st British Division

		Name	Regiment	Appointment
		Maj-Gen Sir James Kempt		Commander 8th Inf Brigade
		Maj-Gen Sir Denis Pack		Commander 9th Inf Brigade
		Col Hon. Alexander Abercromby	Coldstream Guards	AQMG
		Col Sir John Elley	RHGuards	DAG
		Lt-Col. Sir Andrew Barnard	95th Foot	RD Commanding officer
		Lt-Col. Sir George Berkeley	35th Foot	Assistant Adjutant General to Pof O
		Lt-Col. Robert Henry Dick	42nd Foot	RD Second-in-Command
		Lt-Col. Sir Robert Hill	Royal Horse Guards	RD Commanding Officer
		Lt-Col. Hon. Frederick Ponsonby	12 Lt Dgns	RD Commanding Officer
		Lt-Col Charles Rowan	52nd Regt	RD. Second-in-Command
		Lt-Col. Lord Fitzroy Somerset	1st Foot Guards	Military Secretary/DofW
		Lt-Col. Henry Wyndham	Coldstream Guards	RD
		Maj Hon. George Dawson	1st KDG	AQMG
		Maj Thomas Hunter Blair	91st Foot	BM/Adam
		Maj Hon. William Stuart	1st Foot Guards	RD. 3rd Major
		Capt Edward Bowater	3rd Foot Guards	RD
		Capt the Hon. Orlando Bridgeman	1st Foot Guards	ADC/Hill
		Capt Henry Dumaresq	9th Foot	ADC/Byng
		Captain James Fraser	7 Lt Dgns	ADC/Uxbridge
		Capt Charles Gore	Half pay	ADC/Kempt
		Captain John Gurwood	10H	ADC/Clinton
		Capt Robert Hesketh	3rd Foot Guards	RD

			Name	Regiment	Appointment
			Capt Horace Seymour	60th Foot	ADC/Uxbridge
			Capt William Verner	7 Lt Dgns	RD
			Capt Thomas Wildman	7 Lt Dgns	ADC/Uxbridge
			Lieut John Gordon	7 Lt Dgns	RD
			Lieut James Robinson	32 Foot	RD
			Ensign David Baird	3rd Foot Guards	RD
			Ensign George Fludyer	1st Foot Guards	RD
			Ensign Hon. John Montagu	Coldstream Guards	RD

APPENDIX E
The Wedderburn-Webster Affair

The Duke of Wellington was, with Napoleon, the finest general of his age and on the battlefield he was incomparable, but in the salons of Europe's capitals he was definitely a ladies' man. In contrast, James Wedderburn-Webster and his wife, Lady Frances, were an unintelligent and shallow couple, whom Byron accurately described to Lady Melbourne as 'the Blunderhead family'.[1] Between them this foolish pair came perilously close to seriously tarnishing Wellington's reputation at the time of his greatest triumph. It would be wrong to overstate their importance in these great events, but for several weeks in Brussels in 1815 Wellington conducted an ill-advised affair with Lady Frances, which subsequently caused him severe embarrassment in a court case in 1816, while four letters he wrote at the time surfaced many years later and threatened him yet again. What set this episode apart from his many other affairs was that it was the only occasion to give rise to the *allegation* that he had allowed his love life to interfere with his military business and it is for this reason – and since the alleged events took place in Brussels – that this brief affair merits closer examination.

James Wedderburn-Webster
James was the son of David Wedderburn, a Scotsman, whose uncle, James Webster of Clapham, a very successful merchant in the West Indies trade, died in 1796. Under the terms of the Will, David inherited considerable property on condition that he assumed the additional name of Webster. Now named David Wedderburn-Webster, he died in 1801, leaving a widow, three sons and two daughters.[2]

The eldest son, James Wedderburn-Webster, duly inherited his father's estate, and went up to Cambridge where he became one of a circle of hard-drinking undergraduates, which included the young Lord Byron. On going down from Cambridge, Webster's money was sufficient to purchase a commission in one of the most fashionable regiments in the Army – 10th (Prince of Wales's) Light Dragoons. He was commissioned as a cornet in 1809, and promoted to lieutenant in 1810, but his three years military service were spent entirely in England. He was stationed initially at Brighton then at Romford, Kent, from where he spent a very brief spell in London, helping to quell the Burdett[3] riots (16 April 1810) – his only known active service. He then returned to Brighton.

Webster's only claims to fame during his military service concerned wagers. In the first, he won a bet that he could ride from Norwich to London in forty-four hours; he won, completing the distance in forty-two hours. Then, in 1809, he bet 1,000 guineas that Captain Robert Barclay, a noted athlete, could not walk one mile every hour for 1,000 hours. So intense was the interest and so great the sums wagered in side bets, that Barclay carried a brace of pistols and employed a famous prize-fighter as his escort after dark, but he completed the course and collected his money from Wedderburn-Webster. Webster left the 10th Hussars in 1811, whereupon he became a 'man-about-town' and one of the set which included such men as Lord Byron and Scrope Davies, although it would be true to say that they tolerated him for his money, rather than welcomed him for his personal qualities.

Lady Frances

Lady Frances Caroline Annesley, born in 1793, was the second daughter in a leading Irish family, her parents being Arthur, first Earl of Mountnorris and his second wife, the Hon. Sarah Cavendish. Frances led an unexceptional childhood, until 1810 when at the age of 17, and after what was reported to be a very short courtship, she married James Wedderburn-Webster, then still serving in 10th (Prince of Wales's) Light Dragoons. Her brother, Lord Valentia, told Byron in 1811 that 'she married to get rid of her family – (who are ill-tempered) – & had not been *out* two months so that to use a fox-hunting phrase she was "killed in covert." ' She gave birth to a son in 1811 or 1812, who was named Byron, but he died in infancy, whereupon the poet told the father, 'Well I cautioned you & told you that my name would almost damn any thing or any creature.'[4]

The Visit

Frances quickly became disenchanted with her husband, but relished the circles he moved in, which were more adventurous and 'racy' than those her family was used to. In 1813 she invited Lord Byron and his half-sister, Augusta, to stay at the Wedderburn-Webster country residence, Aston Hall. Byron already knew Frances' brother, Lord Valentia, and had known Webster for some years, so he accepted, although Augusta, perhaps fortunately, did not. Byron duly arrived on Sunday 3 October, but immediately found the atmosphere distasteful, since Webster loudly proclaimed his wife's beauty and faithfulness, while becoming instantly jealous if he thought Byron was paying her too much attention – and all the while he was not only carrying on with other women, but also seeking Byron's advice on how to succeed in such affairs.

On the other hand, Frances treated her husband with disdain, Byron reporting to his confidante, Lady Melbourne:

> Every now and then he has a fit of fondness – & kisses her hand before his guests – which she receives with the most lackless indifference – which struck me more than if she had appeared pleased or annoyed.

On another occasion, Webster and his wife had a major disagreement in front of Byron over a trivial matter, making the latter feel embarrassed and out-of-place – and even more so when Frances whispered to him, 'N'importe – this is all nothing', suggesting that it was but one of many such pointless marital arguments.

Webster's attitude and several absences inevitably forced Byron and Frances closer together, with Byron in some trepidation because Frances kept on protesting that they must take care, whilst always seeming to be on the point of giving the game away herself. Eventually, on one night when her husband was away, she offered herself to him, but astonishingly, despite being a renowned rake and lacking in scruple where women were concerned – and even though he considered himself in love with her – Byron felt that he could not seduce his friend's wife in their family home and, as he reported to Lady Melbourne, '. . . I spared her'. A few days later when Webster asked Byron for a private conversation, the latter was convinced that he was about to be challenged to a duel, instead of which Webster took the opportunity to explain yet again how much his wife was in love with her husband. Byron was very relieved to leave on 19 October.

The affair continued for several months, although it is generally agreed that it was never consummated. Byron certainly thought himself to be in love with her and she was a beautiful young woman, although some thought her too pale and thin, while a fellow beauty considered her eyes to be bloodshot. She was 19 at this stage and it appears probable that this was her first affair, so she must have felt triumphant at capturing the heart of the most famous poet of the day, becoming the Ginevra of his sonnets, and the Medora of *The Corsair*. In the end, however, it was she who ditched him rather than vice-versa.

Brussels

The Websters travelled to Brussels at some time in the winter of 1814–15, for reasons not known, although Frances' father, mother and sister were already in residence there, while James's step-uncle, Lieutenant-Colonel Sir William Douglas, was in command of the 91st Foot. Wellington arrived in Brussels on 4 April and appears to have met Lady Frances shortly afterwards, possibly at dinner at the Duke of Richmond's house. The acquaintance seems to have progressed rapidly, since only three weeks later Captain Digby Mackworth recorded on 27 April 1815:

Lord Wellington gave a grand ball yesterday, at which all the principal people in Bruxelles were present. A most magnificent supper was prepared, and the gardens so well illuminated as almost to resemble day. The Duke himself danced, and always with the same person, a Lady Frances Webster, to whom he paid so much attention, that Scandal, who is become Goddess here, began to whisper all sorts of stories, but we are not bound to believe all she says; not but that the well-known bad private character of His Grace would warrant any suspicions whatever. There must have been something essentially bad in the education of the Wellesley family – on the score of gallantry not one of its members, male or female, is *sans reproche* . . .[5]

The more respectable elements of the British colony in Brussels seem to have regarded the Duke with an amused tolerance, always respectful of him as a general and as a man, but sharing Digby Mackworth's views on his social behaviour. Lady Caroline Capel reported to her mother on 2 June:

The Duke of W has not improved the morality of our Society, as he has given several things & makes a point of asking all the Ladies of Loose Character – Every one was surprised at seeing Lady John Campbell at his House & one of his Staff told me that it had been represented to him her not being received for that her Character was more than Suspicious, 'Is it, By ?' said he, 'then I will go & ask her Myself.' On which he immediately took his Hat & went out for the purpose.[6]

Mackworth and Lady Capel were not alone in noticing something amiss, a third being Lieutenant Basil Jackson of the Royal Staff Corps, who recorded many years later:

I was sitting one afternoon in the park [at Brussels] with an elderly Belgian lady, when a very great man walked past us, and immediately after a carriage drew up at an entrance on the opposite side of the park, and a lady alighted, who was joined by the great man. My friend and I, prompted by curiosity, arose to see the result of the junction, following with our eyes the lady and gentleman until they descended into a hollow, where the trees completely screened them. We then perceived another carriage arrive, from which an old lady descended, whom I recognised as Lady M. N., who went peering about as if looking for some one or something, but was completely baffled by the tactics of the lady and gentleman, and left the park *re infectâ*. She was clearly in search of her daughter, Lady F. W., of whom 'busy fame whispered light things'. But I must proceed to matters of more moment . . .[7]

There can be no question that 'Lady M. N.' was the Countess of Mountnorris and the lady who went into the copse – 'Lady F. W.' – was her daughter, Lady Frances Wedderburn-Webster. Although the reference to 'the very great man' is less specific, there can be little doubt that it was the Duke of Wellington.

To add to the gossip, James left for London in May, whereupon Lady Frances moved in with her parents, who kept a much less strict eye on her. He did not return to Brussels until 5 August, and quite why he went to London was never clear; it may have been for business reasons, as he claimed, but it could also have been that his wife wanted him out of the way.

The Letters

Lady Frances attended the Duchess of Richmond's Ball on 15 June, but on this occasion she seems to have created little occasion for gossip, although the Marquise d'Assche certainly saw her talking to Wellington. However, for most of the time Wellington was busy dealing with more military matters and he left the Ball at about 2am.

Wellington left Brussels soon after dawn on 16 June, took part in the Battles of Quatre Bras and Waterloo, and then returned to Brussels at dawn on the 19th to write his despatch and also to visit some of the wounded officers, before returning to the army on the 20th. However, it was rumoured at the time and confirmed many years later, that during this period he wrote two letters to Lady Frances, although, as will be seen there were, in fact, more.

In the early hours of 18 June, whilst at his headquarters in Waterloo village, the duke is known to have written four letters, three of them on professional matters. The first was to the Duc de Berri, the second to the governor of Antwerp and the third a note covering both, which was addressed to Sir Charles Stuart, asking him to forward the first two to their respective addressees.[8] Those first three were timed at 3am, but he then wrote a fourth, timed at 3.30am:

> MY DEAR LADY FRANCES,
> As I am sending a messenger to Bruxelles, I write to you one line to tell you that I think you ought to make your preparations, as should Lord Mountnorris, to remove from Bruxelles to Antwerp in case such a measure should be necessary.
> We fought a desperate battle on Friday, in which I was successful, though I had but very few troops. The Prussians were very roughly handled, and retired in the night, which obliged me to do the same to this place yesterday. The course of the operations may oblige me to uncover Bruxelles for a moment, and may expose that town to the enemy; for which reason I recommend that you and your family should be prepared to move to Antwerp at a moment's notice.

I will give you the earliest intimation of any danger that may come to my knowledge: at present I know of none.
Believe me, &c.,
WELLINGTON.

Present my best compliments to Lord and Lady Mountnorris.[9]

On his return to Brussels on the morning of 19 June, Wellington first completed his despatch and then chatted with various visitors, including the Duchess of Richmond and John Creevey. However, despite having many other matters to deal with, he also found time to write a letter, dated 'Bruxelles, 19th June, 1815, ½ past 8 in the morning:'

MY DEAR LADY FRANCES,
Lord Mountnorris may remain in Bruxelles in perfect security. I yesterday, after a most severe and bloody contest, gained a complete victory, and pursued the French till after dark. They are in complete confusion; and I have, I believe, 150 pieces of cannon; and Blücher, who continued the pursuit all night, my soldiers being tired to death, sent me word this morning that he had got 60 more.
My loss is immense. Lord Uxbridge, Lord FitzRoy Somerset, General Cooke, General Barnes, and Colonel Berkeley are wounded: Colonel De Lancey, Canning, Gordon, General Picton killed. The finger of Providence was upon me, and I escaped unhurt.
Believe me, &c., WELLINGTON[10]

The Duke left again on the 20th and the Allied armies had closed up on Paris by late June and on 4 July a peace was concluded. On 7 July Lady Caroline Capel reported to her mother in a letter that 'Shoals of English are flocking there [to Paris] to see every thing' and that although 'it is I think rather premature for families to go there, – Lady Frances Wedderburn Webster is gone for the purpose of being confined there.'[11] The majority of the Mountnorris family remained in Brussels, however, until James Webster returned from England on 5 August, after which they all moved to the French capital, where both James and Frances were seen by a reliable observer having supper with the duke on the evening of 9 August.[12] Shortly afterwards Lady Frances gave birth to a baby boy, who was christened David Wedderburn-Webster, in tribute to James's father.[13]

The Court Case
The Duke of Wellington was now at the peak of his military glory: victor in Portugal, Spain, southern France, and now Waterloo, he was the leading Allied general in Paris and was being showered with rewards. But, no British hero is allowed to avoid the attentions of the more

scurrilous national newspapers for long and in this case his period of grace was short indeed. There had been gossip in British circles in Brussels about the duke's attentions to Lady Frances and the story inevitably got back to London, where several British newspapers took up the story, particularly the *St James's Chronicle,* whose 3 August edition included the following paragraph:

> It was said at Brussels, that when the Duke of Wellington returned after the battle of Waterloo ... he came to visit the wounded – perhaps the wounded heart was meant. A word to the wise.

Having whetted its readers' appetite with this enigmatic morsel, two days later (5 August) the paper was more explicit:
BRUSSELS, 1815 – FASHIONABLE ALLITERATION

> In the letter W, there's charm half divine,
> War, Wellington, Wedderburn, Webster, and Wine.

The editor, however, placed the related paragraphs at some distance from this heading. They read:

> The cessation of warfare, has, in Paris, enabled scandal to resume her usual influence on the public mind. A report is very prevalent, in the first Parisian circles, that a distinguished Commander has surrendered himself captive to the beautiful wife of a military officer, high in rank. The transaction had been discovered in such a manner as to make a very serious investigation of this event indispensable. But it is hoped, that it will turn out to be nothing more than a tale of malevolence.
>
> The *amour* alluded to in a former paragraph, did not take place at Paris, but at Brussels, a day or two after the battle of Waterloo. The husband has laid his damages at 50,000£, which it is said, the fortunate lover has offered to pay – but the affair is too notorious for composition, or the party injured has too much sensibility to be content with wearing gilded horns.
>
> The Parisian husbands are astonished at this conduct, which they ridicule as strange English prejudice. Each of them wishes that he could have netted his Venus with such a Mars. An orderly-serjeant did the duty, on this occasion, usually performed by a prying chambermaid. He is acquainted with all the circumstances, and will be the principal witness at the trial.

This report was curious in several respects. It refers to a 'military officer, high in rank' which, in view of the subsequent reports, clearly referred to

179

Wedderburn-Webster. But he had left the service some five years earlier in the rank of lieutenant, which was by no stretch of the imagination 'high' rank. It also implies that an army sergeant had found the duke and Lady Frances *in flagrante delecto,* although this report does not appear anywhere else, and was not even mentioned in the subsequent libel trial.

By now many other British newspapers were reporting the scandal and the *St James's Chronicle* returned to the fray on 8 August by quoting from another paper:

> Several of the public prints have, in some particulars, gone too far in their statements respecting a high military character and a blooming bride of 22, and have blazoned their *Crime. Con.* [Criminal Conversation, the contemporary euphemism for adultery] and damages in their usual way. These statements show that they are ignorant of the localities, circumstances, and truth of the case. We cannot dismiss the subject without noticing another absurd report, that a subscription at the head of which is the M. of H. [Marquess of Hertford] for 200, is on foot, to defray the law expenses of the gallant defendant . . . (Evening Paper).

The *St James's Chronicle* then added: 'A very beautiful woman of Irish extraction, is said to be a party to the *amour* at Brussels, which is said to have made so great a noise on the Continent.'

Nor was this all, as the satirical poet, Peter Pinder, published a poem 'Love at headquarters, or a Week at Brussels', which also mocked Wellington and Lady Frances.[14]

As soon as she was in Paris – and despite her advanced state of pregnancy – Frances joined in the social life. She attended a ball given by the Duke of Wellington on 1 August, which was attended by King Louis XVIII and all the Allied leaders. Lady Frances was seen sitting with Lady Caroline Lamb, with a vacant chair placed between them, being saved for the duke, who subsequently joined them, together with Walter Scott.[15] Once Frances had recovered from her confinement, she became one of some half dozen beautiful moths fluttering around the Wellington flame, and prior to the arrival of the Duchess of Wellington in October she was a leader of the group.

Rumours at the time suggested that Webster did, indeed, make representations to Wellington, but that the latter convinced him that it was all unfounded. Webster, however, then saw the opportunity for money in another sphere and he and his wife jointly sued Charles Baldwin, the proprietor of the *St James's Chronicle* for 'a libel charging adultery between the most noble Arthur Duke of Wellington and Lady Frances C.W. Webster, at Brussels after the battle of Waterloo'. The civil action was heard in the Court of Common Pleas on 16 February 1816 and the damages claimed were £50,000 – no mean sum; the judge was Chief Justice Gibbs, with Mr Serjeant Best for the Plaintiff and Mr Serjeant Lens for the Defendant.

None of the principals in the case appeared in person, but the Plaintiffs wheeled out some heavy artillery in the person of the Duke of Richmond, who, in deference to his status and rank, sat beside the judge. In his evidence, the duke painted a picture of a woman of unimpeachable virtue, to whom he and the duchess were most content to entrust their unmarried daughters, even after they had seen the allegations in the British newspapers. Several other witnesses for the Plaintiff were present in court, including Lord Grantley, Lord Arthur Hill, Lord John Somerset, Colonel Sir John Campbell and the Rev. George Stokes, but none was called. Significantly, neither of the Wedderburn-Websters was called either.

The defence stood little chance and from the trial records appears to have given up from the start. Who could expect a British jury to find against the Duke of Wellington so soon after Waterloo, and which of the jury could doubt the sworn testimony, given in person by the Duke of Richmond, a peer of the realm? When Mr Serjeant Lens turned down the opportunity to attack Frances' character or to seek to prove the truth of the allegations, his case was lost. The judge summed up as even-handedly as was possible in the circumstances, and the jury took just thirty minutes to decide that the Defendant was guilty of libel, although they awarded the Websters just £2,000 in damages. This was considerably less than the £50,000 claimed, suggesting that the jurors did not feel that the harm done to Lady Frances' reputation was all that great.

Following the court case, the Websters returned to Paris, where Frances continued her social life, although this was interrupted by the death of her first son in 1816, and the subsequent births of another son, Charles, who was also fated to die in infancy, and later a daughter, Juliana, who survived to adulthood. Meanwhile, James undertook some inconsequential work, including publishing a slim volume of poems at his own expense. Webster seems to have envied Byron's reputation as both a lover *and* as a poet, and he now decided to write his own poem on 'Waterloo' despite having been in England at the time. This was subsequently published, the author having '. . . yielded – contrary to my own wishes & opinions, to the solicitations of some friends, whom I fear have been blind to its numerous errors and imperfections'. The poem on Waterloo consisted of fifty stanzas and a lengthy conclusion, and most of Webster's friends, including Byron and Scrope Davies, were scathing. One stanza will serve to explain why:

> Napoleon! Oh thou baneful shade!
> Yet deign to view the wreck thou'st made;

> Cast but one ling'ring look behind,
> Then give thy Course to the wind . . .[16]

Frances had a brief affair with Scrope Davies, which began in late September 1818[17] and was well under way by mid-November, with Frances informing him that '. . . I shall knock at your door in – an hour – when I shall claim a rehearsal of the Conjugal Tragedy which you promised me . . .'[18] She was a passionate lover, but very impetuous and intense – her letters were written at a breakneck speed with scarcely a single sentence finished before she was into the next – but Davies' problems were exacerbated by the fact that he was also conducting an affair with Lady Caroline Lamb, as reported by their mutual friend, Hobhouse, to Byron on 4 November: 'SBD [Scrope Berdmore Davies] is got into the hands of Lady CL [Caroline Lamb] and is in deep with Lady FW (Frances Webster] . . .' As Lady Caroline and Lady Frances were both fast-living women and are known to have been good friends since their time in Paris, it may well be that neither was entirely ignorant of the other's activities with the hapless Davies.

Not surprisingly, he seems to have failed to stay the course and on 29 November Frances wrote from Chippenham that '. . . your past will be forgotten – as much as is in my power to forget . . .' but by late December it was all over. 'This crumb, my blessing – prayers – hopes and wishes follow you! Adieu Adieu! You know not what you have done! Adieu.'

Her final letter purported to be a suicide note:

> Between the hours of two and three tomorrow I may perhaps be what the chymists call, 'decomposed' – if such should be my lot, remember me with affection for I have loved you to madness – if I should survive then, I pray you, destroy this letter . . . Dear creature adieu – I have destroyed all your letters – The time approaches and I am resolved – Farewell . . .

As a final gesture she cut off a lock of her hair and enclosed it in her letter (it is still there in the British Library, a light brown in colour, and as lustrous and fresh as the day it was cut). Needless to say, after all these histrionics she did not commit suicide, nor did Davies destroy her letters. A lady author discussed this affair some years later with Scrope Davies who told her how Frances had a 'peculiar mode of manifesting preference', which, unfortunately for posterity, the lady author concerned decided 'to suppress'.[19]

The year 1821 was difficult for the Websters. In April James suspected that his wife was having an affair with a friend of his, Lord Petersham, and one night when she went out he assumed that she was going to meet her lover, so he climbed on the back of her coach as she left. The coach entered the yard of an inn where Lord Petersham emerged from the building and put his head through the open window to talk to Frances. At this the enraged Webster attacked the lord from behind and set about him and then, drawing back, ensured that witnesses were within earshot as he hurled a torrent of abuse at the astonished and discomfited Lord Petersham. This was more than sufficient to warrant a duel and the two met at Kingston on 21 April where they, somewhat ignominiously, discharged their pistols into the air and with 'honour satisfied', made up and were friends again.[20]

The couple then returned to Paris, but by September the marriage had so broken down that Frances fled with her daughter, whom she left in a place of safety and then took refuge herself with her uncle, Mr Cavendish Bradshaw, at Boulogne. She then wrote to Lord Sidmouth, a government minister, asking him not to give her husband a warrant to obtain help from the French authorities in finding her daughter, as she had hidden the child for its own protection.[21]

In June 1822 Webster thought that he was about to receive a knight-hood, although quite what meritorious service he had performed to warrant such an honour is impossible to discover. But, as with so many things in his life, matters did not go smoothly and, to his considerable embarrassment, his name was omitted from the *London Gazette* and he had to remonstrate to ensure that it appeared in a later issue.[22]

Matters appear then to have gone downhill and in 1829 Frances appealed to the Duke of Wellington for financial assistance and, surpris-ingly, employment for her husband. The great man delegated to Sir Robert Peel the responsibility for sending a rather brusque and unhelpful reply.[23]

The Mystery of the Letters

Matters rested there for some years. Frances died in 1837 at the early age of 44, and in the following year, shortly after the publication of the first series of the Duke of Wellington's 'Dispatches', a small advertisement appeared in a morning paper offering several letters written by the duke, for sale at a solicitor's office in Lincoln's Inn. Colonel Gurwood, the editor of the Dispatches, was sent to see what was going on and reported back to the Duke that there were five letters in all and that the owner wanted £50 for them.[24] One of them was to Wedderburn-Webster concerning admission to the trial of Marshal Ney and was irrelevant, but the other four were potentially much more serious, all being written by the duke to Lady Frances. Two have already been discussed, those written at Waterloo (18 June), the other at Brussels (19 June), and Gurwood was particularly taken with Wellington's phrase in the latter that '. . . the hand of Providence was upon me'. There were, however, two more, one written from Le Cateau on 25/26 June, the other from Paris.

The duke immediately authorised Gurwood to purchase them for £50, but made so many stipulations about including them in any future edition of Dispatches that Gurwood left them out completely. Despite this, the existence of the letters became public knowledge and, according to one story, the duke read the letters and then thrust them into the fire, remarking, 'I was a damned fool when I wrote those letters.'[25]

When the 'Supplementary Dispatches' appeared in 1863, Volume 10 included the two letters from the Duke to Lady Frances from Waterloo and Brussels (quoted above) and although they appear without explanation, it is clear that they are part of the group bought in 1838, since the second includes the phrase 'the hand of providence'. Thus, either the story of the duke burning them is incorrect, or else he did burn them but the wily Gurwood made copies before he did so. What was in the other two letters and why they were not published cannot be established.

Conclusions

Brussels in 1815 was notorious for its gossip and some of the stories about Wellington and Lady Frances may have been mere tittle-tattle. But Digby Mackworth, Lady Caroline Capel and Basil Jackson were serious-minded people, known for their veracity, and seem unlikely to have fabricated their particular stories.

Also, the story of the two letters was proved, some thirty-three years later, to have been correct. That the duke could have found the time in the early hours of 18 June to write a letter to Lady Frances suggests a close relationship, while the post-script asking for a message to be passed to Frances' father appears mere camouflage. The note written on the 19th is even more curious, since the duke was in Brussels when he wrote it and Lady Frances was living only a few hundred yards distant. The details of artillery captured and of officers lost would almost certainly have been of little interest to a young woman of 21 years, but it may, rather, have been a touch of bravado intended to encourage her to rush round to congratulate her hero. We shall never know. It is also curious that the affair became public knowledge, one possibility being that the courier delivering the letters on 18 and 19 June may have told others of his task and the gossip-mongers (of whom there were many in Brussels) did the rest.

Frances gave birth to a child in August, indicating that she was in her seventh month of pregnancy in June. Ladies' dresses of the time would have tended to disguise this, but, while there is no question that Frances flirted with the duke, it seems unlikely that matters could have progressed much further.

Many questions cannot now be answered, but there are two certainties in all this. First, that the Wedderburn-Websters were a foolish couple, whose only importance lay in their potential to damage others. James was a braggart, the proverbial 'hanger-on', who attached himself to people such as Byron, and, in many of his actions, plain silly. His wife was equally dangerous, being both intensely ambitious and highly strung, and using her undoubted attractions to latch herself onto, first, the leading poet of the day and, secondly, the most famous soldier. There can be little doubt that their combined intent in bringing the court case was to make money for themselves rather than to protect the reputation of either Lady Frances or the Duke of Wellington.

On the other hand, Wellington took chances with his reputation, both by paying so much attention to Frances at public events in Brussels and in writing letters at times when his mind should have been on more important matters. He was a man capable of issuing crushing dismissals and could have ended matters with Lady Frances at any time and with a single sentence had he wished to do so.

There can be no doubt that if the jury in the 1816 trial had found for the Defence (i.e., that there *had* been an adulterous affair between the duke and Lady Frances) then the duke would have been embarrassed, although such was his reputation as a military hero, it would not have ended his career. But, it was due to luck rather than judgment that Frances and her husband failed to sully the duke's reputation.

NOTES

1 Letter to Lady Melbourne dated Aston Hall, Rotherham 5 October 1813.
2 David's widow remarried the following year, her new husband being Robert Douglas, whose brother was Lieutenant-Colonel Sir William Douglas, later to be commanding officer of the 91st Foot at Waterloo. David's daughter Anne subsequently married her stepfather's son by his first marriage, Captain Archibald Murray Douglas, an officer in the 52nd Foot.
3 Sir Francis Burdett (1770–1844), a radical MP had been imprisoned for breach of parliamentary privilege, having published a defence of an imprisoned radical orator.
4 *Alas The Love of Women*, p. 106.
5 *The Waterloo Diary of Captain Digby Mackworth, 7th Foot*, ADC to Lt-Gen. Lord Hill; *Army Quarterly*, October 1937, January 1938.
6 The Capel Letters, p. 102.
7 *Notes and Reminiscences of a Staff Officer*, Basil Jackson, p. 11.
8 *Dispatches*, Volume 12, pp. 476–7.
9 *Supplementary Dispatches*, Vol. X, p. 501.
10 SD, Vol. X, p. 531.
11 The Capel Letters, p. 123.
12 'There cannot be much foundation for the report of legal proceedings which you allude to for the gentleman and lady dined at his Grace's the day before yesterday and his Grace was seen parading about the lady in the evening . . .' Letter from Thomas Sydenham to his brother Benjamin, dated Paris 11 August 1815, *The Waterloo Papers*, Edward Owen (ed.), p. 36.

13 *Gentleman's Magazine*, Vol. 85 Jul–Dec 1815, p. 274. '28 Aug 1815 'At her father's, the Earl of Mountnorris, Paris, r.h. Lady F Wedderburn Webster, a son and heir'.
14 B Lib 32–5.
15 Simpson, J, *Paris after Waterloo*, p. 192.
16 *Waterloo and Other Poems*, J Wedderburn Webster, Esq., Paris, 1816.
17 B Lib Loan 70 Vol. I f.68.
18 ibid. f.70.
19 'Diaries Of A Lady Of Quality From 1797 To 1844, edited and with notes by A. Hayward, Esq, QC,' (2nd edition. London, Longman, Green, Roberts and Green.) pp. 350–1.
20 Mrs Arbuthnot. Volume I, p. 87.
21 PRO HO 44/10
22 PRO HO 44/11 ff 218–19.
23 B Lib Add Ms 40399 f. 320. Correspondence of Sir Robert Peel Home Office 8 Sep. 1829.
24 Letter Gurwood to Wellington, dated 25 August 1838. University of Southampton. Wellington papers 2/53/74.
25 *Edinburgh Review*, Volume CXII, July–October 1860, No. 228, p. 213.

Major-General Maitland's Elopement

It has long been known that in October 1815 Major-General Peregrine Maitland, commander of the Guards Division during the Allied occupation of Paris, eloped with Lady Sarah Lennox, one of the daughters of the Duke and Duchess of Richmond. It is germane to this story of the Duchess of Richmond's Ball, since the romance must have started in Brussels, but the two of them managed to keep it a complete secret, not only from the gossips of the place, but also from the Duchess, who had few greater interests in life than that her daughters should make suitable (and profitable) marriages.

The very word 'elope' has a romantic ring to it, conjuring up visions of a midnight flight using a ladder set against a bedrooom window, a desperate coach journey through the darkness and the lady's father galloping behind, intent on rescuing his errant daughter. What actualy happened in this case has long been a mystery but has now come to light in the correspondence of the Reverend G G Stonestreet, a direct, if somewhat bemused, participant in the events of the night of 16/17 October. Stonestreet was serving as the chaplain to the Guards Division – a post he had occupied for several years – and Major-General Maitland was his military superior officer, but when it came to the choice the steadfast chaplain remained true to his clerical office, despite being placed under great pressure by his general and his ADC. Stonestreet explained it all in letters to a friend in London

Letter I. Reverend G.G. Stonestreet to George Trower, Esq[1]

HQ 2nd Division,
Paris. October 16, 1815.

... I was dining yesterday with Gen Howard and was sitting as his Vice over a Turkey – a là I forget what – when a breathless Aide-de-Camp rushed into the room, saluted nobody, but said Mr S is wanted instantly. It did not seem from his manner that it was a funeral or a baptism or a sickness. He was greatly agitated; I was quite sure I was wanted; and rose with a professional reluctance from my savoury duties, and followed him out. When we reach'd one of the saloons, he said with great earnestness, Take your hat and come with me . . . I was convinced by the anxiety of my aide-de-camp and by the consideration that it was half past seven and quite dark . . .

'They are at the Gate.' 'And who are at the Gate? – 'My General and Lady Sarah Lennox.' 'How at the Gate?' – 'Yes in a fiacre.' I had not time to compare or compound my ideas – no time to be astonished, or vexed, or angry, or cautious, or good humoured or ill humoured. My thoughts came in torrents of a thousand forms, both muddy and opake, I could make nothing at all of it, tho' I knew both the parties – by the time 12 paces more brought me to the carriage in the street. The door flew open – 'Come inside' – the steps fell – I got in. My aide-de-camp put up the steps, shut the door, retreated; and there I was seated in a fiacre with Sir Peregrine Maitland, my own general Commanding the Guards and Lady S Lennox second daughter of the Duke of Richmond. She was sobbing loud 'Here we are' – said the General – 'We have just run away from the Duke's – we shall be pursued – will you marry us instantly?' – What an extraordinary instinct we have – innate, or intuitive or sensitive – I care not what it is call'd, which makes us sensible of our own danger. Those ideas which w^d not amalgamate into a common notion on the outside of the fiacre, now touch'd by the electricity of what in downright honest philosophy I must call self-interest or self preservation – became suddenly condensed into my deepest reasonable good sense. 'What' I said (to *myself*) 'Steal a young Lady out of a Duke's family – the ex-Viceroy of Ireland – the friend of Wellington – the offender too a good staid Widower of near 40; this is a most terrible piece of larceny – I too am to be the accomplice – the 'blacksmith' of Paris[2] – who have received numerous attentions from the Duke's family, and performed so many marriages, where he has taken an active part![3] What a pretty sort of convenience I should become to all the mad capers of intrigues here! All this you know was 'asides'; for it was not pretty to tell him what terms belongs to a Gentleman and what term too to Ladies who do these sort of things – But I told him out – that there was only one course to be pursued. He *must* get me the Embassador's or Wellington's licence (not that the Civilians think that more than waste paper). He said they w^d both refuse. The Duke by this time had warn'd them – That if I did not marry them blood would be spillt. He c^d refuse the Duke of Richmond's challenge as a son-in-law but not otherwise. The Duke might call him villain and only one consequence c^d answer.

I said I sh^d greatly regret such a consequence – that it was independent of my duty; in the exercise of which I might never be terrified by such improper consideration, the mention of which I hinted only [indecipherable] to distress the lady at his side. He said it would be a marriage in the eyes of Heaven! It was only for a few days and then the thing *must* take place in a proper form. But every instant I felt stronger; and at last added that it would draw on *me* the indignation and vengeance of the Duke & justly. That I was too dependant on my profession to risk such a misfortune – and that my sentiments and my interest equally forbade me, painful as it was, to comply with the wishes of persons I so much, on all other occasions, respected! They then ask'd what other Clergy there were: whether French, Protestant or Catholic w^d do it? I assured them: No, marriage here is strictly guarded as a civil contract purely. Whether any Chaplain w^d do it? – It was not likely – the General belonged to my Division and they w^d not interfere. He asked to try – I gave him an address – and jumped out of the carriage – the aide-de-camp jumped in – I thought no more about rain or hats and made my way rapidly across the court and once more joined in the party.

But the turkey was gone! Cheese, a tasteful repast to a ploughman or a cricketer was too vulgar and too mortifying and I reserved my disappointment for ample revenge on the dessert. But Cupid still battled with Bacchus for the control of that hour – and back again came – now my evil genius, the aide-de-camp – he said the Chaplain was gone to England three days ago, and that what another *could* do, I *might* do – that they wanted to speak to me in the carriage again! He would not let me go for my hat but led me again prisoner back. At the porter's lodge however I made a vigorous stand – I would not trust myself in the fiacre again – I thought a gallant General who could steal a Duke's daughter w^d not make much of carrying off a parson and one too *under his command* – so I took up a position in the Concierge's room and there declared that all I could and would do was to give another Chaplain's address who lived in a Village four miles off – Away they went again.

I sent early in the morning to my friend the Chaplain to know what he had done. He said an Officer unknown, of my Division, had applied between eleven and twelve o'clock at night for marriage – which he had refused, without any knowledge of the parties –

This morning Sunday as I went to my field preaching – the aide-de-camp, now at his post, told me in a whisper nothing was yet done! That he had spent the night in calling up French priests and notaries – and St Genevieve was amply called on, I doubt not, in assisting the troublesome Gentleman, in some future journey, to the Diable. However he made a proposition to which of course I assented, namely that I sh^d now go to the Duke of Wellington and after to the Embassador, to ask the consent of one and the licence of the other.

This I did – the Duke of Wellington received with his overbearing stare and abrupt questioning. But I stand bullying very well – it only puts me up – and I brought him too – he gave his consent, because I believe he had talk'd the thing over with the Duke of Richmond, desired me to prepare the licence in his private room – and with a piece of Generalship not very honourable, while I was so occupied, sent for his own Chaplain, told him to take his ceremonials and go to the Embassadors – and marry General Maitland on his arrival. So much for his [indecipherable]; he is a man *who will serve his friends at all costs* ... I dined with him afterwards – a large party, little said . . .'

Letter II. Reverend G.G. Stonestreet to George Trower, Esq[4]

Paris November 23rd.

Dear Trower,
I believe I left off in the middle of my history of the gallant General and the intrepid Lady Sarah Lennox. It turned out the luckiest thing in the world for them that I made so many difficulties; as it gave them time for her Papa's anger to cool and for the Duke of Wellington to take advantage of his actually good nature and affection for his family. I was quite sure from the first moment, that the Duchess, her Mama, as a Complete woman of the world would face the thing, probably say the General was her greatest favourite in the whole world; and that how it was a pity that when people are in love they will not want to let things work their way quietly, but take such violent and odd measures in their heads! Things took just this course. Four days after the Wedding the Bride returned to the World! Made her debut at a grand family dinner, all branches delighted; and nothing was heard of for a week after but that the Embassador was to give the married couple a dinner such a day, Lord Castlereagh such a day, the Duke of Wellington such a day, &c &c. I think I drew my head well out of the scrape ... The Duke of Richmond, however, is in spite of all these gaieties, sensibly hurt; and he said to me with some emphasis and significiancy, he had been long enough in Paris and wish'd himself back, and at Brussels . . .'

So, this particular elopement was certainly dramatic but by no means romantic. Indeed, it was more of a farce, with a responsible and mature major-general, fresh from his successes at Waterloo, and the second daughter of one of England's premier dukes rushing around Paris in the dark and the rain, trying to find a chaplain, a priest – indeed, anyone – who would marry them! And one cannot but feel sympathy for the unfortunate aide-de-camp, being used as the messenger-boy between the would-be happy couple and a series of unbending and uncompromising clerics.

NOTES

1   BLib Add Ms 61808 ff 77, 80. Reproduced by courtesy of the British Library.
2   Presumably a reference to the blacksmith at Gretna Green.
3   I know for certain that Stonestreet solemnised the marriage of Lt Col Berkeley
     (a distant relative of the Richmonds) and Miss Sutton in Brussels, but there
     may have been others.
4   BLib Add Ms 61808 f 80. Reproduced by courtesy of the British Library.

Bibliography

Albemarle, George Earl of; *Fifty years of my Life*; Macmillan, London, 1877.

Altham, H S; *A History of Cricket*; George Allen & Unwin, London, 1962.

'A Near Observer'; *The battle of Waterloo, containing the series of accounts . . . forming an historical record of the operations in the Netherlands in 1815*; J Booth, London, 1815.

Anglesey, Marquess of (ed.); *The Capel letters, being the correspondence of Lady Caroline Capel and her Daughters with the Dowager Countess of Uxbridge from Brussels and Switzerland, 1814–1817*; Jonathan Cape, London, 1955.

Anon; *The important Trial in the Common Pleas, Friday February 16th, 1816. Webster v. Baldwin, for a Libel charging Adultery between the most noble Arthur Duke of Wellington and Lady Frances. C. W. Webster, at Brussels after the Battle of Waterloo*; W Hone, London, 1816.

Anon; *Proceedings on the Trial of a Special Action on the Case, by James Webster Wedderburn Webster, Esq., and Lady Frances Caroline Webster Wedderburn Webster, his Wife, against Charles Baldwin, for a Libel; in the Court of Common Pleas, at Westminster, on Friday, the 16th of February 1816. Taken in short-hand by Mr. W. B. Gurney, James Ridgway*; E Kerby, London, 1816.

Anon (Pinder, Peter); *Love at Head Quarters or a Week at Brussels, a Poem by 'The Author of 'The Royal Sprain'*; J Johnston, London, 1815.

Anon (Captain of a Company in One of the Regiments of Guards); *A Short Review of the Recent Affair of Honor between His Royal Highness the Duke of York and Lieutenant Colonel Lenox, with free and impartial strictures and comments upon the circumstances attending to it*; J Bell, London, 1789.

Anon (An Englishwoman); *Narrative of a Residence in Belgium during the Campaign of 1815*; John Murray, London, 1817.

Bamford, F (ed.); *Journals of Mrs Arbuthnot*; Macmillan, London, 1950.

Barrow, John, FRS; *The Life and Correspondence of Admiral Sir William Sidney Smith*; Richard Bentley, London, 1848.

Beaumont, W; *A History of the House of Lyme, in Cheshire*; P Pearse, Warrington, 1876.

Biddell, Colonel R S; *Memoirs of 10th Royal Hussars (P.W.O.)*; Longman, London, 1891.

Blücher, Princess Elizabeth (ed.); *Memoirs of Prince Blücher*; John Murray, London, 1932.

Brett-James, Antony; *General Graham, Lord Lynedoch*; Macmillan, London, 1959.

Brialmont, General; *L'histoire du Duc de Wellington*; Brussels, 1856.

Bronne, C; *L'Amalgame*; Ad. Gœmære, Brussels, 1948.

Brynn, Edward; *Crown & Castle. British Rule in Ireland, 1800–1830*; O'Brien Press, Dublin, 1978.

Byron, Lord; *The Works of the Rt Hon. Lord Byron*; M Thomas, Philadelphia, 1820.

Carr-Gomm, Francis (ed.); *Letters and Journals of Field Marshal Sir William Maynard Gomm 1799–1815*; John Murray, London, 1881.

Cave, Kathryn (ed.); *Diaries of Joseph Farington, 1793–1821*; Yale University Press, 1984.

Chad, G W; *A Narrative of the Late Revolution in Holland*; John Murray, London, 1814.

Cotton, Sergeant-Major Edward (late 7th Hussars); *A Voice from Waterloo*; B L Green, London, 1849.

Delaforce, Patrick; *Wellington the Beau*; The Windrush Press, Moreton-in-the-Marsh, 1990.

Edgcumbe, Richard (ed.); *The Diary of Frances, Lady Shelley 1787–1817*; John Murray, London, 1912.

Fraser. Sir William Augustus, Bart; *The Waterloo Ball*; F Harvey, London, 1897.

Fraser, Sir William Augustus, Bart; *Words on Wellington: The Duke, Waterloo, the Ball*; J C Nimmo, London, 1889.

Fraser, Alexander; *The Frasers of Philorth*; Privately Published, Edinburgh, 1879.

Gore, John (ed.); *Creevey, Selected and Re-edited*; John Murray, London, 1948.

Grattan, Thomas Colley; *The History of the Netherlands*; Longman, Brown & Green, London, u/d.

Greenhill Gardyne, Lt-Col. C; *The Life of a Regiment, The History of the Gordon Highlanders*; Medici Society, London, 1901.

Gleig, Rev. G R; *History of the Life of the Duke of Wellington from the French of M. Brialmont*; Longman, London, 1860.

_____ *Personal Reminiscences of the First Duke of Wellington*; Blackwoods, Edinburgh, 1904.

Gurwood, Lieutenant-Colonel; *The Dispatches of Field Marshal the Duke of Wellington 1799–1815*; John Murray, London, 1838.

Hardy, Thomas; *The Dynasts. a drama of the Napoleonic wars, in three parts, nineteen acts, & one hundred and thirty scenes*; Macmillan, New York and London, 1904.

Hayward, A (ed.); *Diaries of a Lady of Quality (Miss Frances Wynn) from 1797 to 1844*; Longman, London, 1864.

Heeley, Edward; 'The Journal of Edward Heeley', *Journal of Army Historical Research*, 1985.

Heyer, Georgette; *An Infamous Army*; Mandarin, London, 1992.

Hibbert, Christopher; *Wellington, a Personal history*; HarperCollins, London, 1997.

Juste, Theodore; *Bruxelles en 1814*; Librairie Classique; Brussels, 1884.

Lennox, Lady Sarah; *The Life and letters of Lady Sarah Lennox 1745–1826*; John Murray, London, 1902.

Lennox, Lord William Pitt; *Three Years with the Duke of Wellington in Private Life by 'An ex-aide-de-camp'*; Saunders & Otley, London, 1853.

_____ *Percy Hamilton or, The Adventures of a Westminster Boy*; London, 1851.

_____ *My Recollections, 1806–1873*; Hurst & Blackett.

Liddell Hart, B H (ed.); *The Letters of Private Wheeler 1809–28;* The Windrush Press, Gloucestershire; 2000.

Longford, Elizabeth; *Wellington*; Weidenfeld & Nicholson, London, 1992.

Madan, Beatrice (ed.); *Spencer and Waterloo, The Letters of Spencer Madan 1814–1816*; Literary Services, London, 1970.

Maidment, James (ed.); *Kay's Edinburgh Portraits*; Hamilton & Adams; London, 1885.

Malmesbury, Earl of; *A Series of letters of the First Earl of Malmesbury, His Family and friends, 1745–1820*; R Bentley, London, 1852.

Marchand, Leslie (ed.); *Alas! the Love of Women! – Byron's Letters and Journals*; John Murray, London, 1974.

Mercer, General Cavalié; *Journal of the Waterloo Campaign*; William Blackwood, 1870.

Miller, David; *Lady De Lancey at Waterloo*; Spellmount, Staplehurst, 2000.

Müffling, Friedrich Carl Ferdinand, Freiherr von; *Aus meinem Leben*; Mittler Sohn, Berlin, 1851.

Murphy, Charles Cecil Rowe; *A Mixed Bag*; William Clowes, London, 1936.

Napier, Sir W F P; *History of the War in the Peninsula*; London, 1834.

Norgate, Major-General (ed.); *Paris and the Parisians the year After Waterloo, Being Observations made during a Visit to Paris in the year 1816 by Rev Burroughs T Northgate*; London Literary Society, 1870.

Normington, Susan; *Lady Caroline Lamb – This Infernal Woman*; House of Stratus, London, 2001.

Owen, Edward (ed.); *The Waterloo Papers – 1815 and beyond*; Army Quarterly & Defence Journal Publications; Tavistock, 1998.

Philippart, J (ed.); *The Royal Military Calendar, or Army Service and Commission Book*; T Egerton, London, 1820.

Pocock, Tom; *A Thirst For Glory. The Life of Admiral Sir Sidney Smith*; Aurum, London, 1996

Reese, M M; *Goodwood's Oak, The Life and Times of the Third Duke of Richmond*; Threshold, London, 1987.

Reeser, Dr Eduard; *The History of the Waltz*; Sidgwick & Jackson, London; 1902.

Richardson, Ethel M; *Long Forgotten Days (Leading to Waterloo)*; Heath Cranton, London, 1928

Robertson, D; *The Journal of Sergeant D. Robertson, late 92nd Foot, comprising the different campaigns, between the years 1797 and 1818, in Egypt, Walcheren, Denmark, Sweden, Portugal, Spain, France, and Belgium*; J Fisher, Perth, 1842.

Romberg, J B; *Brussels and its Environs*; Brussels, 1816.

Ross-Lewin, Harry; *With the 'Thirty-Second' in the Peninsular and other campaigns*; Hodges, Figgis, Dublin, 1904.

Russell, Edward Frederick Langley (Baron Russell of Liverpool); *Knight of the Sword. The life and letters of Admiral Sir William Sidney Smith, G.C.B*; Victor Gollancz: London, 1964.

Siborne, Major-General H T (ed.); *Waterloo Letters*; Cassell, London, 1891.

Simpson, James; *Paris after Waterloo*; William Blackwood, Edinburgh, 1853.

Seaton, R C (ed.); *Notes and Reminiscences of a Staff Officer (Basil Jackson)*; John Murray, London, 1803.

Simpson, James; *A Visit to Flanders in 1815*; William Blackwood, Edinburgh, 1815.

Smith, Sir Sidney; *Memoirs of Admiral Sir Sidney Smith, KCB, etc; by the author of 'Rattlin the reefer' &c*; Richard Bentley, London, 1839.

Smola, Baron Carl von, *Das Leben des Feldmarschalls Heinrich Grafen von Bellegarde*; Wien, 1847.

Strickland, Margot; *The Byron Women*; Peter Owen, London, 1974.

Swinton, Hon. Blanche; *A Sketch of the Life of Georgiana, Lady de Ros, with some reminiscences of her family and friends, including the Duke of Wellington*; John Murray, London, 1893.

Thackeray, William Makepeace; *Vanity Fair*; Penguin Books, London, 1994.

Tod, Andrew (ed.); *Elizabeth Grant of Rothiemurchus, Memoirs of a Highland Lady*; Canongate, Edinburgh, 1988

Torrens, Robert; *An Essay on Money and Paper Currency*; London, 1812.

Verner, Ruth (ed.); *Reminiscences of William Verner, 1782–1871, 7th Hussars*; Society for Army Historical Research. Special Publication No. 8; London, 1965.

Webster, James Wedderburn; *A Genealogical Account of the Wedderburn*

Family; author's private press, Nantes, 1819.
_____ *Waterloo and Other Poems*; Archibald Constable & Co, Paris, 1816.
Wellington, 2nd Duke of (ed.); *Supplementary Despatches, Correspondence and Memoranda of Field Marshal Arthur, Duke of Wellington, Volume X*; John Murray, London, 1863.
Wellington, 7th Duke of (ed.); *The Conversations of the First Duke of Wellington with George William Chad*; Saint Nicolas Press: Cambridge, 1956.
Wilson, Thomas, Dancing Master; *A Companion to the Ballroom, Containing a Choice Collection of Country Dance and Waltz Tunes*; London 1816.
Young, Julian Charles (Rector of Ilmington); *A Memoir of Charles Mayne Young, tragedian, with extracts from his son's journal*; Macmillan, London, 1871.

Journals
Costume, No. 34, 2000; The Waterloo Dresses at the Museum of Costume, Batch, Penelope Byrd and Dr Ann Saunders; pp. 64–69.

Reference Books
Army Lists
Burke's Peerage
Dalton, Charles; *The Waterloo Roll Call*; William Clowes, London, 1890.
Der grosse Österreichische Hausschatz, Volume II; Zamarski, Wien, 1856.
Dictionary of National Biography
Gentleman's Magazine (various years)
Wurzbach, Dr Constant von; *Biographisches Lexicon des Kaiserthums Oesterreich*; Zamarski, Wien, 1856.

Index